Come Help Change Our World

Come Help Change the World

Bill Bright

NewLife
PUBLICATIONS
A MINISTRY OF CAMPUS CRUSADE FOR CHRIST

COME HELP CHANGE THE WORLD
by Bill Bright

A Campus Crusade for Christ Book
Published by
HERE'S LIFE PUBLISHERS, INC.
P.O. Box 1576
San Bernardino, CA 92402

Library of Congress Cataloging-in-Publication Data

Bright, Bill.
    Come help change the world.

    "A Campus Crusade for Christ book."
    1. Campus Crusade for Christ. 2. Students — Religious
life.   I. Campus Crusade for Christ.
II. Title.
BV4427.B73   1985   267,.61   85-21931
ISBN 0-86605-157-0 (pbk.)

HLP Product No. 403493

Scripture quotations not otherwise identified are from the New American Standard Bible, © The Lockman Foundation, 1960, 1962, 1963, 1971, 1972, 1973, 1975, and are used by permission. Other Scripture quotations are from the Living Bible, © 1971 by Tyndale House Publishers; used by permission. Additional quotations are taken from the King James Version.

FOR MORE INFORMATION, WRITE:

L.I.F.E. — P.O. Box A399, Sydney South 2000, Australia
Campus Crusade for Christ of Canada — Box 300, Vancouver, B C., V6C 2X3, Canada
Campus Crusade for Christ — 103 Friar Street, Reading RG1 1EP, Berkshire, England
Lay Institute for Evangelism — P.O. Box 8786, Auckland 3, New Zealand
Great Commission Movement of Nigeria — P.O. Box 500, Jos, Plateau State Nigeria, West Africa
Life Ministry — P.O. Box/Bus 91015, Auckland Park 2006, Republic of South Africa
Campus Crusade for Christ International — Arrowhead Springs, San Bernardino, CA 92414, U.S.A.

To those individuals who are and have been a part of the Campus Crusade for Christ staff family, I gratefully and affectionately dedicate this book. They are 20th-century Christian disciples who are committed to changing the world and fulfilling the Great Commission in this generation. This is their story.

Contents

Preface

Some time ago one of America's leading theologians and scholars wrote, "I am at Wheaton College where I am to speak at chapel tomorrow. I arrived late last night tired and eager to rest. However, before I went to sleep I decided to read the first chapter of your book, *Come Help Change the World*, which I had just acquired. It is now 2 A.M. and I have just finished reading the first eight chapters. I have gotten down on my knees to rededicate my life to the Lord Jesus Christ. Thank you for writing this book. It touched my life."

The revision of this book has been around the world in manuscript form many times since I began to rewrite my original book, *Come Help Change the World*. I have written on planes and trains, in hotel rooms and dozens of other places.

The reason that I have felt this book is important enough to sandwich my writing into an already overcrowded schedule is that God is doing so many dramatic, revolutionary things through this ministry that I feel the incredible story of Campus Crusade for Christ needs to be updated.

It is my prayer that God will speak to you, dear reader, and call you to be a part of this or some other similar movement dedicated to helping to change the world through helping fulfill the Great Commission — the greatest challenge ever given by the greatest Person who ever lived.

Bill Bright
Arrowhead Springs

Acknowledgment

I wish to express my deepest personal gratitude to the people who diligently labored with me in the production of this book. Their help has made it possible for me to tell the exciting story of the miraculous workings of our Lord through the ministry of Campus Cruisade for Christ.

Chuch MacDonald was of invaluable assistance to me in this project as he spent long hours researching, updating and polishing the material.

Janet Kobobel's final editing was crucial to the manuscript. So were the efforts of Judy Douglass and other dedicated staff members in the publications department who aided me in revising the original *Come Help Change the World* book which was printed in 1970.

I am also grateful to Frank Allnutt for his wise counsel and for overseeing the entire project to completion.

Erma Griswold, my assistant, is another whose help was so important, as she provided detailed editing of the manuscript.

And finally, I am thankful to my beloved wife, Vonette, who has labored with me in this movement for the past 28 years and whose contributions of love, patience and dedication to the Lord have helped further the impact of this ministry around the world.

Prologue

March 6, 1996. New York City. The United Nations.

Vonette and I were at the press conference for the announcement of the 1996 Templeton Prize for Progress in Religion. As we listened to the remarks of the presenter, a wealth of thoughts and emotions flooded my mind.

Many regard the Templeton Prize as the most prestigious award given in the world—even more so than the Nobel Prize. Begun in 1972 by renowned global investor Sir John Templeton, the prize is awarded each year to a living person who has "shown extraordinary originality in advancing humankind's understanding of God and/or spirituality." Templeton endowed the prize so that it would always be the world's largest annual award, and this year its value exceeded 700,000 pounds sterling, more than one million U.S. dollars. Previous winners included Mother Theresa, Aleksandr Solzhenitsyn, Dr. Billy Graham, and Charles Colson.

Today, although I had received prior notice of the purpose for this press conference, my heart was beating a bit faster than usual as the presenter enumerated several benchmark events of Campus Crusade for Christ's history and concluded:

> …This year, as Campus Crusade for Christ celebrates its forty-fifth anniversary, Bill Bright continues his work with the same steadfastness with which he began. Indeed, though actually reaching the world's six billion people would certainly be an amazing feat, there is also glory in setting it as a goal. For his efforts, Bill Bright has been awarded the 1996 Templeton Prize for Progress in Religion.

Strobe lights flashed and camera autowinders whirred as I moved forward to accept a plaque commemorating the award. Sir John Templeton shook my hand and posed beside me for photos. Vonette, my dear wife and co-laborer since Day One of Campus Crusade's ministry, awarded me with a spontaneous hug and kiss that was documented in newspapers worldwide. The formal presentation would take place in a private ceremony in Buckingham Palace on May 8. The public ceremony followed the next day at the Church of Santa Maria near Rome. But at this March press conference, I felt deeply honored to accept the Templeton Prize on behalf of my Lord Jesus Christ whose cause I serve, and on behalf of my beloved fellow staff, board members, and financial supporters— all of whom He has used so mightily in helping spread the gospel worldwide through the ministry of Campus Crusade for Christ International.

Who would have thought, when in 1951 I felt God prompting me to leave my seminary studies and obey His Great Commission to "go into all the world, and preach the gospel to every creature," that we would be where we are today—poised to help take the wonderful news of God's love and forgiveness to the entire world by the year 2000?

Who could have imagined, during Campus Crusade's humble beginnings in 1951 on the UCLA campus, that forty-five years later God would have enabled us to develop more than forty specialized ministries throughout the nation and in some 165 countries of the world, staffed by more than 13,600 incredible full-time staff and 101,000 trained volunteers? Our "JESUS" film alone, a full-length movie on the life of Christ, has been viewed by more than 766 million people in 365 languages in 218 countries.

Although my co-workers would never accuse me of being a small thinker, I must admit I never dreamed that God would bless this ministry in the way He has.

When we started on the campus of UCLA in 1951, the strategy was simple: reach the campus leaders and influencers for Christ, and you will reach tomorrow's influencers in all of society. Multiply this strategy to as many campuses as possible, and you can influence the course of an entire nation and perhaps the world.

We have never abandoned that core strategy. However, while building evangelism and discipleship ministries on more than 752 university campuses in the U.S. and 750 abroad, God has revealed hundreds of other key ways to accelerate the spread of His message throughout the nations of the world. He has brought us the full-time staff and volunteer help needed, and blessed their faithful efforts as literally millions of people worldwide have indicated that they have received Jesus Christ as Savior and Lord.

Indeed, it has been four and a half unbelievable decades. Yet, I know that without God's supernatural guidance, empowerment, and blessing, all of our labors would have been in vain. If Vonette and I had not consciously turned every thought, possession, and desire over to Him, we surely would have followed our own materialistic path instead of His way of true abundance. Had we not built the ministry on a strong foundation of prayer and continued to emphasize the importance of humbling ourselves before God and obeying His Word, we surely would have realized neither the positive results nor the multitude of blessings with which He has enriched our lives.

Since I knew that the Templeton Prize press conference would receive global coverage that night and the following day, I had prayerfully considered my acceptance statement. I wanted my words to bring honor and glory to God, to briefly explain why I count it a privilege to serve Jesus Christ by telling others about Him, and to make clear that I wanted to donate the financial award to help bring spiritual revival to the United States and the world. Below are excerpts from my press conference acceptance statement. Other comments are included in my acceptance address printed in the back of this book.

> I am deeply humbled and greatly honored to receive this prestigious Templeton Prize which, to me, because of its nature, is to be desired above every other prize given for whatever purpose.

> I would like to thank and commend Sir John Templeton for establishing the Templeton Prize, which emphasizes the most important aspect of life—the spiritual dimension—upon which all other considerations of life find fulfillment.

> I receive this prize in the name of our wonderful Lord whom I have served for more than fifty exciting years and on behalf of my beloved wife, Vonette; our wonderful sons, Zac and Brad; fantastic fellow staff members; board of directors; and a great army of faithful and generous supporters. I feel that I am the most privileged and fortunate man in the world to be associated with such a remarkable team.

> This money from the Templeton Prize will be used to educate leaders of the church worldwide to the spiritual benefits of fasting and prayer. I believe that fasting with biblical prayer is the most enriching and energizing of all the Christian disciplines and can accomplish the glory of God and ensure His blessing upon the peoples of the earth more than anything else we can do.

> Again, I am deeply grateful and honored for this recognition, and I give all the honor and glory to the One to whom it is due—the Lord and Savior Jesus Christ, who is risen, and who lives today in the hearts of all who love, trust, and obey Him.

> I invite all others who share my hopes and concerns for the world to join with me in proclaiming His great and desperately needed message of love,

> forgiveness, peace, and eternal life to the ends of the earth.

That evening's TV and radio news, and the next day's newspapers, all carried the story of the Templeton Prize. Paul Harvey's News and Comment splashed it on the radio airwaves. Congratulatory phone calls and letters poured in to our ministry headquarters in Orlando, Florida. In the whirlwind weeks that followed, dozens of media requested follow-up interviews.

On May 8 Vonette and I were flown to London, treated as royalty, and presented the actual award in a private ceremony with Prince Philip at Buckingham Palace. Then it was on to Rome, where on the evening of May 9 close to 900 dignitaries and guests gathered for the public convocation at the Church of Santa Maria, Trastevere. On this worldwide platform I was privileged to present a formal acceptance address in which I sought to share the gospel and give God all the honor and glory. Considering the influential worldwide audience, the speech was one of the most important messages and testimonies I have ever given and, as I spoke, I sensed a special strengthening within me. Afterward I learned that 102 of our staff back in Orlando, and hundreds more around the world, had been on their knees praying as I spoke that God would anoint me in a special way.

While I am both thrilled and honored at receiving the Templeton Prize, the award and all the attention it brings is also humbling and sobering. God's Word tells us that "it is required that those who have been given a trust must prove faithful" (1 Corinthians 4:2, NIV). Vonette and I and our other ministry leaders know in our hearts that we have accomplished nothing apart from God—that every positive result of our labors is only because of His blessing and supernatural work in people's hearts. We are only His instruments, trying to remain faithful to His calling. If we should ever make the prideful mistake of thinking we can do it by ourselves, He could quickly remove His hand of blessing from us. God uses the humble, broken, obedient heart, not the proud, boastful one. Therefore, we know that now more than ever we must be on our knees before Him in a spirit of confession, humility, and obedience to His will. Now more than ever, as the world's spotlight is on this ministry because of the Templeton Prize, we must exercise careful, godly stewardship of the time, finances, and manpower God has given us.

To this end, I appointed a committee of godly men to oversee the stewardship of the Templeton Prize money to assure that every penny is carefully and wisely used for the special purpose to which I felt God wanted me to donate it: to encourage and facilitate genuine, humble prayer and fasting among Christians worldwide so that 2 Chronicles 7:14 may come true in our generation: "If my people, who are called by my name, will humble themselves and pray and seek my face and turn from their wicked ways, then will I hear from heaven and will forgive their sin and will heal their land."

God has truly blessed us, but to whom much is given, much is required. There is no way we can or will rest on the achievements of the past. With the guidance and enabling of the Holy Spirit, the leadership and staff of Campus Crusade are committed to not only continue and improve our existing ministries worldwide but also to develop and implement exciting new strategies designed to "step up the pace" toward the fulfillment of the Great Commission. Working hand-in-hand as teammates with other Christian organizations, Christian denominations, and independent churches, we are dedicated to using the most strategic, efficient means available to give every resident of Planet Earth the opportunity to say "yes" to Jesus Christ. There simply is nothing more important for Christians to be doing.

The pages that follow tell the incredible story of how God raised up, blessed, and multiplied the ministry of Campus Crusade for Christ. I do not, and cannot, claim one ounce of credit for what He has done. I have simply dedicated myself to trying to live a life obedient to Him. As a ministry, we've come a long way, learned through our victories and mistakes, and seen miracle after miracle. But I am convinced that our most exciting days lie ahead—just around the corner!

Come Help Change the World is merely my human attempt to document some wondrous things God has done through men and women who want to help change their world through His message of love, forgiveness, peace, and eternal life. I wish our language had the words to truly convey my deep sense of awe, reverence, and love for our Lord, or to describe His supernatural working in the hearts of people with whom we have come in contact. But I have tried in these pages to share some benchmarks of the adventure with you, and I hope you catch at least a taste of the excitement we have experienced through the years.

I share this story to give God praise for what He has done, and to encourage you to ask how He wants you to make your life count the most for eternity. Because of the vision and strategies He has given Campus Crusade for the next decade, we are praying for 100,000 sharp Christian men and women to join us full-time in the task of saturating our neighborhoods, cities, countries, and continents with God's message of love and forgiveness. So let me warn you: As you read the Campus Crusade story, you just might catch a bit of the personal excitement Vonette and I and our staff have felt during our forty-five years of ministry! You may find yourself wanting to ask how your own background, skills, and talents could be used of God in a cutting-edge outreach such as the one He has entrusted to us. If so, do not worry about inexperience, lack of training, or funding; if God should lead you to join us, remember that we all started out inexperienced and unprepared. Some of the most outstanding Christian men and women in the world stand ready to train and help you. All we require is a genuine commitment to Jesus Christ as Savior and Lord, a heart for God, and a teachable spirit.

Indeed, the fields are ripe unto harvest. There is growing evidence that revival fires are starting to burn across America and around the world. Millions of people are realizing the futility of life apart from God and are turning from their wicked ways. More hearts and doors are open now than ever before in history. As we humble ourselves before God and obey His command to share Christ in the power of the Holy Spirit, revival fires will burn brighter and brighter in the days ahead. The world is primed and ready for the Good News of Jesus Christ, but as the apostle Paul asked, "How can they believe in Him if they have never heard about Him? And how can they hear about Him unless someone tells them?" (Romans 10:14, TLB).

There is no nobler calling, no better investment of one's life, than telling others how to know God personally and enjoy Him forever.

Revival is coming! We look forward to being part of it. We want you to be part of it, too! Will you join us in this exciting adventure?

Will you come help change the world?

Bill Bright
Orlando, Florida
July 1, 1996

CHAPTER ONE

EXPLO '74 —
An Awesome Experience

My heart quickened as I stepped to the microphone. This was the most awesome responsibility and most exciting challenge of my life. I looked out upon an ocean of people stretching as far as I could see to the left of me, to the right of me and in front of me. Officials estimated 1.3 million people had gathered in Seoul, Korea, for this evening meeting of EXPLO '74, an international congress on evangelism sponsored by Campus Crusade for Christ.

My message was based on Ephesians 2:8,9, and I wanted to explain that salvation is a gift of God which we receive by faith. After each sentence that I spoke to the crowd, I paused, allowing Dr. C. C. Park, one of the leading pastors in all of South Korea, to translate my statements into Korean. At the completion of my message, I asked all of those who wanted to receive Christ, or who, as a result of my message, had gained assurance of their salvation, to stand.

All over Yoido Plaza, people began to stand from where they had been sitting on the asphalt of this converted airstrip. Grandmothers, teenagers, businessmen, farmers, merchants and children stood quietly as the EXPLO choir, some 8,000 voices in number, sang softly.

I could hardly believe my eyes as hundreds of thousands of people stood! I wanted to make sure they understood what I had said, so I repeated my invitation again, slowly. Still more people stood!

Midnight Call

About midnight, I answered a phone call from Dr. Joon Gon Kim to report on the evening's activities. Dr.

Kim is the director of Campus Crusade's movement in Korea and has been my beloved friend and co-laborer for Christ since 1958. He and his staff were responsible for calling together this remarkable gathering.

"I have exciting news," he said. "When you gave the invitation tonight, our staff determined that about 80% of the estimated 1.3 million people in attendance stood. Do you realize that more than one million people indicated tonight that they received Christ or that, for the first time in their lives, they were assured of their salvation?"

It was some time before I could respond, because I was so overwhelmed. Even now I cannot quite grasp it. I know it happened only because of God's supernatural, miraculous working, for what greater miracle is there than the miracle of a new birth?

This was just one of the many momentous moments I witnessed during EXPLO '74. Night after night I was filled with awe and praise to God as I stood on the elevated platform and looked out over a sea of faces.

I was deeply moved to learn that these were the largest Christian gatherings in recorded history. At least one of the evening mass rallies exceeded 1.6 million people, according to official police estimates.

Record-setting Gathering

Besides this amazing "first" in the history of the Christian church, Dr. Kim later told me of some 24 other firsts in connection with EXPLO '74, some of which, even five years later, were unmatched. They included:

1. The largest number of Christians trained in discipleship and evangelism during one week (a total number of 323,419 registered, representing some 78 nations).

2. The largest number of decisions for Christ in a single evening.

3. The largest all-night prayer meetings in the history of the Christian church (prayer meetings occurred six

nights in a row, with several hundred thousand in attendance each night). The night before EXPLO began, my wife, Vonette, spoke to more than 100,000 women gathered for prayer.

4. The largest personal witnessing campaign ever conducted (more than 420,000 heard the gospel in one afternoon and a record 274,000 indicated salvation decisions for Christ).

5. The largest number of Christians to appropriate the filling of the Holy Spirit at one time (an estimated 70% of the 1.5 million audience one night responded to this invitation).

6. The largest number of Christians to commit their lives to the fulfillment of the Great Commission at one time (a response of 90% was estimated among the final Sunday crowd of 650,000).

No number of human beings nor group of organizations could ever have accomplished what happened at EXPLO '74. All the glory, honor and praise must go to God.

Supernatural Living

I am reminded of the words of our Lord recorded in John 14:12, which have been a constant source of wonder and challenge to me since my early days as a Christian: "Truly, truly, I say to you, he who believes in Me, the works that I do shall he do also; and greater works than these shall he do; because I go to the Father."

From the beginning of my Christian experience, I have interpreted that verse to mean that God wants His children to live supernaturally, especially in the area of living holy lives and bearing much fruit, since that is the reason that our Lord came to this world. God's Word reminds us, "The Son of Man has come to seek and to save that which was lost" (Luke 19:10). Jesus explains in John 15:8, "By this is My Father glorified, that you bear much fruit, and so prove to be My disciples."

Through the years, I have prayed that my life and the ministry of Campus Crusade would be characterized by the miraculous and supernatural. I have prayed that God would work in and through us in such a mighty way that all who see the results of our efforts would know that God was responsible and give Him all the glory.

Now as I look back on EXPLO '74 — surely one of the most exciting and meaningful memories in the history of our movement — I remember earlier days which were also characterized by praise and glory to God, even though I was not privileged to speak to millions, or even thousands. At one point in our ministry, about the only understanding listener I could turn to was my wife.

But let me take you back to those days, to the beginning of the Campus Crusade story and that moment when God revealed to me the ministry I was to undertake for Him.

CHAPTER TWO

In the Beginning

It was the spring of 1951, my senior year at Fuller Theological Seminary. For two exciting and happy years I had been married to my home town sweetheart, the former Vonette Zachary. Vonette had accepted a teaching position in the Los Angeles school system, and we found ourselves living a busy and eventful life.

Once or twice a week, in addition to regular meetings at church, I had the privilege of leading a deputation group of more than a hundred dedicated college and post-college age young men and women who wanted to become disciples for the Lord Jesus Christ. We covered approximately 30 assignments each month, visiting the local jails and hospitals, skid row missions and wherever we felt we were needed. I soon discovered that we had to wait our turn to go to jail services and skid row missions because there were many other churches covering this area of service. One day it occurred to me that there were no waiting lines to reach college students or the top executives of the city. Here were the neglected leaders of our world, both today's and tomorrow's.

Contract With God

By this time Vonette and I had become increasingly aware that living for Christ and serving Him was our major goal in life. As a result of this awareness, we decided we would sign a contract with the Lord. No one had ever suggested this; it was just something we decided to do together. Both of us had been very ambitious and materialistic and had lived selfishly prior to becoming Christians. Now the Lord had changed us and had given us a love for Himself and a desire to serve Him and others.

One Sunday afternoon, Vonette went into one room in our home in the Hollywood hills and I into another, and we made a list of all the things we had wanted out of life. When I had first proposed to Vonette, we had once talked about a honeymoon in Europe, about securing the finest voice teacher to develop her already beautiful singing voice and about living in the fabulous Bel-Air district of Los Angeles. But now all that had been given to Christ. Such ambitions had become secondary for us, there was no longer a great appetite for them. So, we made a new list of the things we wanted.

Similar Lists

Our new lists, surprisingly alike, included: (1) to live holy lives, controlled and empowered by the Holy Spirit; (2) to be effective witnesses for Christ; and (3) to help to fulfill the Great Commission in our generation. We were also concerned for a Christian home, and we suggested two to four children (we have two sons). We thought it would be convenient to own two cars. Today we don't own any, but God has provided us transportation through the generosity of a friend who is also interested in helping to reach the world for Christ. And, we mentioned in our lists, if the Lord be pleased, we wanted a home nice enough for entertaining the President of the United States and modest enough that a man from Skid Row would feel comfortable in it.

By now we had begun to respond to the command of our Lord: "But seek first His kingdom, and His righteousness" (Matthew 6:33). We believed that God's will was better than our own. The more we knew of God's love for us, of His wisdom, power and grace, the more we could trust Him. So we signed our names to these lists as a formal act of commitment to Christ and His cause. This was an especially significant commitment inasmuch as we were doing it together as a young husband and wife. There was no particular emotion involved. It was simply a transaction of the will. Of course, we had been motivated to do this on the basis of the Spirit of God working in us, as explained through the apostle Paul, "For it is God who is at work in you, both to will and to work for His good pleasure" (Philippians 2:13).

What was to happen as a result of this commitment we did not know, but I am sure that God did; and, within a few short weeks, as we continued studies, teaching, deputation work and business, His plans began to unfold.

Birth of a Vision

One evening at about midnight, during my senior year in seminary, I was studying for a Greek exam. There was nothing unusual about the setting or about the circumstances. Vonette was asleep in a nearby room. Suddenly, without warning or without any indication of what was going to happen, I sensed the presence of God in a way I had never known before. Though it could not have lasted more than a few seconds, I suddenly had the overwhelming impression that the Lord had flashed on the screen of my mind His instructions for my life and ministry.

It is difficult to talk about such experiences for fear of being misunderstood or causing others to seek similar experiences; but I think I know a little something of what the apostle Paul experienced when he met the Lord in such a dramatic way on the road to Damascus. In any event, this was the greatest spiritual experience of my Christian life. At this time and in a very definite way, God commanded me to invest my life in helping to fulfill the Great Commission in this generation. I was to begin by helping to win and disciple the students of the world for Christ. How to do this was not spelled out in detail;

that came later as the Lord gave additional insights for the implementation of the original vision. I awakened Vonette, and together we praised God for His direction and promised that with His grace and strength we would obey Him.

Counsel From Mature Christians

Though my heart was filled with praise and thanksgiving to the Lord for this remarkable revelation of what I was to do with my life, I still needed the counsel of more mature Christians. The next day I went to see one of my favorite seminary professors, Dr. Wilbur Smith, famous Bible teacher, scholar and author of many books. As I shared with him what God had revealed to me, he got out of his chair and paced back and forth in his office, saying again and again, "This is of God. This is of God. I want to help you. Let me think and pray about it."

The next morning when I arrived for his seven o'clock class in English Bible, Dr. Smith called me out of the classroom into a little counseling room and handed me a piece of paper on which he had scribbled these letters, "CCC" after which he had written "Campus Crusade for Christ." He explained that God had provided the name for my vision.

Since that spring night experience, it has been my passion and concern to be obedient to the heavenly vision that God had given me. The first major decision I made was to drop out of seminary with only a few units remaining before graduation. I became convinced, and remain convinced today, that God did not want me to be ordained. Though I have a great respect and appreciation for clergy, layman status has often worked to a great advantage in my ministry with students and laymen.

The next move was to look for an advisory board of outstanding men and women of God to advise and coun-

sel me in the establishment of this ministry. Dr. Wilbur
Smith was the first I approached. Then I asked Henrietta
Mears, Billy Graham, Richard C. Halverson, Dawson
Trotman, Cyrus N. Nelson, Dan Fuller and J. Edwin Orr,
to serve in this capacity. All of them readily agreed to
be part of this new facet of God's strategy.

The events of the days that followed were framed in
prayer and meditation. "Lord, where do You want us to
launch this ministry?" was a prayer that Vonette and I
and our friends uttered frequently in the spring and
summer of 1951.

The Target — UCLA

Increasingly, the University of California at Los
Angeles became the focus of our attention. It seemed so
right to begin there, at a university that in 1951 had a
strong, radical minority which was exercising great influence and was causing a number of disturbances. It
seemed that this would be one of the most difficult campuses on which to begin, and that if our venture for
Christ could succeed there, it would be likely to succeed
on any campus.

After our meeting with university officials to share
our plans and request the necessary approval to work
with the students, we looked for a place to live near the
UCLA campus. Rents were high, and nothing was available in the immediate vicinity. But we kept searching
and praying that God would lead us to the right location.

One day as I was going over the files with a local
realtor, he turned past the listing of a large home only
one block from the campus with a rental of $450 per
month, which in 1951 was astronomical. Our budget
indicated that we would be able to spend up to $200,
though that was more than we could realistically afford
to pay. Yet as the realtor flipped past the card of the
listing of this house, I told him rather emphatically,
"That's the house. I want to see it."

"Why?" he asked. "They are asking more than twice the amount you are willing to pay."

But I continued to press him. "How long has the house been listed?"

"For several months." Then he explained that two sisters who lived in the house were planning to take a South American tour. "As a matter of fact," he observed, studying the card, "they leave next week."

I asked permission to go to see them, and I found the house ideally suited for our needs. It was located approximately one block from sorority row and had plenty of room, in particular a spacious living room where I could visualize us holding large group sessions. I explained to the owners our interest in reaching the students of UCLA for Christ, and that we would not be able to pay more than $200 a month rent. They said that they would think about it and would call us. By the time I returned to our home in Hollywood, they had called. Impressed with our mission and wanting to have a part in it, they agreed to the $200 a month rent if we would pay an additional $25 a month for the gardener. This we agreed to do, and shortly thereafter we moved into our new home in Westwood.

Chain of Prayer

Our first spiritual effort was to organize a 24-hour chain of prayer divided into 96 periods of 15 minutes each and invite people to pray around the clock that God would do a unique thing on the UCLA campus. Next, we began to recruit and train interested students and to organize them into teams to visit the various fraternities and sororities, dormitories and other groups on the campus. The teams presented personal testimonies of their faith in Christ, after which I gave a brief message in which I explained who Christ is, why He came and how they could know Him personally.

I remember well our first sorority meeting. It was at

the Kappa Alpha Theta sorority, which was known then as the "house of beautiful women." Apparently the pledges were selected, among other reasons, for their good looks and personalities. In any event, when I finished my message and the challenge was presented to receive Christ, many girls remained behind to talk to us and ask further questions. It was a new experience for me. For more than a year we had gone into various fraternity and sorority houses on local campuses prior to the time that God gave the vision of this ministry; yet we had never seen one single person commit his life to Christ. To our knowledge, no one had ever received Christ as a result of any of our meetings.

Overwhelming Response

At the conclusion of the first sorority meeting following the vision God had given, I was amazed to see such a large group of young women standing in line to express their desire to become Christians. One after another they came (more than half of the original 60 girls present), communicating in various ways, "I want to become a Christian." It was a humbling experience, seeing God work in this marvelous way. This was a dramatic confirmation to me that the vision to help fulfill the Great Commission and to begin by going to the collegians of the world was truly from God. Unsure, stepping carefully, speaking reservedly, we had been cautious until then; but God seemed to be urging us forward, filling us with badly needed confidence and assurance that, having called us to this ministry, He was with us.

We invited the girls to join us the next evening for a meeting in our home nearby, and several of the young women brought their boyfriends. It was a memorable and exciting night. The men were skeptical, but they came with the girls from "the house of beautiful women," and many of them made decisions for Christ, too.

This, then, was the beginning of a movement which is now touching the lives of millions.

CHAPTER THREE

Growing Up

The days that followed demonstrated again and again the fact that God's hand was upon us and upon our ministry. In meeting after meeting — in fraternities, sororities, dormitories and with student leaders — the phenomenal response was the same as that at our first meeting. In the course of a few months, more than 250 students at UCLA — including the student body president, the editor of the newspaper and a number of the top athletes — committed their lives to Christ. So great was their influence for Christ on the entire campus that the chimes began to play Christian hymns at noonday.

By this time the news of what God was doing at UCLA had spread to other campuses, and students, faculty, laymen and pastors in various parts of the country were asking, "Will you help us? We would like to start Campus Crusade at our school."

At this point, I had to make a very important decision. The vision that God had given to me originally embraced the whole world. If I were to stay at UCLA and devote all of my own personal energies to reach only one campus, I would be disobedient to that heavenly vision. I loved the students and could easily have spent the rest of my life serving Christ on that one campus. Yet there was only one thing for me to do — recruit and train other people to help reach collegians of the world with the good news of God's love and forgiveness in Christ.

Search for Staff

As in any expanding business, we needed new personnel. We needed dedicated, qualified staff who could articulate their faith; and we needed many of them. I assumed that they would be available by the hundreds. The standards we established were high, of necessity. The first requirement for potential staff was that they be fruitful in their witness for Christ; second, that they be seminary graduates; and third, that they be sympathetic with what we were attempting to accomplish in winning, building and sending men to help evangelize the world for our Savior. Vonette and I prayed much about the urgency to expand to other campuses.

Finally, it was agreed that she would remain in charge of the work at UCLA while I went from campus to campus on a recruiting tour which took me to many of the leading Christian schools and seminaries of the nation, looking for new staff people.

Imagine my disappointment when I discovered that in those days there were just not many individuals, with or without degrees, who were fruitful for Christ and available. And there were practically none with bachelor of divinity degrees who were effective in their witness for Christ and who wanted to be a part of our ministry. Consequently, we were forced to change the requirements for our staff. We concluded that we would accept for campus staff those with college degrees who were otherwise qualified and who had teachable spirits and a willingness to learn how to introduce others to Christ.

New Recruits

After considerable recruiting, we did find six choice people. Two of them, Dan Fuller and Calvin Herriott, had been fellow seminarians and had just recently graduated. There were also Roe Brooks, a seminarian in his middle year; Gordon Klenck, who was just graduating from college; and Roger Aiken and Wayne Arolla, both of whom had college degrees.

Gordon Klenck was the first of these staff members to arrive in Los Angeles. He still needed to complete one course, which he was doing by correspondence, before he would receive his coveted degree. I had interviewed him on campus and was impressed with his sincerity and his dedication to Christ, though he did look extremely young. He was actually 20 years old but didn't look a day over 17.

Somehow in our correspondence we had failed to give him our telephone number and our home address. He had only a post office box number for Campus Crusade. Thus, when he arrived in Los Angeles, he didn't know how to get in touch with us. We were still such a small organization that we had not even listed Campus Crusade in the telephone directory. Our dining room was our office, and our dining room table doubled as my desk. So Gordon checked in at the YMCA and mailed a card to us, saying that we could find him there. He told us that if he was not in the "Y," he would be in the library completing his correspondence course. Following his instructions, when we could not locate him at the "Y," we proceeded to the library, where we spotted him immediately in the main reading room.

Gordon returned home with us, and as soon as we had walked into the house he asked for a card table, insisting that he must finish his correspondence course before we began our staff training. He must have sensed that he would never get back to his own work once we began to train him for staff. As he set his typewriter on the card table and continued his studies, I remember Vonette commenting to me, as she noted his youthful appearance, "Do you expect to change the world with people like that?" I am sure that Gordon must have looked at us and wondered at the same time if he hadn't made a serious mistake in coming to help us!

Family Atmosphere

Roe Brooks was the next to join us around the family table. "Family" is the right word to use, because we were a family, not only a family in Christ, but also a family in experience. We ate together and we shared together; and our love for each other was very real. Vonette tried to cook for all of us and was never sure how many guests there would be for dinner. But somehow we managed, cutting pork chops in two or adding a can of soup to the stew. Amazingly, no one ever seemed to go away hungry.

Among other things, since we held so many meetings in fraternities, sororities and dormitories, it was important that all of us observe proper etiquette, be well-mannered and understand proper eating procedures. Therefore, Vonette and I began to conduct a training course for the staff. Vonette was the chief drill instructor, and we had some very profitable (and often humorous) times together.

From the very beginning of Campus Crusade we have strongly emphasized the Lordship of Christ, assurance of salvation and the importance of the ministry of the Holy Spirit — how to appropriate by faith His power for a holy life and fruitful witness. We have also considered it very important that each staff member understand how to communicate his faith in Christ to the student world in the most effective way possible. So we began to explore together ways to accomplish these objectives. During that first summer, Vonette and I spent several weeks giving these young men intensive training, the pattern of which has been amplified and developed throughout the succeeding years.

In the fall of 1952, we established the ministry on additional campuses, including San Diego State, University of Southern California, University of California at Berkeley, Oregon State and the University of Washington.

Staff members were to be paid a salary of $100 a month for nine months only. During the other three months, they would receive no remuneration at all. Obviously, they had not come because of a large salary, but because they wanted to be part of something bigger than themselves; they wanted to help change the world. For the first several years, Vonette and I received no remuneration from Campus Crusade; instead, we were giving of our finances to help accelerate and expand the ministry.

New Housing

There were many opportunities to trust the Lord. One day a wire came from Brazil from the owners of the home we had leased for a year, stating that even though only six months had passed, they were ready to return home. Would we be willing to relinquish the house? As I was sitting at the table reading the wire, the telephone rang. Dr. J. Edwin Orr, internationally-known evangelist and author, was calling to ask if I knew of anyone who would be interested in living in his home during the next year while he would be on worldwide evangelistic tours. It just happened that I did know someone! We made Dr. Orr's house our headquarters for three semesters, and although it was two miles from campus, it proved to be ideal for the next phase of our UCLA ministry.

But as we continued to hold many fraternity, sorority and dormitory meetings, confronting thousands of students on several campuses with the claims of Christ, many were responding. Once again we were pressed for space.

Day after day, on my way to the campus, I passed a large home of Moorish castle-style architecture with a "For Sale" sign on the lawn. This home happened to be located in the famous Bel-Air district of Westwood Village directly across Sunset Boulevard from the UCLA campus. I had promised Vonette when we were married that one day we would live in fabulous Bel-Air, so I was tempted again and again to stop and inquire about it. However, I rejected the idea as being a personal, selfish desire until one day I became convinced that perhaps God did want us to acquire this property, inasmuch as it was located only about three minutes from the heart of the UCLA campus. I decided to stop and investigate the property. The price was far more than we could afford, so I decided to put the idea out of my mind.

Help From Dr. Mears

However, shortly after my conversation with the owner, our good friend, Dr. Henrietta Mears, learned of our interest in the property and told us that she had been interested in and had actually negotiated for the purchase of the house some years previously. Now, she would like to purchase the house, provided we would come to live with her, carrying our share of the expenses, of course. She explained that since the recent death of her sister, Margaret, with whom she had lived for many years in a large, two-story home near the UCLA campus, her house was much too big for her alone. Dr. Mears and Vonette accompanied me as I visited the "castle" again, and we unanimously agreed that this would be ideal for all of us — for Dr. Mears, for Vonette and me, and for the ministry of Campus Crusade. The house was large and so designed that we all had our privacy, yet could be together for our meals and whenever else we wished. Once again, God had provided for our needs!

The house was purchased, and soon we were happily and comfortably established in our new home and headquarters. Within days, students were pouring into 110 Stone Canyon Road. As many as 300 students could be packed into the spacious rooms with all of the furniture pushed aside. Many students were introduced to Christ in our various meetings and especially in the little prayer room off the foyer.

Sharing the Bel-Air home with Dr. Mears was made all the more meaningful to us because she had played such an important role in introducing both Vonette and me to Christ.

Perhaps I should elaborate a bit more about Dr. Mears and the part she played in my life. Apart from my mother's life and prayers, Dr. Mears, more than any other person, was responsible for my becoming a Christian. Also, except for her, Vonette may never have taken that spiritual step through which I have had the benefit of her love, counsel and encouragement through the rich, exciting and fruitful years of this ministry.

Vonette and I grew up in the same little Oklahoma town, Coweta, a wonderful community of approximately 1,500 people. She was most attractive, intelligent and personable. She came from a fine family, and I was much impressed with her. She was also very active in the church, and I assumed that she was a vital Christian.

Decision to Enter Seminary

However, since she was four years younger than I, I had never had any romantic interest in her until I moved away and was established in business in Los Angeles. Then, through a series of rather unusual experiences, I got in touch with her, fell in love, proposed, and before I knew it, we were planning the wedding date. Yet, there was one thing that bothered me: the question of her dedication to the Lord. I had decided to enter seminary, and I remember a trip that I made to Oklahoma en route to Princeton Theological Seminary in the fall of 1946 in order to discuss this with her.

During our time together, I made the statement that God would have to come first in our marriage, and this annoyed Vonette. "I'm not sure that's right. I think a man's family should be his first concern," she bristled. I began to mount an argument but then dropped it, thinking that there would be plenty of time to iron out this difference later.

In the fall of 1947, I transferred from Princeton to Fuller Theological Seminary in California — in order to be closer to my business (a fancy food line called Bright's

California Confections) — and was proceeding toward a degree when the matter of Vonette's personal relationship with Christ began to trouble me again. I became increasingly concerned for her spirituality. Yet I was a young Christian and too immature to help her because of our emotional involvement.

Not a Christian

By this time, we had been engaged for more than two years, but a gnawing question persisted in my mind: Was it true, as I had originally been impressed to believe, that God had chosen Vonette to be my wife? If God rules in the affairs of men and nations, and not even a sparrow falls to the ground without His knowledge, it seemed to me that God does have one particular mate for us. Although I had dated many girls prior to our engagement and had been infatuated with some, I had never proposed to anyone else. I had been impressed, I felt, by the Lord and was confident even before our first date that Vonette was the one with whom I was to share my life and my ministry for Christ. Yet, since my proposal and her acceptance, we had both become aware that she was not a Christian. Since she had never received Christ as her Savior, she could not possibly share my vision and concern about introducing others to Christ.

This was one of the greatest conflicts of my life. What was I to do? I had committed my life to Christ and His service. My one great desire was to live and, if need be, die for Him. Now I was in love with and engaged to a girl who, though a good church member, was not even a Christian. Obviously, we could not marry if she did not become a Christian, and yet, I had been so sure. This conflict continued to persist until we decided that perhaps we should explore the possibility that God might have other plans for us. So we both began to date other people. I dated girls who were vitally interested in living for Christ; Vonette, I suppose, dated fellows who were less interested in the Lord. But we kept in touch through frequent letters and telephone calls from Los Angeles to Denton, Tex., where she was attending college.

California Visit

Finally, the day of graduation came for Vonette, and she received her degree in home economics from Texas Women's University. I suggested that she visit her brother, who lived in southern California. She apparently thought this was a good idea, a sort of do-or-die time when we would decide either yes or no. Vonette, as she later told me, confided in a girlfriend before she left college, "I am either going to rescue him from this religious fanaticism or come back without a ring." She did neither.

While in California, Vonette went with me to a meeting of several hundred students at a College Briefing Conference at Forest Home, the famous conference center for Christian leadership established by Dr. Mears. Even though I had been able to help many others find Christ, I felt inadequate in introducing Vonette to Him. Someone else would have to help me, and Dr. Mears was the logical choice. She had counseled with thousands of young people and knew how to communicate with individuals with inquiring and scientific minds.

By this time, Vonette had begun to doubt the Bible and even the existence of God, so I felt that she needed help from someone who knew more than I. Also, because of the emotional involvement, I was afraid that I might be able to get from her a verbal commitment to Christ but not a commitment of the will to Him. She might say yes to Christ with her lips in order to please me and not mean it in her heart.

We arrived at the beautiful mountain setting where thousands of lives had been changed by the power of Christ. Vonette could not help but be impressed with so many vibrant lives. She liked the quality of life they possessed but was bewildered by their expressions of faith. After a couple of days, she decided that they were enthusiastic about Christianity just because it was so new to them. After all, she had been reared in the church and did not see anything about Christianity to get excited about. She thought their enthusiasm would soon wear off. She did not want to stand in my way and suggested that since she felt this would not work for her perhaps we should break our engagement. It was then that I asked her to talk to Dr. Mears, who had played such an important role in my own spiritual birth and growth.

Joyful Reunion

While Dr. Mears and Vonette talked, I paced back and forth outside the cottage, praying. Time dragged — 15 minutes, an hour and more. Suddenly the door burst open, and Vonette came bounding into my arms. There were tears of joy on her cheeks and an indescribable look of joy on her face. She did not need to say a word. I knew what had happened, and tears of gratitude filled my eyes, too.

Vonette later wrote her impressions of that day:

> Dr. Mears was one of the most vibrant, enthusiastic personalities that I had ever met. She was waiting for me, and the entire conference staff, without my knowledge, had been praying for my conversion. Dr. Mears explained that she had taught chemistry in Minneapolis, and that she could understand how I was thinking. (I had minored in chemistry in college, and everything had to be practical and workable to me. This was one of the reasons I had questioned the validity of Christianity.) As she explained simply to me from God's Word how I could be sure that I knew God, she used terminology very familiar to me. She explained that, just as a person going into a chemistry laboratory experiment follows the table of chemical valence, so it is possible for a person to enter God's spiritual laboratory and follow His formula of knowing Him and following Him.
>
> During the next hour, she lovingly proceeded to explain to me who Christ is and how I could know Him personally. "Dr.

Mears," I said, "if Jesus Christ is the way, then how do I meet Him?" Dr. Mears responded, "In Revelation 3:20, Christ says, 'Behold, I stand at the door and knock; if any one hears My voice and opens the door, I will come in to him, and will dine with him, and he with Me.' Receiving Christ is simply a matter of turning your life — your will, your emotions, your intellect — completely over to Him. John, chapter 1, verse 12, says, 'But as many as received Him, to them He gave the right to become children of God, even to those who believe in His name.'"

When Dr. Mears finished, I thought, "If what she tells me is absolutely true, I have nothing to lose and everything to gain." I bowed my head and prayed. I asked Christ to come into my heart. And at that moment, as I look back, my life began to change. God became a reality in my life. For the first time I was ready to trust Him. I became aware that my prayers were getting beyond the ceiling. I found that I had control of areas of my life that I had not been able to control before. No longer did I have to try to love people. There just seemed to be a love that flowed from within that I did not have to create. God had added a new dimension to my life, and I found myself becoming as enthusiastic as Bill, Dr. Mears and other students were, and eager as they were to share Christ with others.

Soon after the purchase of our present headquarters at Arrowhead Springs, Calif., Dr. Mears came to see the property and participated in our first institute by offering a special prayer of dedication to the Lord for us and for Arrowhead Springs. This was especially meaningful to us because of the important role which she has played in our personal lives and in the ministry of Campus Crusade. Since Vonette and I had shared her home in Bel-Air for 10 years, both as our own home and as a headquarters and meeting place for our campus ministry at UCLA, and since she was now prepared to retire from her ministry with the First Presbyterian Church of Hollywood as director of Christian education, we invited her to come to live with us at Arrowhead Springs. This she was prayerfully considering when the Lord chose to take her home — a great loss to us and to the cause of Christ, yet we know that He does all things well and our confidence is in Him. Multitudes from around the world have been spiritually blessed and have benefited, even as we have, through the great ministry of Henrietta Mears.

CHAPTER FOUR

Moving Out

From UCLA, our training headquarters was moved to Minnesota. In the fall of 1956, a long-distance call came from Mound, Minn., from Bill Greig, chairman of the Midwest Keswick. He wondered if Campus Crusade would be interested in receiving a gift of a five-acre tract of land in Mound, on the shore of beautiful Lake Minnetonka. Since his group could no longer use the property, they were looking for an organization that would utilize it effectively for the glory of God. "Come out and look it over," Bill said. "If it fits your needs, it's yours."

I expressed gratitude for the offer, but only when I saw the site did I fully appreciate the gift. Though the buildings were old and mostly run down and there was only a rough foundation for a new chapel-dormitory building, the place offered great promise. It was a breathtakingly beautiful site. I knew it would be ideal for a training center for our staff and students, so we gratefully accepted title to it. In the summer of 1958, we completed a beautiful chapel and dormitory combination which, together with existing facilities which we had also remodeled, enabled us to train approximately 150 people at one time.

That first summer we had that number and more. We also had our troubles trying to get the buildings completed. Carpenters, masons and electricians were everywhere. The staff and local volunteers were still painting and building partitions in the dormitories when the students arrived. As a matter of fact, the students joined with the staff in finishing the job. There were problems, too; more than I care to remember. But even these problems served to draw us closer together, so great was the challenge and excitement of moving into our beautiful new training center.

A Successful Pitch

One of our speakers for staff training that summer was a Christian layman who was an outstanding sales consultant, a man who had taught thousands of salesmen how to sell. One of the main points of one of his addresses was that to be a successful salesman a man must have a pitch. In other words, a man who is a good automobile salesman tells every potential customer basically the same things, and the better he communicates, the more successful he is as a salesman. But the danger, he explained, is that when a man becomes weary of hearing himself make the same presentation, he develops presentation fatigue. When this happens, he often changes the message and loses his effectiveness.

Zeroing In

He compared the witnessing Christian to the secular salesman. To be effective in our ministry for Christ, we must have, in his words, "a spiritual pitch." He illustrated his remarks by telling how several well-known Christians had their own special pitch. He spoke of a famous minister who always said basically the same thing; no matter what the problem, his emphasis was the same. He told of a woman, an outstanding Christian leader, who always prescribed the same spiritual solution for whatever problem was presented. He cited successful evangelists who always preached the same basic message under different titles. Then he zeroed in on me and said, "Bill Bright, who works with students and professors and outstanding business executives, as well as with prisoners and men on Skid Row, thinks that he has a special message for each of them. But the fact of the

matter is, though I have never heard him speak or counsel, I would be willing to wager that he has only one
pitch. Basically, he tells them all the same thing." To say
that I objected to such a suggestion is to put it mildly.
The very thought that a man needed to resort to what I
considered Madison Avenue techniques to do the
spiritual work of God was repugnant and offensive to
me.

The longer he spoke, the more distressed I became. I
resented anyone suggesting that I or anyone else who
truly desired to serve the Lord had to depend on gim-
micks, or that we were not led of the Spirit in such a
way that the Holy Spirit was able to be original through
us to the various individuals with whom we worked,
according to their various needs. Furthermore, I resented
his using me as an example before the rest of the staff.

So, when it was all over, and I was licking my wounds
(the most serious of which was a lacerated ego), I began
to reflect on exactly what I shared with the various ones
with whom I worked, young or old, management or
labor, Episcopalian or Baptist, students or professors, or
the men in jails or on Skid Row. That afternoon, I wrote
down my basic presentation and, to my amazement, my
friend was right. I had been sharing fundamentally the
same thing with everyone without realizing it!

God's Plan

What I wrote that afternoon (and later polished) is
now known as "God's Plan for Your Life," from which I
later wrote "The Four Spiritual Laws." I asked each staff
member to memorize it. We all began to share this presentation in personal interviews and in various team meetings on the college campus. Because of this one type of
presentation alone, our ministry was multiplied a hundredfold during the next year.

For those who are not familiar with God's Plan, I
should explain that it is a positive, 20-minute presenta-

tion of the claims of Christ: who He is, why He came and how one can know Him personally. It does not contain any startling new truths. It is a simple statement of the gospel. However, God has used its presentation by our staff, in the power and control of the Holy Spirit, to draw countless thousands more to Himself.

God's Plan was our first written how-to evangelistic material. The how-to approach spells out the specific steps involved in a concept or activity of the Christian walk. There has been a tendency in certain academic and theological circles to play down the simple approach to living the Christian life and sharing our faith with others. "Such an approach is simplistic and anti-intellectual," some have said. It required several years and considerable front-line spiritual combat experience in my work with students, professors and laymen, for certain great concepts to begin to come into focus. The longer I worked with the intelligentsia, the more I realized the necessity of developing simple how-to's for the Christian life.

Need for How-to's

For five years, shortly after I became a Christian, from 1946 to 1951, I studied in two theological seminaries under some of the greatest scholars of the Christian world, to whom I shall always be indebted. I learned many things about the Christian life. But like many other seminarians — and other Christians, for that matter — I was unable to put together the pieces of the spiritual jigsaw puzzle. I did not know the how-to's of the Christian life.

As Campus Crusade grew and how-to materials were developed, we found that the 20th century counterpart of "the masses who heard Jesus gladly" responds with great joy and enthusiasm to our presentation of certain how-to's (or "transferable concepts").

Four Spiritual Laws

Though we had found the 20-minute presentation of God's Plan to be extremely effective, we realized that we needed a much shorter version of the gospel in order to communicate quickly, clearly and simply to those whose hearts were already prepared to receive Christ. I prepared a condensed outline of God's Plan, complete with Scripture verses and diagrams and asked the staff to memorize it. For several years, we wrote it out as we were sharing Christ in witnessing experiences. Then, as more and more people became involved in the training program of Campus Crusade, it became apparent that we needed to make the Four Spriritual Laws presentation available in printed form to insure faithfulness to the content and uniformity of presentation. Thus, the booklet was born.

As the name suggests, there are four basic truths to the Four Spiritual Laws: (1) God loves you and offers a wonderful plan for your life. (2) Man is sinful and separated from God, thus he cannot know and experience God's love and plan for his life. (3) Jesus Christ is God's only provision for man's sin. Through Him you can know and experience God's love and plan for your life. (4) We must individually receive Jesus Christ as Savior and Lord; then we can know and experience God's love and plan for our lives.

Originally our first law emphasized man's sin. but the Lord impressed me to emphasize God's love. This change was made just before we went to press. I had done my final editing and had left Vonette and the girls to finish the typing. As I had been traveling a great deal and it was quite late, I had gone upstairs to bed. In fact, I was in bed just at the point of going to sleep, when suddenly there came clear as a bell to my conscious mind the fact that there was something wrong about starting the Four Laws on the negative note of man's sinfulness.

Last-minute Revision

Why not start where God starts, with His love? I had been drawn to Christ originally because I was overwhelmed with God's love. The love of God had been the basis for my presentation of the gospel ever since I had become a Christian. I wanted everyone to know how much God loves him and that God offers a wonderful plan for the life of everyone who will accept His plan. I felt that few people would say "No" to Christ if they truly understood how much He loves them and how great is His concern for them.

So, I got out of bed, went to the head of the stairs and called down to Vonette and the girls to revise the presentation so that the first law would be, "God loves you and has a wonderful plan for your life," instead of "You are a sinner and separated from God." We moved the statement of the fact of man's sin and separation from God, making it Law Two. Thus, the Four Spiritual Laws started with the positive note of God's love and plan.

Some time later, one of the girls said to me, "I was so distressed over your change in the presentation that I wept that night. I was afraid that you were beginning to dilute the gospel and that you were no longer faithful to the Lord, because you placed such a strong emphasis on the love of God rather than on man's sin. Now in retrospect, I realize of course that this is one of the greatest things that has ever happened to the Campus Crusade ministry." Now many millions of people all over the world are being told, through the presentation of the Four Spiritual Laws, that God loves them and offers a wonderful plan for their lives. At last count, more than 250 million copies have been printed in 100 major languages of the world. It is believed that many millions have received Christ as a result of the Four Spiritual Laws.

Each of these four laws is illustrated by portions of Scripture and diagrams. We have discovered that most people believe the first three laws. However, many people need counsel and assistance in regard to the fourth law. Though most people believe that Jesus Christ is the Son of God and realize their need of Him as Savior, they do not know what to do about it. So, the simple presentation of the Four Spiritual Laws helps honest inquirers, which most people are, to know what to do.

Impact of the Booklet

This little booklet is so simple that one marvels at its effectiveness. I could tell hundreds of stories — thrilling stories — of how God has used it to reach people who have not responded to previous presentations. I think, for example, of an assistant minister whose senior pastor had come to Arrowhead Springs for training. The senior pastor was very excited about the Four Spiritual Laws presentation. He went back to share his enthusiasm with his church and with his assistant minister.

The assistant minister was turned off by the Four Spiritual Laws booklet. He had a dislike for tracts, and this looked like just another tract to him. He tossed the booklet aside on his desk.

A few days later a woman who was a city official came by to inspect the facilities of the church plant. As the woman was about to leave following the inspection tour, it suddenly occurred to the man that he had not talked to her about Christ. He looked around quickly, and the only thing he saw was this little Four Spiritual Laws booklet, which he had tossed aside in disgust some days previously and had not bothered to read. He reached for the booklet to give it to her, as the pastor had suggested, thinking it would certainly not do her any harm.

"Read this," he said, meaning that she should read it when she got home. She misunderstood, however, and began to read it aloud in his presence. She read every word, and by the time she got through Laws One, Two and Three and began to read Law Four, tears were streaming down her cheeks. She came to the prayer and prayed aloud, leading herself to Christ.

By this time, the assistant was so overwhelmed that he vowed to go to Arrowhead Springs and to find out for himself how he could use the Four Spiritual Laws. He decided that it was far more effective than anything or any other method he had ever employed.

The Town Atheist

A missionary friend in Japan shared a heartwarming experience of his use of the Four Spiritual Laws. There was a man who was greatly admired in his home town, though he was not a Christian. In fact, he was known as the town atheist. Whenever there was any kind of evangelistic meeting in his city, the pastors, evangelists and laymen would "witness" to him, but he would never respond. My missionary friend, whose parents had been befriended by this man, felt indebted to him and was also concerned for his soul. After obtaining a Four Spiritual Laws booklet, the missionary decided to call on his friend and read it to him.

As he finished reading, he asked, "Does this make sense?"

The atheist replied in the affirmative.

"Is there anything that would keep you from receiving Christ?"

"No," was the reply.

The two men knelt together and prayed, and the "atheist" invited Jesus into his life. When they arose, my friend was rejoicing with the man, who then stunned him with this question, "Chuck, is this what you and all the other Christian leaders have been trying to tell me for years?"

When my missionary friend nodded affirmatively, the man continued, "Well, why didn't you tell me? Any man would be a fool not to receive Christ if he really understood what is involved."

Obviously, others had been trying to communicate the gospel but had been unsuccessful. The Four Spiritual Laws presentation had cut right through the barrier of skepticism and indifference so that the professing atheist got the message.

We have found that the average person does not need to be convinced that he should become a Christian; he needs, rather, to be told how to become a Christian. I should hasten to explain that it is the Holy Spirit who uses this presentation as He empowers the one giving the witness and enlightens the one who hears and responds.

There is no magic in the Four Spiritual Laws booklet. God blesses its use because it contains the distilled essence of the gospel, especially when it is used by men and women who are controlled and empowered by the Holy Spirit.

Being Filled With the Spirit

The second most important how-to in our training explains how to be filled, controlled and empowered by the Holy Spirit. Like many other sincere seekers after the "deep things of God," I had sought for many years to understand the Person and work of the Holy Spirit. For many days at a time, I had fasted and prayed in my attempt to discover new depths of meaning in my Christian experience. Though I had on numerous occasions enjoyed a wonderful fellowship with the Lord and even had several experiences when I knew the Holy Spirit had touched my life and used me, I knew nothing of how to appropriate the fullness and power of the Holy Spirit by faith, nor of how to live under His control. I made a special study of the Person and work of the Holy

Spirit, which included almost every book on the subject on which I could lay my hands. I was hungry for all that God had for me. I longed to be a man of God, whatever the cost, and I knew that this desire could be fulfilled only through the ministry of the Holy Spirit in my life.

One summer in the early years of the Campus Crusade ministry, Vonette and I were invited to spend a few days in the Newport Beach home of Dr. and Mrs. Charles Fuller. Dr. Fuller, a famous evangelist, conducted the "Old Fashioned Revival Hour" on the radio and was the founder of Fuller Theological Seminary. He and his family were very dear to us, and we accepted the invitation gratefully. Vonette and I were both very tired. Our schedule had been extremely busy and crowded, with no vacation for several years, and we could think of nothing more inviting than having a few days to sleep, lie in the sun and swim in the ocean. The midnight hour had come and gone by the time we had arrived and unpacked. Some time near one o'clock in the morning we wearily climbed into bed and fully expected to be asleep by the time the light was out.

Midnight Revelation

But God had other plans. As I turned over to go to sleep, I found my mind flooded with truths concerning the Holy Spirit. Fearful that I might forget them if I didn't write them down, I got up to look for pencil and paper and found several shirt boards. After filling the shirt boards, I found some brown wrapping paper and continued to write furiously.

That night God gave me the truths concerning the Person and work of the Holy Spirit that have been basic to the ministry of Campus Crusade through the years. This material has now been incorporated into our Bible study course, Ten Basic Steps Toward Christian Maturity, and the Transferable Concepts, which are being used by many churches and various Christian organizations around the world.

This basic and revolutionary concept of how to be filled with the Holy Spirit has been condensed into a small booklet comparable to the Four Spiritual Laws presentation and entitled, "Have You Made the Wonderful Discovery of the Spirit-filled Life?" This Holy Spirit booklet has also been printed by the tens of millions and is being used by many thousands of Christians all over the world to help lead carnal Christians into an abundant and fruitful life in the Spirit as well as to help new Christians understand their spiritual heritage in Christ. Like the Four Laws, this brief presentation of the ministry of the Holy Spirit is having revolutionary results.

CHAPTER FIVE

Arrowhead — A Fabulous Dream

By 1960 our staff numbered 109, and we were serving Christ on 40 campuses in 15 states. Furthermore, we had established ourselves in Korea and Pakistan. We had also begun a weekly radio broadcast which was carried on several local stations without any cost to Campus Crusade.

It had long since become obvious that we had outgrown our facilities at Mound, Minn., and we had begun to intensify our search for a solution to our expansion problem. We knew that we must either build or purchase larger facilities in the Lake Minnetonka region, or find more adequate facilities elsewhere. It was then that word came from a long-time friend, George Rowan, president of the R. A. Rowan Company in Los Angeles, that the famous Arrowhead Springs Hotel and Spa which had been closed most of the time for four years was for sale at "a greatly reduced price."

I agreed to look at Arrowhead Springs in the foothills above San Bernardino, Calif., assuming that this beautiful hotel would have deteriorated considerably from the plush days when it was hosting some of the biggest names in the entertainment and business world. To my surprise, it was all in amazingly good condition. Except for a little peeling paint on the outside of the six-story building, there seemed to be little wrong with it. One could not haggle too much over a little paint!

"This is a fabulous place, and it would be an ideal headquarters and training center for us," I told George, "but I am sure that it is far beyond our means. What is the lowest price the owner would take?"

Two Million Dollar Price Tag

"He is asking two million, firm," George replied. I swallowed hard. This was an incredible amount for our organization, which had never had an extra dollar in its 10 years of existence. Now, even though we had expanded to the point that we had to have more and larger facilities, I could not truthfully conceive of any way that we could raise the kind of money that would be needed to make such a large purchase.

The two million dollar figure was a good one — only a fraction of the property's true worth. It had been appraised at $6,700,000. The beds were even made; spare linens were in the closets; china, silverware and cooking utensils (about $450,000 in inventory) were ready and waiting for guests. "All we would have to do would be to move in," I thought. The place didn't look as though it had been closed most of the time for four years.

Meanwhile, I did a little research and learned several interesting things about the famous resort. For example, I learned that various Indian tribes had come to this spot through centuries, bringing their sick and wounded for healing in the natural hot mineral springs. They called the place "holy land," and all weapons of warfare were laid aside here.

The first hotel and spa was built on the property in 1854 by Dr. David Noble Smith and was widely advertised as a health resort. When the original hotel was destroyed by fire, two others followed.

They too, in turn, were destroyed by fire, and the present structure of concrete and steel was built in 1939, financed by a group of Hollywood film stars. It opened in December of that year. Present for the gala opening were some of the biggest names in Hollywood and the business world. Rudy Vallee, Al Jolson and Judy Garland entertained on that first night.

Arrowhead Springs became a popular retreat for the

movie colony and for top executives in the business world. Only a short distance from the heart of Los Angeles, world-famous movie stars streamed toward Arrowhead Springs for relaxation and revelry.

White Elephant

However, when transportation developed to the point that the stars could easily travel further afield, they were attracted to Las Vegas and Palm Springs, and Arrowhead Springs turned into something of a white elephant. Several different owners tried to restore the property to the status it had once enjoyed but without noticeable success. Finally, Benjamin Swig, owner of the Fairmont Hotel in San Francisco and the historic Mission Inn in Riverside, Calif., acquired it from the Hilton Foundation. He operated it briefly before concluding, as had his predecessors, that it had limited profit potential, and then he closed it down. Though different groups tried to purchase it from Mr. Swig, and one or two parties used it for a brief time, it was closed more than it was open during the approximately four years before my visit.

I was immediately enchanted by the remoteness and beauty of the property. Following a winding road into the hills above San Bernardino, I was reeling with the grandeur of this famous place before I ever stepped out of Mr. Rowan's automobile. I was even more impressed as I walked about the spacious grounds and examined the many buildings.

Below me, a couple of miles away, spread the populated valley, feverishly at work — industry clanging and pounding, cars and trucks rumbling in every direction. But all I could hear was the song of birds, the rustle of date palm leaves as the wind filtered gently through them and the sound of rushing water from a stream as it made its way from many artesian springs, tumbling wildly down over the rocks into Strawberry Canyon.

But even these sounds were muted. In a way, an

ethereal quality permeated the place, and more than once I found myself almost whispering to Mr. Rowan as we walked the grounds, 1,735 acres in all. There were 10 private bungalows, dormitory facilities for several hundred, an auditorium which could accommodate 700 people, a recreation house, four tennis courts, a stable, two big swimming pools and the 136-room, six-story, concrete and steel hotel. Without too much imagination, I could see as many as a thousand people here at one time. This was breathtaking in comparison to Mound, where approximately 150 people were all we could crowd in at one time, even with wall-to-wall people.

Talking With the Lord

Could this be the answer to our dilemma — our need for larger training facilities? I wondered. Constrained to be alone to talk with the Lord, I asked Mr. Rowan and the caretaker of Arrowhead to excuse me while I went into the hotel.

Past the unattended reception desk, through the empty lobby, out into the glass-enclosed Wahni Room I moved, the click of my shoes echoing as I walked. There was a shiny bar, empty of customers. Behind it the glasses were neatly stacked, awaiting business. The shelves, where a goodly supply of bottles once stood, were now empty. Tables and chairs were grouped in intimate clusters so that holiday visitors could look out on the city, which I could imagine would be a starry wonder at night. But it was broad daylight at that moment, and I had not come there for a drink or to see the panoramic view, but to share with the Lord the dream that was working overtime in my head.

Falling to my knees, I bowed my head and began praying and listening, "I am overwhelmed, Lord. This place is so big and beautiful. True, we've been asking You to direct us to new facilities, the best place in the country, and I know that You will; but if this is it, where will we get two million dollars to buy it? It seems too impossible to even consider. Yet I keep hearing in my heart Your voice, and it suggests that this is the place You have chosen for us. If it is, then You are going to have to make it crystal clear. How can I know for sure?"

Then, though not in an audible voice, God spoke to me as clearly as if there had been a public address system in the room. Unmistakably I heard Him say, "I have been saving this for Campus Crusade. I want you to have it, and I will supply the funds to pay for it."

With tears running down my face, I said, "God, I don't know how You intend to work this miracle, but I know You can, and I thank You for this gift. I claim this property in Your name."

CHAPTER SIX

Story of a Miracle

I came away from that memorable visit to Arrowhead Springs convinced that Campus Crusade would one day occupy those beautiful facilities. The impression that God wanted this facility for Campus Crusade was so real that almost every day I found myself expecting a telephone call from some person saying that he had heard about our interest in Arrowhead and that he would purchase it for us.

I felt certain the Lord did not want me to write letters inviting people to invest, believing instead that God had a plan already working. Vonette and I and other members of the Campus Crusade staff purposely limited our concern to prayer. For 14 months, we prayed that if God wanted us to have Arrowhead Springs, He would provide the funds in some supernatural or unusual way.

Increasingly, I knew that God wanted us to move to Arrowhead, though there was no tangible evidence of that fact. That is not to say that our faith never wavered. Sometimes the thought came, "What if someone else buys the property?" Then deep down in my heart I knew that it would eventually be ours. Still, I frequently prayed that God would not let us have Arrowhead Springs unless it was His perfect will for us. I well knew that unless this was truly God's will, to become involved in raising money for such a big project could well sabotage our spiritual ministry and destroy Campus Crusade in the process.

While we were praying, we were also working. Among other things, we did a feasibility study of the property, a careful cost analysis of what was involved in operating the grounds, figuring the cost of maintenance and repairs and the operation of the various facilities. After several weeks of careful analysis, various factors convinced us that if money could be raised for the capital investment, we could carry the load and operate in the black from the very beginning. The factors included such items as our office rental in Los Angeles, our expenses for the various training conference grounds which we rented from time to time, and the fact that the headquarters staff would be living on the Arrowhead Springs campus and thus would pay rent there. Our conviction was strengthened by a dedicated staff willing to work long hours and without thought of personal remuneration or glory.

Negotiations Begin

Then it happened. The telephone rang. Henry Hanson, the father of two students who had been influenced for Christ through our ministry, was on the line. Through him negotiations were begun with the owner, Benjamin Swig. Mr. Swig proved to be most cooperative, helpful and generous.

Though we had not asked for financial help from our supporters during the 14 months of waiting and praying, I now felt, after my conversation with Mr. Swig, that the Lord wanted me to share this opportunity with some of my close friends. Outstandingly successful men who were also dedicated to Christ and vitally interested in the ministry of Campus Crusade came to look over the property and talk with me. Many of our close friends, however, were far from being of one mind concerning the wisdom of making the purchase. Some were convinced that it would be a foolhardy move and poor stewardship of the Lord's money, while others believed that Campus Crusade needed training facilities such as Arrowhead Springs would supply. On the basis of God's previous blessing on the ministry, this was another opportunity for us to trust Him for even greater things. A few individuals supported their convictions with offers to help make the down payment.

Property Purchased

After careful and prayerful consideration of loans and gifts, the board of directors, acting upon the advice of these men who were interested in helping us, advised us to make an offer to Mr. Swig. The offer was a $15,000 deposit toward a two million dollar purchase price, with an additional $130,000 to be paid within 30 days after we signed the contract. Amazingly, the offer was accepted. With an empty bank book we were buying a two million dollar property! It was the greatest act of faith I had ever seen or in which I had ever had a part. We borrowed the $15,000 needed for the deposit, and on the weekend of December 1, 1962, Campus Crusade for Christ International moved from its Westwood headquarters in Los Angeles to Arrowhead Springs.

We still did not have the necessary $130,000 for the next payment, but several friends had agreed to help and, interpreting this as God's will, we took the first step by advancing the $15,000 as a deposit. Thirty days later at the last minute an additional $130,000 had been given by interested friends. I dashed off to San Francisco to see Mr. Swig and make the payment to consummate the purchase. The monthly payment schedule was a very stiff one, and there followed a series of financial cliff-hanging experiences that forced us to depend wholly upon the Lord. Every financial move was a precarious one for months — indeed, for several years. God used the faith, work and prayer of a dedicated staff to make Arrowhead Springs possible.

Lives Transformed

From the start, God blessed and used the headquarters in a spiritual way that surpassed all our expectations. Hundreds of young men and women, and adults as well, came to Arrowhead for training that first year, and their lives were transformed. We had the assurance that the day would come when God would send a thousand people per week to Arrowhead Springs for training. That goal was soon exceeded, and so many staff, students and laymen began to respond to our training that scores of conferences are now held each year not only at Arrowhead but also on university campuses, in conference facilities and in hotels across America.

The decision to acquire Arrowhead Springs as our international headquarters and institute for evangelism for our worldwide ministry was to be one of the most significant ones that we had ever made.

When Arlis Priest, outstanding Phoenix businessman, visited Arrowhead prior to its purchase, he volunteered, "If God should make this property available to you, I would like to give my services for one year without salary to help you get the headquarters operating efficiently." His life had been greatly affected in one of our day-long institutes in Phoenix, and this was his way of thanking us. Imagine his surprise a few weeks later when I took him up on the offer. "How soon can you come?" I asked over the phone. "We are now ready to move to Arrowhead Springs, and we need a manager."

"I'll call you back later today and give you an answer," he said. Within a matter of days he was with us; God used him mightily to help organize the offices and get the long-closed facilities operating efficiently. I do not know how we would have done it without him and his lovely wife, Nadine, who was not only a great help herself but also was willing for Arlis to work day and night to help us get into operation. The dedication of the entire headquarters staff was a joy to behold. A normal day ran 10, 12, 15 hours — all with a joyful spirit — as we all were responsible for many different jobs.

Dedication Service

May 17, 1963, found several hundred friends of Campus Crusade gathered for our dedication of Arrowhead Springs as our international headquarters and conference center. Dr. Walter Judd brought the dedication address, which was one of his characteristically inspiring and challenging messages. The mayor and many outstanding local officials were present. The mayor stated, "The finest thing that has ever happened to the city of San Bernardino is the coming of Campus Crusade for Christ to Arrowhead Springs." Participating in the program were Dr. Bob Pierce, president of World Vision; Dr. Dick Hillis, president of Overseas Crusade; the Rev. Armin Gesswein, director of Pastors' Revival Fellowship; Dr. Walter Smyth, vice-president of the Billy Graham Evangelistic Association; Dr. Carlton Booth, professor of evangelism, Fuller Theological Seminary; Dr. Roger Voskyle, president of Westmont College; and Dr. John MacArthur, Sr., leading evangelist and radio pastor.

Also present at the dedication service that day were Mr. and Mrs. Guy F. Atkinson. Mr. Atkinson was one of the world's leading builders of roads, dams, bridges and other multimillion dollar construction projects. He was then 89 years of age — sharp, alert and very astute — and had come primarily to hear Dr. Judd. He inquired what we planned to do with the property and asked more questions about the ministry of Campus Crusade at Arrowhead Springs than any group of people had ever asked me in its history.

Some months later he expressed interest in helping, but before he did anything he wanted to send his attorney to look over our financial records and our corporation structure, including the bylaws. Of course we were very happy to have him do this. After several days of careful study of the organizational structure, policies and financial records by himself and his attorney, Mr. Atkinson announced that he would like to give $300,000 if we would raise the balance of the then $1,570,000 still due on the two million dollar purchase. This was an exciting challenge. He gave us exactly one year to raise that amount, and we set forth with great enthusiasm and determination to raise a sum so great that I could hardly even comprehend the amount. It might as well have been a billion dollars. Yet, we were confident that God would help us.

Slow Progress

With the passing of the months, however, it seemed that we were not going to be able to reach our goal of $1,570,000 to qualify for Mr. Atkinson's $300,000 pledge. We had an additional challenge of an offer from Mr. Swig to discount $100,000 from the balance due, plus a savings of $120,000 in interest. All this meant, with Mr. Atkinson's pledge of $300,000, a total gift and savings of $520,000. But we were becoming aware of the fact that we were faced with an impossible task. We asked Mr. Atkinson if he would still be willing to pledge his $300,000 if we raised part of the balance by selling some of the land. He agreed to do this with the understanding that we would not sell more than 400 acres of our 1,735-acre total.

Arlis Priest and I had interested a group of 20 laymen in the idea of purchasing one million dollars worth of our land from us. It was estimated that by selling approximately 400 acres we could raise that amount. When Mr. Atkinson agreed that we could sell one million dollars worth of land and raise the balance through gifts, we took new courage and approached the deadline of June 30, 1965, with confidence. In the meantime, we were devoting considerable time to contacting potential contributors in an attempt to raise the balance.

In spite of the additional encouragement, we found that we would still fall short of the amount needed. I had made a commitment to the Lord that I would not

allow Arrowhead Springs or the raising of funds to inter-
fere with my spiritual ministry or the ministries of any
of our campus staff. In fact, none of the field staff were
ever asked to become involved in raising funds at any
time, because we felt that it was a tangible expression
of our trust in the Lord to put our spiritual ministry first.
We were confident that if we sought first the kingdom
of God, the Lord would meet our financial needs.

One Week Left

Thus, in the last week prior to the deadline, I found
myself speaking at very important conferences several
times a day and unable to make any significant contribu-
tion to the raising of funds. Dr. Raymond V. Edman,
president of Wheaton College, came to speak for an
educators' conference at the same time a Campus
Crusade student conference was in session. He shared
with Vonette and me a very meaningful verse that God
had given him that morning while he was praying for
our needs. The verse was especially appropriate: "He
that putteth his trust in Me shall possess the land, and
shall inherit My holy mountain" (Isaiah 57:13). We will
always be grateful to Dr. Edman for his special concern
and prayers for us during those urgent days of crisis, as
well as for the great ministry of his life and witness with
us.

On the evening of the deadline, I met with Arlis
Priest, just before I was to bring a message to the conference then in session. He informed me that we still needed
$33,000 and that every possible source of revenue had
been exhausted. There was nothing more, humanly
speaking, that we could do. After the completion of my
message at about 9 in the evening, I inquired again as
to our progress. Though several members of the staff
were gathering and praying, working and hoping, the
situation remained unchanged. I assumed that there was
nothing more I could do personally so I went to our

cottage, too weary to give further thought to the matter.

Deadline Approaches

I was dressing for bed when Vonette returned with the boys from a youth meeting. "All of the money must be in or you wouldn't be going to bed," she said.

I told her that was not the case, adding, "I've done all I know to do. I will have to leave the rest in the Lord's hands."

"Honey, I have never seen you give up so easily," Vonette said.

"If the miracle is going to happen, the Lord will have to do it right away," I replied.

It was then about 10 p.m., and we had two hours to go before the deadline. We had been praying for months, but as Vonette and I now knelt with our two sons, Zachary and Bradley, we prayed with a new urgency. I prayed first, then Vonette and then Zac. But it was Brad's prayer that I remember. He was only seven years old, but he spoke to the heart of the matter. "Lord, we need this money, and we ask You to send it right away."

After all of us had prayed and the boys had gone to bed, I reached for my Bible to read before turning out the light. As I did so, I saw a scrap of paper I had brought home from my office. It had memos on both sides. I had read only one side; now I saw the other side. There was a telephone number on it. Gerri von Frellick had called me the day before and had asked me to call him back. I had failed to get the message.

More Help

I checked my watch and by now it was 10:30, which meant that it was about 11:30 at his home in Denver, Colo. I debated whether I should return his call at such a late hour. "Maybe Gerri wants to help," Vonette suggested. I finally decided to call him even though it was very late. He answered the phone sleepily, and I apologized for waking him up. "How are you getting along with your fund-raising campaign?" he asked.

I told him that we had an hour and 30 minutes to go and still lacked $33,000. He said that he wanted to send us $5,000 if it would help us meet our goal and would send it the next morning. Gerri had already given generously when we first moved to Arrowhead Springs; now he was giving again. This, of course, was encouraging, and yet at that point I did not think that $5,000 was going to make much difference, but I thanked him warmly and hung up. "You were right, Vonette," I said. "He did have some money for us. Now we need only $28,000."

Property Offered

Suddenly it occurred to me that a month or so before, a businessman in Arizona had given us a piece of property not far from Denver, for which we had been offered $17,000 by a local attorney. If he would pay us $20,000 for the property, that would reduce the balance to only $8,000, and there was still a possibility that we could meet that amount. The more I thought about it the more excited I became, so I placed the call to the attorney in Colorado, who I realized was also probably in bed asleep.

Shortly the attorney was on the line. I reminded him that a month ago he had offered $17,000 for the property and that we would be willing, because of a particular need, to take $22,000 for it. He countered with $18,000 and said he would wire it the next morning. I accepted his offer. Now we were within $10,000 of our goal.

I called the switchboard at the hotel and reported the good news. I heard a big cheer when staff and friends who were waiting prayerfully and expectantly learned we were within sight of our goal.

In the meantime, members of our staff were gathered in the lobby of the hotel, praying and giving generously of their own limited funds — not because they were asked, but because they were impressed by the Lord to do so. Arlis Priest recalls that dramatic evening: "It was getting late. Nadine and I were both in bed when some of the staff began to knock at our door. This happened several times. Each time some staff member would hand me an envelope with money in it. The first few I looked at were $25, $200 and $250. A peace came over me, for I knew God was doing something special. These dedicated staff members who had hardly enough money to live on were giving the widow's mite."

Final Minutes

With less than 30 minutes before the deadline, we had $10,000 more to raise. We were all getting increasingly excited. Surely God was going to answer our prayers and meet our need.

About 15 minutes before midnight, Dr. Walter Judd, who had come to Arrowhead Springs to address one of our conferences, returned from speaking at a local medical association meeting and called to inquire as to the progress toward our goal. "Have Bill call me," he told the switchboard operator.

When I called, he said that he would like to give the last $5,000, and I should call him back if his money was needed. In the meantime, Vonette (her mind working overtime) reminded me that Al Curtis, our business manager, at my request, had put aside some months previously a $5,000 gift from Mr. Atkinson, money which had been given to be used wherever we felt it was most needed. We had agreed then that the money should be held for this very deadline in case of need. Yet, at the moment I had temporarily forgotten about it. I called Al, who had just returned to Arrowhead from Los Angeles and a futile attempt to raise funds. He verified the fact that we had $5,000. "Get it ready," I told him.

This meant that we only needed Dr. Judd's gift of

$5,000. At two minutes till midnight and our deadline, I called him to make sure that I had understood his offer. "I will pledge that amount," he repeated, and a minute later I called the hotel lobby and an anxious, waiting staff to announce that God had worked another miracle.

By this time Vonette and I and the members of the staff were so excited and filled with gratitude to the Lord that we decided to meet immediately in the International Theater to thank Him for this miracle. We quickly dressed and rushed to the hotel. The International Theater was packed to overflowing with grateful staff and friends.

For the next couple of hours we sang and worshipped the Lord. The office girls, some of them in pajamas and housecoats with their hair in rollers; faculty, who were there for an educators' conference; and other workers all came together. It was a beautiful experience, one of the highlights of my spiritual life. Never have I heard the doxology sung with such vigor. Never did the lyrics, "Praise God from whom all blessings flow. . ." hold so much meaning.

CHAPTER SEVEN

The Trial of Faith

The good news of what God had done had to be told. I could hardly wait to inform all of our friends of the miracle God had performed. Soon a letter was dispatched to thousands on our mailing list and to personal friends and supporters, telling them that the deadline had been met and that Campus Crusade had been able to pay off the total indebtedness against the Arrowhead Springs property. In part I wrote:

> Rejoice and give thanks to the Lord with us. The miracle has happened! God has answered prayer! Exactly two minutes before the June 30 deadline, at 11:58 p.m., the goal of $1,570,000 was reached which qualified us for a $300,000 pledge, and the future of Arrowhead Springs as our International Headquarters and International Institute of Evangelism was assured (sale of the land involved in the transaction is to be consummated in approximately sixty days). The details of how it happened are far more dramatic than words could ever describe. We had prayed that God would provide the needed finances in such a way that the end result would cause all men to acknowledge His supernatural provision and that all honor, glory and praise would go to Him. God has answered this prayer, for no man could have planned the final days prior to the deadline as exciting, dramatic and fruitful as He had arranged them . . .

The letter was sent, and calls and letters of congratulations came back from all over the country.

Disturbing Development

But the story was not ended. Ten days later the appraisers announced that the acreage required for the one million dollar sale of the property was approximately 120 acres more than we had thought would be needed. The 20 friends who had agreed to purchase the land were going to borrow the one million dollars from an insurance company, purchase the land and later sell or develop it and give any profits to Campus Crusade. But to borrow that amount, it was necessary for the value of the land to be at least double the amount of the loan, which meant that two million dollars worth of land had to be made available to the men to secure a one million dollar loan.

When I informed Mr. Atkinson of these developments, he was disturbed. He said he wanted to see me immediately. When he arrived from his La Canada home, he reminded me, as we sat in my office, that his original agreement called for our raising in contributions and pledges the entire amount of $1,570,000 to match his contribution of $300,000 in cash. When it was discovered that we were not going to be able to raise that amount, he had agreed to our selling 400 acres of land.

"I remember when land in nearby Orange County was selling for a few dollars an acre and some of it is now selling for as much as $50,000 an acre," he said. "You would be foolish to sell at this price. Whatever you do, don't sell it. And if you do, I withdraw my pledge of $300,000." I realized that Mr. Atkinson, because of his warm friendship and interest in the ministry, was seeking to prevent us from making an unwise move. Nevertheless, this was a crushing blow, and as I took him from my office to his car, I could hardly wait to get back to my office before my emotions took charge. Back in my office, I closed the door behind me, fell on my knees and wept.

Crumbled Dreams

The miracle had become a mirage. All of our hopes and dreams had suddenly crumbled. In the attempt to meet the challenge of Mr. Atkinson's pledge, all of our fund-raising efforts were designed to raise the money for this project. Now, since we had failed to meet this goal, we were in an impossible position financially. Not only could we not write off the debt, but also we would actually lose the property unless God intervened immediately. This possibility seemed rather remote in those bleak moments of discouragement. Furthermore, I would have to write the thousands of friends who had read only a few days before that God had worked a miracle and tell them that there had been no miracle at all. There was personal humiliation involved, of course. But worse than that, the cause of Christ would suffer, and many Christians would be confused.

What was I to do? I got out my Bible and looked for help and assurance. We are admonished and assured, "God causes all things to work together for good to those who love God, to those who are called according to His purpose" (Romans 8:28). I read, "Without faith it is impossible to please Him" (Hebrews 11:26), and "The righteous man shall live by faith" (Galatians 3:11). I read a command from God which I had discovered some years before and which on various occasions had proved very meaningful to me: "In everything give thanks; for this is God's will for you in Christ Jesus" (1 Thessalonians 5:18).

"Thank You"

Since the righteous are to live by faith and since "all things work together for good to those who love God," I didn't know of a better way to demonstrate faith than to say, "Thank You." So I got back down on my knees and thanked God for what had happened. I thanked Him through my tears. I thanked Him that in His wisdom and love He knew better than I what should be done and that out of this chaos and uncertainty I knew would come a far greater miracle. There on my knees while I was giving thanks for this great disappointment, God began to give me the genuine assurance that this greater miracle really was going to happen.

Even so, the next day I began drafting the letter that

would inform our friends that "our miracle" had been only a mirage. For some reason, however, I felt strongly impressed to delay mailing the letter.

Saving the Land

A week passed. Ten days. Then Mr. Atkinson called and said that he would like to see me again. He said he had been talking to Arlis Priest and had an idea he thought might solve our problem. As soon as he arrived at Arrowhead Springs, he came directly to my office. "I would like to suggest," he said, "that Campus Crusade borrow the money as an organization from the same insurance company that had offered to loan the money to the original 20 men. Then we should invite the men who had originally agreed to purchase the land to sign the notes as guarantors. If you like this idea, I will still give Campus Crusade the $300,000 originally pledged."

I was overjoyed at his offer. This meant that we would not have to sell our prized land, which we would one day no doubt need because of our rapidly expanding training program. The 20 men agreed to this new arrangement, for they had no interest at all in promoting their own financial gain, and they signed the note. Jess Odom, the president of the insurance company, a wonderful Christian and good friend of Campus Crusade, approved the loan at the lowest legal interest rate allowable.

The second miracle proved to be greater than the first. We still saved a large portion of the interest. Mr. Swig generously discounted his note $75,000 instead of $100,000 as he had originally offered because of the lapse of time which now had taken place. So I tore up the letter of apology to our friends and supporters and in its place sent another explaining all that God had done.

I shall be forever grateful to the Lord for Mr. and Mrs. Atkinson and for their encouragement in so many ways. After Mr. Atkinson went to be with the Lord, memorial gifts from his family and friends were used to build the beautiful Guy F. Atkinson Memorial Chapel at Arrowhead Springs which has been dedicated to his memory.

Prior to and following the purchase of Arrowhead Springs, it has been our prayer that everything God would do through Campus Crusade and through our own personal lives would be characterized by the supernatural and the miraculous. We have asked Him to do things in such an unusual and wonderful way that men would have to say that He was responsible, and that they would give the glory to Him instead of to man. God has answered that prayer on many occasions.

Exhausted Water Supply

A few months after our arrival, we faced a particular crisis that demanded a miracle. I received a call early one morning from Arlis Priest, stating that our large water reservoir was exhausted, that the water had disappeared mysteriously overnight, and that now, with a large staff and student group of 450 gathered for several weeks of training, there was absolutely no water for them. When we purchased the property we had been assured that there was plenty of water, but now we discovered that there was not enough water, at least not for us. This was one of the greatest of all the crises that had arisen for us at Arrowhead Springs.

The students and staff had paid thousands of dollars to come from far distances to be present for the training, and now our only alternative would be to send them home unless God worked a miracle to supply water. To return the students' money would be financially disastrous, for we had actually anticipated the revenue of the summer in making preparations for their coming. The maintenance and repairs for the facilities and the purchase of food took all the money; there was none left with which to reimburse them. Once again we were faced with the kind of crisis that could have meant the loss of this property and quite possibly the destruction of this ministry.

My first impulse was to panic; then, remembering again the admonition to give thanks in all things as an expression of faith, I fell on my knees, saying, "Lord, thank You for this crisis. I thank You that You will again demonstrate Your power and wisdom in our behalf."

While on my knees, I felt impressed to call George Rowan, who in drilling for steam had discovered large quantities of hot water on the property, and to ask him if he had any idea of how we could convert the hot water well into drinking water. We had not used any of the hot water from the big well because we had been told that a cooling tower would cost at least $20,000; and since we didn't have even $20 extra, this expense was far beyond our capabilities.

George informed me that he did not know how to cool the water but that he would check immediately with a friend of his, the president of a large geothermal corporation, who very likely could give us the information we needed.

Cooling Tower

Within a matter of a few minutes, his friend called me and told me over the telephone how a simple, inexpensive wooden cooling tower could be built. With the most rudimentary blueprint in hand, I rushed to the maintenance department and explained how the cooling tower could be built. Immediately, several staff members and a host of other volunteers, professionals and amateurs alike, began to work. By two the next morning, cool water was running through the tower. Again God had heard our prayers.

One of the most beautiful parts of the whole experience, however, was the attitude of the staff and students about the crisis. They gathered in meetings, large and small, to thank God as an expression of their faith for this crisis in obedience to the command of 1 Thessalonians 5:18. During the next 24 hours, a most remarkable spirit of cooperation and of cheerfulness pervaded the entire campus. Individuals were going to San Bernardino to buy small jugs of water and supplying their own needs and the needs of others. It was a beautiful experience of what happens to men who trust God and of how God honors faith. What better way to demonstrate faith than to thank God for whatever He does.

Growing Faith

But these have not been the only times of testing. Such times are still frequent and almost continuous. But faith is like a muscle; it grows with exercise. The more we know of the trustworthiness and faithfulness of God, His grace, love, power and wisdom, the more we can trust Him. I think of my own faith; how, in the beginning years of the ministry, I could believe God for a few dollars and, on occasion, a few hundred. More recently I have been asking God for millions.

For example, early in the ministry I discovered one day that we had an urgent need for $485. It was a Saturday morning, and I was alone in the office. I was on my knees praying for this $485 when the mailman came knocking on the door with a registered letter. I reached the door just as he was leaving, and he said, "It's a good thing you were here, or I wouldn't have been able to leave this letter." I signed for it, went back into my office to pray, but decided I would open the letter first. Inside, I discovered a bank note for $500 sent by a friend from far off Zurich, Switzerland, whose entire family had become Christians through our ministry.

Need for $48,000

At another time, an additional $48,000 was desperately needed to meet one of our annual payments on the loan. This kind of money does not come easily. We had prayed much and worked hard to raise the money but to no avail. Our deadline was only days away when a lawyer friend who knew of our need introduced me to a friend who agreed to loan the amount needed for 60 days. I was in the lawyer's office ready to sign the necessary papers when my office called to tell me that Dean Griffith had called from Chicago and wanted me to contact him right away. Within minutes I reached him at his Chicago office. "I have been praying about your need for $48,000," he said, "and my father and I would like to send you a check for that amount today." Needless to say, I was grateful. As a matter of fact, I got down on my knees and thanked the Lord that He had answered our prayers, and then I went out to share with our friends the good news that the loan was no longer needed. I offered to pay for the costs and inconvenience involved, but my offer was refused.

The purchase of Arrowhead Springs was a giant leap of faith. This facility accommodated several times as many as could be housed at our training grounds on beautiful Lake Minnetonka in Minnesota. However, we soon found that it was not big enough. The first summer of 1963 found the big hotel and most of the other facilities filled, and by the second and third summers, we were overflowing during the summer peaks. By 1966, we knew we would have to expand our facilities. Projections indicated that we would one day be training many thousands each week during the summer months, and there was no place to train them, as present facilities were already taxed to capacity.

Facilities Expansion

What were we to do? I called together a group of outstanding businessmen, planners and builders for counsel. Norman Entwistle, our very able architect, drew up elaborate plans. One member of the board of directors agreed to chair an emergency fund-raising campaign called Operation Explosion. We needed large sums of money to provide these new facilities as well as to meet other emergency needs resulting from the rapid growth and expansion of the ministry. Warren Bradley, an outstanding Los Angeles building contractor and dedicated Christian, agreed to construct whatever facilities we chose to build without profit to himself or to his company. We were under the pressure of deadlines. If we did not start building at once, it would not be possible to complete construction in time for the summer invasion of thousands of students.

So it was decided by the committee and the board of directors, that, for emergency needs, we would build a simple, inexpensive board-and-batten frame construction with a tar paper roof. We soon discovered we were building in an area where fire insurance premiums would be extremely high, and upon the recommendation of Warren Bradley and his brother, Elmer, it was decided we would be well advised to build with slump stone and a tile roof. Norman Enwistle designed a beautiful complex of four dormitories and a dining-auditorium area that would accommodate a minimum of 480 and a maximum of 640, depending upon the number of people assigned to each room.

Though no funds were available for the construction of these buildings, the urgency of their completion was upon us, and after much prayer, we felt impressed to proceed with the building in the assurance that God would supply the funds to pay for their construction. The bulldozers had cleared the site, the foundations were being poured, and some of the walls were beginning to rise when a newcomer (who has since become a very good personal friend and strong supporter of Campus Crusade) appeared on the scene. He and Arlis Priest visited the building site, and as they surveyed the hustle and bustle of the busy scene with workmen rushing to and fro hastening the construction of these urgently needed buildings, my friend turned to Arlis and said, "Who is going to pay for these buildings?"

Funding the Program

Arlis said, "God impressed me to share this need with you."

Our friend dropped his head as if in silent prayer and meditation and then said, "I think I would like to be responsible to provide the funds for the building of these four dormitories. I need to talk with four of my associates and see if they are in agreement."

A short time later he came excitedly into my office to share his idea. He explained that he had been down to look over the site of the new Arrowhead Springs Village development and that he had felt impressed of the Lord to encourage his associates to join with him in paying for the project. "How much money will it take?" he inquired. "Approximately $550,000," I responded. "I think we can swing it," he said, "if we can work out a plan which will enable us to pay a certain amount each month over a period of years."

Soon he was on the telephone contacting his associates, and before long they were in unanimous agreement that this would be a good investment for the Lord's money which He had so graciously and so generously given them. They were being good stewards. Here they saw a chance to multiply their dollars a hundredfold so that the tens of thousands of men and women who would be trained in this beautiful new addition would join with them to help take the claims of Christ to the entire world.

Giving God the Glory

Later, I said to my friend, "What you are doing is such a challenging and inspiring example of Christian stewardship that I would like to prepare a plaque so that other friends of Campus Crusade will see what God has done through you and your associates. How would you like the plaque to read?"

Whereupon he responded, "My associates and I want to give God all the glory for the gracious way He has met our needs. Therefore, we would like the plaque to read. ARROWHEAD SPRINGS VILLAGE, DONATED BY FIVE BUSINESSMEN WHO WANT TO GIVE GOD ALL THE GLORY."

Later, a beautiful dining-auditorium building was constructed at a cost of $286,236, which amount our anonymous friends asked the Lord to enable them to underwrite as well. Thousands of students and laymen from as many as 50 countries have been trained to be disciples for the Lord Jesus Christ in these beautiful facilities.

This gift is a true example of Christian stewardship — an example to other Christians to "lay up . . . treasures in heaven, where neither moth nor rust destroys, and where thieves do not break in or steal" (Matthew 6:20).

CHAPTER EIGHT

Training: Repeating the Basics

I believe that there are three basic reasons why God has blessed the Campus Crusade ministry in such a phenomenal way: (1) dedication to exalting Jesus Christ and His cause in every circumstance; (2) a strong emphasis on the ministry of the Holy Spirit in the life of the believer; and (3) special, detailed, comprehensive training for every staff member, student and layman in how to live holy lives and share their faith in Christ with others.

The training ministry of Campus Crusade insures that the staff, students, laymen, pastors and all persons associated with the ministry receive adequate instruction in the various training programs in which they are involved. The instruction includes principles of Christian living, principles and methods of evangelism and follow-up, as well as biblical and theological training.

Importance of Repetition

In this ministry, a strong emphasis is placed on the basics, which are reviewed again and again without apology. Repetition is one of the major factors in learning.

Some time ago I had occasion to explain to our staff why we repeated the same basic messages and materials again and again as a part of our training. At the close of the meetings, one of our directors, a seminary graduate and former Presbyterian pastor, said, "I would like to share with you a good illustration to help support your emphasis on the necessity of repetition. Years ago I was a member of a good church where the pastor repeated the basic Christian doctrines several times each year, much to the benefit of us all. Recently, after nine years away, I returned for a visit and was encouraged to know that the pastor is continuing to preach and teach these same basic truths which made such an impact on my life.

"Later," he shared, "I was associated with a very scholarly minister who polished each message like a beautiful gem. He never spoke on the same subject twice. You will be interested to know that I could not tell you one thing I learned from this great, eloquent preacher, but much of what I know about Christ and the Bible I learned from my first pastor who believed in and practiced repetition."

Training Makes the Difference

We have discovered that when we truly train people, they are inspired to a height of dedication that one cannot possibly experience through inspiration alone. It is my strong conviction that true inspiration is the result of a very strong training program. From the inception of this ministry, our major thrusts have been to first build disciples and then, after training, to send them forth for Christ. Even in a conference in which a number of non-Christians are present, if the majority of those present are Christians, almost all of our messages are designed to build the Christian in the faith and challenge him to become a disciple. We train defeated, discouraged, unfruitful Christians to become spiritual, joyful, fruitful Christians, teaching them the difference between walking in their own power and walking in the power of the Spirit. We show them how to share their faith in Christ more effectively with others. The end result is that within a matter of a few hours after the carnal Christians have become spiritual Christians and have learned how to communicate their faith, they begin to share Christ with the non-believers at the conference or institute. Soon they, too, receive Christ. Thus, more people come to Christ through the awakened Christians than we could ever hope to reach for Christ through directing all of our messages toward non-Christians. Of course, the Christians are forever changed through their experience of introducing others to Christ.

These basics of training are repeated again and again in each of our ministries. But although our experience and tested methods are transferred to each kind of outreach, every ministry is also unique — with a special appeal to each unique group of people.

Initial Training Program

With this basic commitment to training and building disciples, Campus Crusade has first of all placed a strong emphasis on training the staff. We began this during the second year, when Vonette and I met with our six staff members at Forest Home and planned our training program for the coming year. There we began the preparation of materials for evangelism and follow-up. The second and third years our training program was held in the Campus Crusade lodge at Forest Home. Then we graduated to the beautiful campus of Westmont College. As the staff continued to grow, however, we found it necessary to secure still larger facilities, and in 1956, our training was conducted near the UCLA campus. Ultimately, of course, the training has been given at Arrowhead Springs, and now additional conference sites across the country are being utilized.

Our commitment to the necessity of training has led to the establishment of several effective programs, including:

Institute of Biblical Studies: This is a three-summer course of study, lasting four weeks each summer. The entire curriculum is centered on the Bible and has been developed to provide solid biblical training that will help to equip Christians for roles in spiritual leadership in a world of crisis.

Leadership Training Institute: Hundreds of week-long and weekend training sessions held around the world each year are designed to teach students how to experience a revolutionary Christian life and how to communicate it effectively to others in the power of the Holy Spirit.

Christian Living Seminar. Laymen are encouraged to become more vital and fruitful in their lives and witness for our Savior in their local churches, families, businesses and professions.

Through the years we have developed an entire series of how-to's or transferable concepts, which have helped to make this a dynamic ministry. These concepts contain the distilled essence of the Christian life. For example, our experience has proved that we can teach these transferable concepts in a very short period of time to any sincere Christian who wishes to know them.

A transferable concept is a truth that can be communicated to another, who, in turn, will communicate the same truth to another, generation after generation, without distorting or diluting the original truth. This is what the apostle Paul was saying to Timothy, his spiritual son in the faith, when he wrote, "For you must teach others those things you and many others have heard me speak about. Teach these great truths to trustworthy men who will, in turn, pass them on to others" (2 Timothy 2:2, Living).

A "transferable technique" is the vehicle, such as a tape, film or booklet, which is used to communicate a transferable concept. For example, the Four Spiritual Laws booklet is a transferable technique. The message contained in the Four Spiritual Laws booklet is a transferable concept.

When Jesus gave the disciples the command to "Go therefore and make disciples of all the nations, baptizing them . . . teaching them to observe all that I commanded you" (Matthew 28:19,20), He was referring to certain truths which would enable His disciples to be more vital in their lives and more fruitful in their witness for Him.

Since like begets like and we produce after our kind, we cannot disciple others until we ourselves grasp certain important principles. I do not know how one can build a disciple without including all of the following transferable concepts:

1. How to be sure you are a Christian.
2. How to experience God's love and forgiveness.
3. How to be filled with the Holy Spirit.
4. How to walk in the Spirit.
5. How to witness in the Spirit.
6. How to introduce others to Christ.
7. How to help fulfill the Great Commission.
8. How to love by faith.
9. How to pray.
10. How to be an effective member of the Body of Christ.

It is true that no one can ever master these transferable concepts. I feel like a beginner myself after all of these years. Yet, it requires only a few weeks or months for any one who desires to be used of God to learn these concepts and techniques well enough that they begin to be a part of his own life and he is able to pass them on to others. It is our objective to help train tens of millions of Christians around the world to experience and share the abundant life in Christ so that they can help to fulfill the Great Commission. These transferable concepts will help to accomplish this objective.

Today, the title "Campus" Crusade for Christ is, in a sense, misleading. From our beginning in the early 1950's, the need for more expanded and specialized ministries has been seen again and again. In response to that need, our field ministries have grown over the years to include college, executive, high school, international, lay, military, athletic, music, prayer, prison and special ministries both in the United States and overseas.

Each of the U.S. field ministries is staffed by godly men and women who are committed to the same objective: to help saturate the United States with the claims of Christ on a continuing basis. Throughout the world our goal is to bring this good news to everyone in our generation.

Now, I should like to spell out more about the individual development and strategies of the field ministries to show how they each fit into Campus Crusade's objective of becoming "all things to all men" that we might be used to "save some" in order to help fulfill the Great Commission of our Lord.

CHAPTER NINE

A Strategy for Colleges

Upon my arrival at a large midwestern university, it was announced that I was to have dinner and speak in the leading fraternity on campus. There was no time to check into the hotel nor to get ready for the meeting. I was already late, and consequently I rushed to the fraternity house.

As I entered the living room, the fellows scattered as though I had leprosy. I wondered what was wrong and was puzzled by the coldness and indifference of the men who remained in the room. Apparently someone had invited me without knowing who I was or anything about the nature of my message. No doubt they had decided in a subsequent fraternity bull session that they had no interest in a religious speaker, and my invitation to speak had been a mistake.

The president of the fraternity hardly spoke to me during the dinner hour. Obviously, he did not want any of his brothers to think that he was interested in religion. Finally, it became his painful duty to announce that there would be a "religious" meeting upstairs in the living room following the dinner hour. Without introducing me, he simply mentioned (in a tone that indicated he was not interested, and anybody who was, was foolish) that a speaker from California would be speaking to those who were interested in religion.

Not a Religious Speaker

I knew, as I observed the attitudes of the men, that there would be no one present to hear me unless I acted fast. So I asked the president for permission to say a few words. Reluctantly, he granted me a few moments, and I said to the men, "I have observed from your reaction that you are no more interested in religion than I am, and I want to put your minds at ease at once. I am not a religious speaker, nor am I here to talk to you about religion. As a matter of fact, I am opposed to religion. History records that religion has done more than any other one thing to keep man in ignorance and fear and superstition through the centuries."

This group of cold, indifferent, even antagonistic men had suddenly come alive. Some of them were dumbfounded. A few well-chosen words had captured their attention. By this time, the men appeared ready to listen to anything I had to say, so I invited them to meet with me upstairs in the living room if they wanted to hear more.

Some of the men began to quiz me. "We thought you were a religious speaker," they said. "You don't sound very religious. What are you going to say?" Others, I discovered later, rushed to the telephone and called their friends in other fraternity houses and dormitories. They invited them to come and hear me speak, saying, "We have a religious speaker at our house tonight who doesn't seem to be very religious. Come on over." By the time we gathered upstairs for the meeting, the room was packed. Many additional men had come out of curiosity to learn what I had to say.

"As I mentioned earlier," I began, "I am opposed to religion. But let me explain what I mean. By way of definition, religion is man's best effort to find God through his own good works, whereas Christianity can be defined as God's search for man and the revelation of Himself in Christ. Because of man's many efforts to find God through the centuries, he has even resorted to criminal means, such as the Inquisition and the Crusades. The superstition of reincarnation and the belief that certain animals are sacred beings have caused masses of human beings to starve while animals survived.

"I am not here to talk to you about religion, but I am here to tell you how God became a man and visited this planet in the person of Jesus of Nazareth. I am here to share with you how you can have a personal relationship with God made possible through the most remarkable Person who ever lived — the God-man who changed the course of history: B.C., before Christ; A.D., *anno Domini*, in the year of the Lord."

Speaking About Jesus

For the next 45 minutes, I talked about Jesus — who He is; why He came to this earth; what He taught; the miracles He performed; His death on the cross for our sins; His resurrection; His message to men through the centuries; and His relevance to the collegian of today. When I finished, no one seemed to want to leave. As usual, a good percentage expressed their desire to receive Christ.

Multitudes of students in fraternity, sorority and dormitory meetings on campuses across the country respond similarly when staff members of Campus Crusade present the Person of Christ — not religion, not Christianity in the broad general sense, not even the church, but a living, dynamic Person.

How do we account for this remarkable response on the part of students? In addition to the spiritual emphasis, part of the answer is planning and strategy. Since the inception of this ministry, our slogan has been, "Win the campus to Christ today, win the world to Christ tomorrow." Our strategy for accomplishing this is to expose men and women to the gospel, win them to Christ, build them in the faith and send them forth to proclaim with us throughout the world the good news of the gospel.

For example, many years of experience have shown

us that an average of one-fourth to one-half of the non-Christian students in "team" meetings are interested in making their commitments to Christ. Though not all of the ones who offer to pray a prayer of commitment give evidence of new life at that time, many thousands do.

Interested in Christ

Many adults automatically assume that college students are not interested in religion and in the church, and in this assumption they are correct. However, the average student is interested in the Person of Jesus Christ, and for many years we have made this distinction in our presentation.

We do not talk about religion or the church, though we believe in the church and require that every staff member become an active member of a local church within 90 days after arriving at his permanent assignment. We also encourage all the students to become active church members.

However, at our first encounter our message emphasizes the Person of Jesus. Students are sometimes antagonistic when we first arrive, assuming that we are going to give them the bit about religion and the church, which they have long since rejected.

I remember one such experience when I arrived with a team to speak in an outstanding fraternity house. We arrived in time for dinner, as per the invitation, and it was arranged that we would make our presentation following the dinner hour. While I was sitting beside the president during the meal he revealed to me that he was faced with a very serious problem. Though he was not a Christian, he was sympathetic with our cause and felt that he should warn me that several of his brothers were planning to embarrass us and cause us to leave the fraternity house in defeat and humiliation. The ringleader of this plot was one of the outstanding students on campus, a moral reprobate who had an unholy disgust and dislike for anything religious or Christian. He was determined to make us the laughingstock of the campus and had rallied several of his fraternity brothers to his cause over the objection of the president.

As the president and I conferred, I felt impressed to recommend to him that he exercise his authority as president and require that every member of the fraternity attend the meeting and that he leave the rest to us. Though I did not tell him so, I was leaving the rest to the Lord. The brothers were somewhat disgruntled when the president announced that their attendance at the meeting was required.

Anticipating their disgruntlement and unhappy presence, we greeted them with a bit of humor then proceeded to explain to them that we were not there to play games. We were there to talk about the most revolutionary Person the world has ever known, a Person who made revolutionary claims for Himself and revolutionary demands upon all who would follow Him. We made it clear that there were a lot of people who did not have the intestinal fortitude to be His followers and asked all of those who felt that they had the potential to be His followers to put aside their preconceived ideas and listen to what was being said as though their lives depended upon it, as indeed their eternal lives did.

Responsive to the Gospel

The whole atmosphere of the house changed. The men responded to the challenges, and when the opportunity was given for those who wished to receive Christ, over half of the men, including the president and the leader of the original plot to embarrass us, marched with me into the fraternity den. There we had the opportunity to explain to them further how they could know Christ. We had prayer with them and made plans for the beginning of a weekly Bible study. Different members of the team made appointments with those who had responded, as well as with other members of the fraternity who had attended the original meeting. Throughout the remainder of the week these appointments were kept, and further commitments to Christ were made.

Appointments for subsequent personal interviews are usually made by a member of the team approaching a member of a house and asking, "What did you think of that meeting?" The response is usually, "Great! Wonderful! I've never heard anything like it." The next questions is, "Did it make sense?" "It sure did," is the reply. "Would you like to get together and talk about it?" The answer is almost always in the affirmative.

Often, when there is no rush to leave, a team member will pursue the matter further, if the individual responds that what he heard made sense. The team member will ask if he would like to talk about it at that point, and together they consider the Four Spiritual Laws and then pray together. Thousands of students have been introduced to Christ following meetings of this kind. It is also an approach that many laymen use following church services or similar meetings which non-Christians are invited to attend.

Saturated With Prayer

A meeting of this kind is always bathed in prayer. The team members meet one hour before the time of departure for a special briefing on what each team member is to say and how he is to say it; to check each other on the way they are dressed; and then, finally, to pray for God to work in the hearts of the students. They are conscious of the fact that unless God speaks through their lips there can be no spiritual harvest, for Jesus said, "No man can come to Me, except the Father, who hath sent Me, draw him." By faith, each team member acknowledges his dependence upon the Holy Spirit and appropriates the fullness of God's power, and the group is on its way, in joyful anticipation of what God will do.

In addition to these thousands of team meetings, individual students are also contacted by staff through random surveys taken casually over a cup of coffee or a Coke in a dorm, student center or fraternity. The random survey is an evangelistic tool containing questions which provide an opportunity to share the Four Spiritual Laws.

Unpressured honesty characterizes all appointments. Staff are not so concerned that a student make an immediate decision to accept Christ as they are that each student has a clear understanding of how he can establish a personal relationship with Him.

College Life meetings are another evangelistic opportunity, as they give staff a chance to interact with students. Held each week on hundreds of campuses across the nation, these meetings are attended by as many as 300 on some campuses and on special occasions by several thousand. The program includes singing, entertainment, a main speaker — usually a Campus Crusade staff member — and refreshments. Afterwards, trained staff members and students are on the alert for visitors and guests who are interested in Christ's promise of new life.

"Aggressive" Evangelism

Campus Crusade is committed to "aggressive" evangelism. By aggressive evangelism, I mean going to men with the good news of our living Christ and His love and forgiveness, not in argumentative tones nor with high pressure techniques, but taking the initiative to tell (as the apostle Paul wrote) all men everywhere about Christ.

We realize that this can best be accomplished by multiplication (teaching witnessing disciples to make other witnessing disciples) rather than through addition (simply leading others to Christ one by one). This is the reason training is so important and has been since the inception of this ministry. Each week on hundreds of campuses, Leadership Training Classes are held in which thousands of students learn how to share their faith, how to study the Bible and how to disciple other students.

Those who participate in the classes are encouraged to become involved in smaller action groups. It is the purpose of these action groups to put into practice the training received in the Leadership Training Classes. As these groups of a half dozen or so encourage one another in their Christian walk and witness, their lives are enriched for Christ and their relationship with one another is beautifully enhanced. Because of these small action groups and Leadership Training Classes, there develops a great bond of Christian love and camaraderie reminiscent of first-century Christians, whose love for one another has been extolled.

Thousands of students are being introduced to Christ through team meetings, personal appointments, College Life meetings, and through special meetings with Andre Kole, Josh McDowell, and our various athletic teams and singing groups. It all adds up to a busy schedule for our more than 1,200 campus staff members who are presently working on hundreds of campuses across the United States.

Bal Week

An additional strategy that has proved tremendously successful in working with college students has been to involve them in a ministry during times when they are not in school. This strategy was first put into practice in 1965 during Bal Week, Easter vacation at Balboa and Newport Beaches in southern California.

Approximately 30,000 students from California and surrounding states crowded the sunny beaches during this time of year. For years Bal week had been one of the biggest headaches for the local police as thousands of students became involved in all kinds of delinquencies, including sex, drugs, drunken brawls and vandalism.

The staff believed that something should be done about taking the claims of Christ to these thousands of students. So a strategy was developed. It called for taking several hundred of our staff and students into the Balboa area where they would live in the homes of adult friends. The morning hours would be spent in training the students to understand how to live in the control and power of the Holy Spirit of God and how to communicate their faith in Christ effectively with these thousands of beach-goers. The afternoons and evenings were to be spent in personal and group contacts with the students.

Startling Results

The results were startling and phenomenal. Contacts were not hard to make. There were plenty of people who had nothing to do but sit and listen. Trained students with clipboards, student surveys, evangelistic booklets, Van Dusen letters and Four Spiritual Laws booklets would sit down in their swim trunks and proper beach attire next to a sun-baked coed or young man. Thousands of students responded. The impact was so great that delinquency and vandalism were greatly lessened, and before the end of the week, the police were giving the violators of the law the alternative of going to jail or talking with a member of the Campus Crusade team.

In a converted bar called The Hunger Hangar, several members of the team were available to provide refreshments and to give personal counsel to hundreds of lonely students who were looking for someone to talk to about the things of God. Across the front of the temporary summer headquarters was hung the banner, CHRIST IS THE ANSWER. On the other side of the street, a group of fraternity men reacted to our banner by hanging a sign from their apartment which read, BOOZE IS THE ANSWER. But in the course of the days that followed, these men made their way one by one to our headquarters, at first out of curiosity and then from a genuine interest that developed as members of the team talked to them about Christ and introduced them to the Savior. Eventually all of the young men met Christ, and the BOOZE IS THE ANSWER sign came down.

From its beginning at Balboa and Newport Beach, the ministry soon spread to other beaches. Daytona Beach, Ft. Lauderdale, Panama City, Ocean City, Lake Tahoe, Cape Cod, Santa Cruz, Colorado River and other resort areas became the scene of Campus Crusade activity, as thousands of staff and students invaded these areas to give witness to the living Christ.

Modern-day Prodigal Son

One day, just after I had arrived at my hotel room, where I was to speak to the students at Daytona Beach, a young man knocked on the door of my room and asked if he could retrieve his key. It seemed that he had tossed his key from the patio area on the ground to the third floor, but he had missed the third floor, and his key had fallen on my terrace on the second floor. Knowing that God makes no mistakes and sensing that here was a lad whom God had prepared, I invited him in and he found his key. Then I asked him if he had a few moments to talk. As we chatted together, I explained to him the love of God and His forgiveness made possible through faith in Jesus Christ, as contained in the Four Spiritual Laws booklet.

When I finished, he told me this moving story: "I grew up in the church. My mother and father are very devout Christians. But I have rejected Christianity. For some reason I have not found satisfaction and fulfillment in the church. My parents did not want me to come to Daytona. They knew I would be involved with the wrong crowd. But, in violation of their wishes, I came anyway. And now, of all the places in the world, you should be here to confront me with what my mother and father have told me all these years. Surely, God has arranged this meeting."

We knelt together and prayed, and this young modern-day prodigal who had been running from the Lord surrendered his heart to the Savior.

Expansion to Other Resort Areas

The success of these outreaches prompted the expansion of the format to involve students in a similar type of program for an entire summer. The summer projects gathered students together in various vacation spots around the country to help them grow in their Christian walk. The plan is a simple but effective one. A selected team of students comes to the resort area, locates jobs and settles into a normal work routine. At the same time, a Campus Crusade staff team comes to live with the students for a portion of the summer months. Often the Christians find housing together. Usually they secure a common meeting ground to sponsor outreaches.

After work hours, the staff members spend time with the students, helping them acquire effective evangelistic skills. The constant influx of tourists and vacationers in most spots provides ample opportunity for students to practice one-to-one evangelism.

"The lasting impact this project makes is phenomenal," commented one staff member from the South Lake Tahoe project. "Church members are ecstatic to see us back each summer. Employers beg us to send students to work for them because of the quality of life evident in these young Christians. Scores of people at work, on the beaches and in the parks come to know Christ personally each summer through the witness of the students."

Projects Overseas and in the Inner-city

Summer projects are also held overseas and in the inner-city. In Detroit's inner-city, students and staff capitalized on a city ordinance that permitted city streets to be roped off for parties, with the consent of the residents. They moved a truckload of recreational equipment like basketball hoops, volleyball nets, ping-pong tables and other sports equipment into the area. "The street was turned into a playground," said the project director, "and we found the atmosphere very conducive to sharing the gospel."

In addition to ministering to American college students, a number of our staff work almost exclusively on campus with international students. There are some 260,000 international students studying in the United States, representing nearly every country in the world. Students studying in the United States are generally more open to the gospel than they are in their home countries. Also, they represent the potential leadership of the countries from which they have come. International students reached for Christ and discipled for Christ here in the U.S. can return to their home countries where they can be a powerful influence for Christ.

One man whom I met during a recent tour of the Middle East had earned his Ph.D. from a midwestern university where he was very much involved in the Campus Crusade ministry. He now plays an important role of leadership in the business and Christian communities of his country, where Christians are in a decided minority.

Our campus staff also minister to people of varying ethnic backgrounds including blacks, Mexican-Americans and American Indians. One of our staff members began ministering to Asian-American students on the campus of the University of California at Berkeley. His ministry expanded to the point where he had a direct or indirect influence for Christ on the lives of 60 Asian-American students. We also have staff ministering full time on a number of black college campuses.

Many thousands of students are being led to Christ

and discipled by our staff on the college campuses. These dedicated men and women are committed to the objective of helping to fulfill the Great Commission in this generation. And they realize that the college campus represents the greatest source of manpower immediately available to accomplish this objective.

CHAPTER TEN

Berkeley —
A New Kind of Revolution

In 1967, Berkeley was synonymous with worldwide student riots, demonstrations and radical movements of all kinds.

As Christians and as members of the Campus Crusade staff, we became concerned that so little was being accomplished for Christ on this campus, the fountainhead of the radical movement. So, at one of our campus strategy sessions, we decided to call together 600 of our staff and students from across the nation and saturate the University of California with the good news of Christ through a week-long convention. Our theme was "Solution — Spiritual Revolution."

A syndicated news release from Berkeley carried this story:

> A new kind of revolution talk was heard today on the steps of Sproul Hall on the campus of the University of California at Berkeley. This site has been the scene of student protests and demonstrations and unrest for several years, but today about 3,000 students gathered to hear about a different kind of revolutionary leader — Jesus Christ. The occasion was a rally put on by the Berkeley chapter of the Campus Crusade for Christ, an organization which is having its national convention this week in the Berkeley student union building. While other students passed out handbills for and against the firing of the University of California president, Clark Kerr, and others distributed buttons reading "Impeach Reagan," a folk singing group sang gospel songs with a contemporary sound and the Campus Crusade leader proclaimed a new kind of revolution. The students were asked to trust Christ as the One who has the answers to all the problems of today and the One who can bring spiritual revolution and change to the world. They claimed that the Christian message is revolutionary because it has changed history, creating vast social reforms through reshaping the lives and

attitudes of individuals. The Campus Crusade rally on the Sproul Hall steps came at a time of special turmoil and tension on the Berkeley campus because the day previously the Board of Regents had fired President Clark Kerr. As a result, newsmen and television cameras were on hand for the rally assuming that students were planning a major demonstration over the firing of Kerr. Instead, they were greeted by the Campus Crusade revolutionaries who had reserved this area some weeks prior to the firing of President Kerr. Inasmuch as they had the use of the air, it was impossible for the radicals to drown out the demonstration, and both of the major television networks commented on the fact that Berkeley was the quietest campus in all the University of California system because of the influence of the Campus Crusade for Christ on the Berkeley campus.

Student Leaders Respond

The week at Berkeley began Sunday afternoon with an athletic banquet. All Cal athletes were invited, and some 400 responded to hear famous athletes give their testimonies. I presented additional good news of Christ to these men and invited them to receive Him as their Savior. A number of Berkeley's outstanding athletes responded to the invitation.

The following morning 125 student leaders of the university's student government attended the student leadership breakfast where two leaders shared their faith in Christ, and I followed with a salvation message explaining who Christ is, why He came and how to know Him personally. A number of these leaders also responded.

During that week, many additional meetings were held on and off campus. Christ was presented at 28 separate dinners given for international students, and many of these were introduced to Christ. Meetings continued from noon until after midnight in the Forum of Telegraph Avenue, a hangout for the radical students, the street people and the hippies at Berkeley. Approximately 40 of these radicals received Christ during that week. In addition, each evening another 1,400 students gathered in the Berkeley Community Theater to hear Campus Crusade staff present the claims of Christ.

Billy Graham was with us for the last day of the meetings. That last Friday morning a special breakfast was held for approximately 300 of the faculty in the Student Union. Billy gave a powerful presentation of the gospel, and I explained the purpose of our week at Berkeley.

Threat of Cancellation

We had scheduled a great rally at noon at the Greek Theater, where Dr. Graham and I would both be speaking. Dawn had greeted us with a downpour of rain that continued all morning. As we met in our various sessions, we prayed God would stop the rain in time for the noon rally. There was no other place to meet, and the Greek Theater had no roof. Thus, thousands who would otherwise come would be forced to miss hearing the gospel through Dr. Graham's message. As we continued to pray, the rain continued to pour. What were we to do? Surely God had not brought us to this great week of witness for Christ and finally to the grand climax meeting for us to fail.

"Whatever we ask in prayer believing we shall receive . . . If we ask anything according to His will, He hears, us, and if He hears us, He answers us . . . God is not willing that any should perish but that all should come to repentance." These and many other promises of Scripture were claimed as we asked God, the Creator of heaven and earth, the One who controls men, nations and nature, to intervene for the salvation of souls. As we prayed, dramatically and abruptly it happened — the rain stopped. A spontaneous song of praise flowed from our hearts, for we realized that the rally in the Greek Theater would take place as planned.

More than 8,000 students and faculty joined us in the Greek Theater. I greeted them with a brief message and introduced Dr. Graham. Following his clear-cut presentation of the gospel, he invited the students to commit their lives to Christ. Long after the meeting was over, 600 staff and students counseled and prayed with those remaining behind to learn how to become Christians. God had done a mighty work at Cal, but this was only the beginning.

Follow-Up Program

After most of us left Berkeley, those remaining began a follow-up program designed to preserve and increase the impact that had been made. All the students who had invited Christ into their lives, and those who expressed interest in knowing more, were contacted during the first week after the convention. Approximately 200 of those who had just received Christ attended a retreat to learn more about how to live the abundant Christian life. Many of those who expressed interest in Christ also responded.

One local newspaper described the "invasion" at Berkeley this way:

> Unparalleled organization. Campus radicals, accustomed to being hailed the best student organizers, looked on in amazement as the extensive Campus Crusade for Christ campaign got under way in an attempt to evangelize the entire student body at Berkeley. Teams of delegates spoke and shared their faith in Christ in more than 70 dormitories, fraternities, sororities and nearby student residences. Other groups spoke and sang in restaurants, coffee houses and similar gathering places for "free speech movement" advocates, and other teams of delegates conducted a door-to-door campaign in the entire area adjacent to the campus just to make sure that no one was overlooked in the crusaders' effort to give each of the 27,000 students an opportunity to hear the claims of Christ on their lives.
>
> In addition to the regular convention schedule of morning and evening addresses, daily Bible exposition and prayer sessions, staff members also spoke in nearby churches and in church related meetings.
>
> More than half of the students in most of the fraternities, sororities and dormitory meetings indicated that they would

like to know how to become Christians. A young man from Hawaii who was visiting Berkeley made his decision in a restaurant after a third Crusade delegate, during that one week, had talked to him about his personal relationship with Christ.

During that week at Berkeley, I met by appointment with one of the leaders of the radical movement on campus — a brilliant, dynamic, personable individual. Reared a Jew, more recently this person had become a dedicated atheist and card-carrying Communist. It has been my practice for years to ask Muslims, Hindus, atheists and Communists, "Who is the greatest person who has ever lived?" When I asked the radical leader this question, there was a long, awkward silence. "I guess I would have to say Jesus of Nazareth," was the reluctant reply. This leader was one of thousands who came face to face with the Master that week.

Radical Movement Broken

Dr. Hardin Jones, a well-known scientist and professor at Berkeley for 40 years, shared with me that the back of the radical movement was broken at Berkeley that week. He also said that since then there was more talk about Jesus Christ on campus than about Karl Marx. There is power in the gospel. Satan cannot withstand it. When he is confronted with men and women who trust and obey God, he releases control of occupied territory.

By the time the week-long convention had ended, more than 700 had made commitments to Christ, and approximately 2,000 other students indicated that they would like to know more about Jesus Christ and how they could also commit their lives to Him.

On another campus, a similar "invasion" of our staff and others confronted a strong group of student activists. It was the fall of 1970 at the University of Texas that brought us another tremendous opportunity to bring glory to God.

Operation Alternative

Campus radicals planned anti-war rallies on the Austin campus that week in October, as we sent 400 Campus Crusade-trained students and staff, working with 100 Navigators, to present an alternative plan for peace. The main thrust, called Operation Alternative, centered on two big free speech rallies during the weekend, but also included two marches on campus, massive use of literature and radio and TV news coverage.

As Christian students and staff began to arrive from Arkansas, Oklahoma and throughout Texas, they took speaking assignments in every campus dining area.

The next morning everyone went on campus to distribute flyers, carry signs, mass for a march and hold a rally on the Main Mall, which Campus Crusade students had reserved weeks before.

About 1,000 gathered as Josh McDowell, traveling representative for Campus Crusade, began telling what Christ meant to him. Other speakers and a number of students followed him.

During the free speech time, students and some professors blasted Christianity and proclaimed political radicalism. At the close, a Cuban student strode to the mike and said, "You don't know what you're talking about. I've been through two revolutions — the one on Cuba and now the one in Jesus Christ." As this student described both, he pointed out that only Christ is the answer.

On Saturday, several thousand students and visiting parents witnessed a similar rally on the West Mall. "The atmosphere was electric," the Campus Crusade director at UT later told us. "Hundreds stopped and listened on their way to the football game. Among other results, Christians at UT have never been as bold or as united as they are now. And students at UT really know that the Christians are alive!"

One radio station described the week on its news broadcast, "Campus Crusade for Christ smashes Student Mobilization Committee."

These wonderful experiences of God's power have been high points in our Campus Ministry. They have revealed to the world that the light of Jesus Christ is more powerful than darkness. As I think back on these times, my prayers increase for God to do it again and again throughout the entire world. Wherever the light of God's love and forgiveness meets the darkness of atheism head on, His light overcomes.

CHAPTER ELEVEN

Here's Life America

A dentist from Cape Kennedy, a businessman from New Jersey and a man with a young family in California — all have been a part of the Here's Life America ministry of Campus Crusade. What brings them together? As one staff member explains, "My wife and I were typical church members. We were traditional, mediocre, a lukewarm kind of Christian. Now that we have experienced a vital personal relationship with Christ, have helped others to find this same exciting relationship and seen entire churches come alive, we want to spend the rest of our lives serving Him." That same desire unites the 320 Here's Life America staff across the United States and Canada, in spite of the variety of backgrounds and education. Directed by Alan Nagel, this ministry is having a dynamic ministry across this country.

This ministry to lay men and women began as a direct outgrowth of the Campus Ministry. As God continued to do a mighty work in the lives of thousands on many college campuses, laymen began to ask, "How do you account for the miraculous results of the ministry of Campus Crusade among students? Can't you give us the same kind of training you give your staff and students?"

Day-long Institutes

Thus it was that in 1959 I began to speak at many day-long Lay Institutes for Evangelism (since renamed Christian Living Seminars) in various cities throughout the nation. From early in the morning until late at night, I presented the basic messages and seminars on how to live the Christian life and share our faith in Christ more effectively. Hundreds of laymen and pastors came for the entire day to hear this seminar presentation. Shortly after that, the Lay Ministry (now Here's Life America) was born, and it has since produced some of the most exciting results that we have seen.

The day-long institutes for evangelism soon became week-long and spread city-wide, encompassing hundreds of churches and thousands of laymen who responded to training.

The greater the response to the training, the more we realized the need for our Lay Ministry to become more than a training institute. From the beginning, the local church has been the most important part of God's strategy to help fulfill the Great Commission. Now we were discovering how to serve the local church more effectively. We became even more committed to the fact that local pastors and laymen are the key to evangelizing communities. If properly trained with an understanding of how to share their faith in the power of the Spirit, they could be used of God in a revolutionary way, even as were the first-century Christians.

Assisting Church Leaders

Here's Life America staff function in two areas to serve the local church. First, they assist pastors and laymen in developing discipleship ministries. Second, they develop movements of spiritual multiplication within some of the leadership groups of the community such as business and professional people, lawyers, doctors, educators and entertainers.

In their church-related ministry, lay staff assist church leaders in causing discipleship methods to become a way of life. In addition to this plan, national conferences called Christian Living Seminars are made available to pastors and laymen. These seminars include courses on discipleship, Lay Institutes for Evangelism and management training. The management course helps pastors break away from the "I don't have time" syndrome and provides pastors and church leaders with priority-oriented administrative procedures as well as training in discipleship and evangelism.

As one pastor put it, "Management training filled the missing place in my church work and in my life. To know the how-to's — how to set clear goals and objectives, set priorities, write job descriptions and divide the work load — will help us succeed in building a Christian community."

Witnessing Assignments

An integral part of our Christian Living Seminars is a laboratory training program. Less than 24 hours after the delegates arrive for an institute, they have already been told how to witness and have spent a few hours in the field seeking to communicate their faith to others. The results are startling and revolutionary.

Many, and one could probably say most, go out on this first witnessing assignment with their fingers crossed. Many are frightened. As one woman said to me, "I won't go. I refuse to go." I assured her that she did not have to go, that it was strictly voluntary, and that she should not feel under any pressure to go. She kept saying, almost as though she were in a state of shock, "I won't go. I won't go." And I kept assuring her that she didn't have to go.

Finally, I suggested that maybe she should go with someone and listen. Reluctantly, and with a face white with fear, she agreed to accompany a staff member. Two hours later she returned bubbling with enthusiasm, overjoyed. She took my hand in both of hers and said, "I'm so glad that you encouraged me to go. What a great loss if I hadn't. My life was forever changed this afternoon when I saw God transform the lives of those who received Christ."

Renewed Life

In one large city, I was speaking at a meeting to which several hundred laymen and students had come from throughout the entire state, some from as far away as 500 miles. At the conclusion of one of my lectures, a leading layman came running down the aisle. He said, "This is the greatest thing I have ever heard in my life. Today I have been liberated. I am now on 12 boards of various Christian organizations, including a couple in my church. I have been trying to serve God so diligently that I practically ignored my business and my family.

"Now you tell me that the Christian life is not what we do for God, but what we allow Him to do in and through us. You say the Christian life is a supernatural life, that no one can live it but Christ, and that this life is by faith through the power of the Holy Spirit. I have been trying to serve God in the energy of the flesh. I understand now why I have been so miserable and so unproductive!"

He telephoned his wife, explained to her how he had made the discovery of being filled and controlled by the Holy Spirit by faith and insisted that she come at once to join in the training. Even though she had made previous commitments, she canceled all her engagements and came. That night at the banquet, following my final lecture, they both stood to tell how the course of their lives had been dramatically changed that day through the new concepts they had heard.

At another institute, I had just finished one of my lectures on the ministry of the Holy Spirit when a pastor approached me. He was rejoicing in the fact that he now knew he was filled with the Holy Spirit by faith, but he was also distressed by the fact that with all of his theological training and his years of preaching, he had never once personally introduced a person to the Savior. He was rightly concerned. As we talked and prayed together, I felt impressed to ask him if he would like to be used of God that very day to introduce someone to Christ. He looked at me in amazement as if to say, "How foolish! I've never led anyone to Christ in all these years. How could I possibly expect to lead anyone to Christ today?"

I suggested that we pray together and then that he go door-to-door in the area where his church was located, using our Community Religious Survey, and present the gospel as explained through the Four Spiritual Laws. This he agreed to do. We asked God that He might honor his efforts.

Imagine his elation and my joy when he returned that afternoon so excited he could hardly speak. In the very first home he visited, he met a 19-year-old student who was rope for the gospel, and upon the simple presentation of the Four Spiritual Laws, this person invited Christ into his life. Needless to say, this was a revolutionary experience for this young pastor.

Mediated Training

A giant step forward in the Lay Ministry was taken in 1974, when this key training that had been used to revolutionize the lives of hundreds of thousands of people was put into an exciting new format, developed by Dr. Norman Bell, a Christian professor of communications at Michigan State University. Dr. Bell is an active adviser, consultant, teacher and friend of the Campus Crusade ministry. During one of my visits to the campus to speak to the students, I met Dr. Bell and learned of this revolutionary new concept in communications called mediated training. As we discussed the concept, it became apparent that it applied to our basic training. We could train tens of millions of Christians around the world — instead of the tens of thousands whom we were then training. So I asked Dr. Bell and Chuck Younkman, then the director of our Mass Media Ministry, and his staff to help me adapt the basic training which had been so effective for more than 20 years into this new format.

This format utilizes slides, 16mm film and cassette sound track. Tests have shown that in similar training sessions 80% of the people who attend retain 80% of the material, as compared to the customary lecture method where retention is frequently no more than five percent.

At the time that God impressed us to pray toward the goal of seeking to help saturate America with the gospel by the end of 1976, we didn't understand how He would do it. We had the capability to train many people to be effective in reaching others for Christ through the staff of Campus Crusade, but we saw no way to be able to train the hundreds of thousands of workers who would be needed to help reach our nation for Christ.

When I first heard the idea of putting our training into the mediated format, the Holy Spirit confirmed that this was a portion of the answer to my prayer for the salvation of millions in the United States. Such revolutionary concepts as "How to Be Filled With the Spirit" and "How to Witness in the Spirit," plus how-to's of evangelism, could now be made available to millions of Christians. We would no longer be limited to our staff as trainers, but laymen and pastors could train others by using the mediated training presentation.

Training Produces Results

At first there were many questions and much skepticism. Many wondered if mediated training could really communicate better than a live teacher. Larry Marks, a Methodist layman from Athens, Ala., expressed the feeling of the people who have taken the training. "I was amazed at the amount of information I gained and could recall when I needed it," he said.

Marks also tells the story of Jack, a layman in his

church, who had always thought that he could witness only by his style of living. After taking mediated training, however, his mind changed. He made a list of 10 friends whom he wanted to introduce to Christ and soon saw six of them receive Christ as Savior.

Ken Kirby, pastor of Bryant Street Baptist Church in Yucaipa, Calif., has also been enthusiastic about the benefits of mediated training. "It gets results," he says. "I couldn't recommend it if there hadn't been any real change in my laymen's lives, but there has. I've seen the Lord use mediated training to equip my men boldly to share their faith."

Those people who have been trained through the mediated training in a Christian Living Seminar do not go out to convert people to their way of thinking or to their philosophy of life or even to their religion. They go with new boldness to share the most important news the world has ever received: the good news of God's love and forgiveness in Christ Jesus. As thousands respond — not to their words but to His Spirit — they have the joy of knowing that their lives are truly counting for eternity.

It occurs to me that there are many, like Peter and John of the Bible, who have "fished" for men for years and are wearied and discouraged. They have never caught anything, never introduced another person to Christ. There is a solution. One needs simply to bow in prayer and ask the Holy Spirit to control and empower his life as he surrenders it to Christ and then receive training in the how-to's of sharing one's faith. The Holy Spirit provides the ability to learn how to communicate Christ more effectively with others.

The time is now: Men and women have never been more ready to hear the good news of our Savior. And the opportunity is now: Christian Living Seminars are held each year across the nation to help lay men and women and pastors fill their nets and to challenge them to forsake all and follow Him.

CHAPTER TWELVE

Special Ministries

Of all the outreaches Campus Crusade employs to reach men and women everywhere, there is probably none so unusual as the methods of our special representative, Andre Kole. As America's leading illusionist and foremost inventor of magical effects, Andre has spent the last 20 years pulling coins from the air, sawing his assistant in half, turning flaming scarves into canes and escaping "The Table of Death."

But his most recent 22 years of performances around the world have been for the sole purpose of using the fantasy of illusions to gain a hearing for the reality of Christ.

At the age of 25, Andre was a success in the fields of business and magic. He was married, had a family and owned a new home and car which were paid for. In addition to doing between 20 and 30 shows each month, he was in charge of the state-wide operation of one of the largest corporations in Arizona, was co-owner of a ranch and a number of real estate buildings and directed several enterprises in show business.

Then he was challenged to consider the miracles of Jesus Christ and what He had to say. "At that time, I took great pride in my reputation as a magician," Andre recalls. "I have never been fooled by any other magician, and I had no intention of being deceived by any first-century trickster — if this was all that Jesus really was."

Unshakeable Proof

The fulfillment of biblical prophecy, the evidence for the resurrection and the dynamic Christian lives that he saw finally compelled Andre to let Christ take control of his life. But it wasn't until he spent two days on campus with the late Elmer Lappen, then our staff director at Arizona State University, that Andre caught a vision of the intriguing new life that lay before him. He developed a presentation to illustrate the Four Spiritual Laws with illusions and convinced that it would work, Andre joined the staff of Campus Crusade in 1963.

Today, he spends more than 60% of each year on tour, has performed in person in 73 nations and has been seen by more than 78 million on television in one year alone. To date, he has addressed more than 2,600 separate university audiences, and some 400 copies of his two films are now circulating worldwide.

Wherever Andre goes, his performances and message never fail to capture the minds and hearts of his audiences. In a recent three-month Asian tour, he found that "the people were open everywhere. I performed 100 times before 110,000 people, and as a result over 10,000 responded to the gospel. Now, staff, students and laymen in that area are following up the young Christians."

A three-week tour through Latin America in 1973 resulted in 14 invitations for Andre to perform on TV programs — nine of which were over national television, and all of which were aired free of charge as a public service. Simultaneously, capacity crowds jammed each stage performance.

His popularity continues to grow on American campuses, too. During a recent school term, he appeared before an average of one million people each week through stage and TV performances. Among the thousands who have come to Christ through Andre's ministry is a student leader in Taiwan who said, "Mr. Kole, when you mentioned that most people are laughing on the outside and crying on the inside, you described me perfectly. Not only is this a picture of my life, but of the life of every student I know on this campus. I only wish I had heard you a week ago or even a day ago." Another said: "I have been a Christian for 11 years but I closed Christ out of my life when I came to college. About a year ago I attempted suicide. I saw nothing worth living for. Since then I have been seeing a psychiatrist, but after tonight I won't need him any more. Thanks to you, I now know I have Christ. Thank you for showing me my need."

From his investigations in 73 countries of the world, Andre has learned that most tricks and illusions attributed to the supernatural (witchcraft and occult) are produced by very natural means. The one thing Andre has found that men can't reproduce, though, is the exciting reality of a personal relationship with Jesus Christ. That is why he is thrilled to be able to use his magical medium for an eternal purpose. Everywhere he goes, he challenges men and women in all walks of life to let their lives count for Christ. "I've always felt that God is likely to use those whom the world considers the most unlikely," he says. "After all, if God can use a magician to accomplish His purpose, He can use anybody."

Ministering to Large Audiences

Like Andre, God has used the ministry of staff member Josh McDowell to minister to large audiences. During a 12-year period, Josh traveled to 539 campuses in 53 countries and spoke to an estimated five million people.

A graduate of Talbot Theological Seminary, Josh keeps the students interested in his message with well-documented historical, scientific and biblical evidences for the Christian faith. And he puts his whole personality into his delivery. Roaming the platform and gesturing enthusiastically, he'll treat his listeners to a joke or let them in one a personal incident from his past. His rhetoric is direct, and he doesn't mince words when exposing faulty thinking.

His messages rarely miss their target. Commented one student after hearing "Maximum Sex," "It presented dating and sex in a healthier light than I've ever heard it before."

On one occasion, 4,500 students came out to hear Josh speak on "Maximum Sex" at Kansas State University. This crowd represented approximately one-third of the student body. Some 400 students checked comment cards indicating that they had invited Christ into their lives that night.

At Louisiana State University, a total of 9,000 students came out to hear Josh during his stay on campus, with 900 of them marking comment cards that they had accepted Christ.

Preparation and Prayer

Successful outreaches like this do not come without a large amount of student participation and prayer. LSU students staged a campaign to build momentum for Josh's appearance on campus by entering a classroom, writing "Josh is coming" on the blackboards, then walking out. This went on for nearly two months before he actually arrived on campus to speak.

The blackboard campaign was followed by ads in the local newspaper announcing "Josh in January." Then, following Christmas, as registration for the next semester's classes took place, students posted 150 hand-painted signs and hung banners saying, "Josh is Coming January 21, 22 and 23."

Several days before Josh arrived, his identity was revealed. Teachers were contacted about speaking engagements in classrooms, student leaders were invited to a banquet, and all the details of his visit were publicized.

Despite the organization, last-minute problems provided the workers with numerous opportunities to trust God for the seemingly impossible. A scheduling error for the athletic field house appeared to thrust the Wisconsin series out in the cold. As others prayed, the student in charge of coordinating the lecture series spoke with the athletic director who decided to cancel women's basketball and junior varsity basketball so Josh could use the facilities. The contract was signed just two days before he arrived.

At the University of Illinois, the assembly hall was already booked for another event, and the rental price of $1,000 a night was far in excess of the budget for Josh. Yet there was no other facility on campus which could accommodate the expected student turnout. Prayer proved to be the answer.

"As we prayed about the situation," said an Illinois student in charge of the physical arrangements, "God unbooked the assembly hall, and He got it for us free! We simply had to say, 'Okay, God, You do it' and that's what He did. It was a real faith builder for me."

In addition to his campus lectures, Josh now speaks frequently to lay audiences. He has written several books, including *Evidence That Demands a Verdict* and *More Evidence That Demands a Verdict* which have both been on the Christian books' bestseller list. Also, he has been involved in the production of an inspirational film, "The Secret of Loving," which was broadcast on television in a number of cities across the nation.

Drama Ministry

Another of the specialized ministries of Campus Crusade is the drama ministry. Formed in 1974 by staff member Jeff Taylor, the drama ministry performs in churches, on campuses and in street theater evangelistic outreaches. Past productions include "Changing Faces," a testimonial performed by one of the drama staff; "O Virginia," which portrayed the life and Christian faith of Revolutionary War patriot Patrick Henry; "The Toy Shop" and "The Pandemonium Parables," a dramatization of several New Testament parables.

Drama ministry staff performed before some 3,000 students during a month-long tour of Ireland in 1978. The performance of "The Pandemonium Parables" at Carysfort Teacher Training College was one of the highlights of the tour. Nearly one-third of the college population attended the Thursday evening presentation. The show was stopped several times by applause, and all available copies of the Four Spiritual Laws were used. There were many opportunities to talk individually with students, and some of the discussions continued for several hours.

Presenting the Gospel by Multimedia

The Paragon Experience is another ministry that reaches large groups of people. A 45-minute multimedia production, Paragon is an effective presentation of the gospel and a dynamic tool for evangelism and follow-up. Nine projectors flash rapidly-changing images, synchronized to the lyrics of contemporary music, on three screens.

Because they are "still" shots rather than a moving picture, they can be more abstract, jumping from one scene to the next, allowing the viewer to fill in the gaps with thoughts and experiences from his own background.

The shows confront audiences with questions of life, death and Jesus Christ. "If I Should Die" tells the story of a young couple's carefree existence suddenly shattered by a head-on collision with death. "How's Your Love Life?" begins by laughingly commenting on the games of love. The story traces a student's agonizing search for fulfillment in life from the break-up of an "ideal" love relationship to the resulting depression that culminates in suicide.

Together, "If I Should Die" and "How's Your Love Life?" were presented to more than a quarter of a million people in the first three and a half years of Paragon's existence. More than 27,000 viewers indicated first-time commitments to Jesus Christ during that time.

Fulfillment of a Dream

Helmut Teichert first dreamed of evangelistic slide shows after becoming a Christian during his freshman year of college. During his junior year, with the help of three others, Teichert set to work on his production. The slide presentation dealt with the topics of Vietnam, drugs and ecology — and offered a solution in Jesus Christ. The following summer the Paragon Experience crew worked hard to produce a second show, which was the backbone of the current "If I Should Die." After college, the group premiered a third show at EXPLO '72 in Dallas to a crowd of 5,000.

Teichert and his wife, Laney, continued to develop Paragon at home while working on their dairy. At many of their showings they saw 25% of the audience respond to Christ. Seeing the great need to begin discipling these Christians, which Helmut and Laney could not do alone, they realized that Paragon needed to be part of a ministry like Campus Crusade that could provide the essential follow-up.

After applying for staff and being accepted, the Teicherts were assigned to Special Ministries to work on their own Paragon Experience. Since the development of the shows, they have toured the United States and Canada with presentations being viewed not only on several campuses but also in churches, high schools, camps, prisons and on military bases.

Individuals come to grips with the issues presented during the shows. One student commented, "For 19 years I've been looking for someone to love me. Tonight I know I finally found it. I know that Jesus has come to live in me now." Another responded, "As a Christian I had always known what I was saved for, but I never

thought about what I was saved from! I realized tonight
I've got to start telling the people I love about Jesus, even
though it's not easy for me."

CHAPTER THIRTEEN

Student Venture — A Ministry to High School Students

Scott Phillips was an enthusiastic, outgoing, rambunctious high school student at Princeton High in Cincinnati, Ohio. In most people's eyes he was a success. A ferocious goalie on the school's soccer team, Scott also played on Princeton's tennis team and was involved in other school activities.

But he was involved in less desirable activities, too, including frequent use of alcohol and marijuana.

"I was pretty wild," Scott says. "When I was almost arrested for possession of marijuana, I became disillusioned with my lifestyle. I saw that I wasn't headed in the right direction."

Some of his friends came to Christ through the high school Campus Crusade Student Venture group, and he began to take notice. After a period of five months he grasped the fact that he did not know Christ.

"It took me a month after that to let go of everything and come to Christ," Scott says.

Student Venture staff member Russ Bannister began to help Scott lay the foundation for Christian growth in his life. And he took it to heart. In later years Scott would return home from college each summer and take on leadership in a ministry which included sixty high schoolers. He led a delegation of students to a Student Venture conference in the Rocky Mountains, and he discipled several students, including his brother.

Individuals like Scott reveal the potential of high school students in making an impact on their world. And it's a world with grim realities: More than 5,000 teenagers commit suicide each year. A survey conducted by the University of Michigan revealed that nearly 62 percent of the teens are involved in some kind of drug use, while 38.7 percent reported having five or more drinks in a row within a recent two week period. According to the Guttmacher Institute, 49 percent of all 15-to 19-year-olds are sexually active.

After fifteen years of fruitful ministry with college students, Campus Crusade's official entrance into this troubled, turbulent mission field occurred in 1966. At this time many college students who had been reached for Christ through Campus Crusade were returning to their home communities and seeking to start Campus Crusade meetings among the high school young people. Thus, across the nation, high school Campus Crusade groups were starting unofficially. We had no control over them nor any opportunity to serve them unless we developed a special organizational program.

To avoid possible conflicts and misunderstandings, I met with Bill Starr, president of Young Life, and Sam Wolgemuth, president of Youth for Christ. They were warm and gracious. I remember Bill Starr's statement, which I believe expressed Sam Wolgemuth's thinking as well. "Bill, let me say to you that we are reaching perhaps only one percent of the high school students of America. It would be naive of us to say that there is no room for Campus Crusade to reach high school young people. We just ask that you cooperate with us, that you work with us, that you move carefully into what you are doing so as not to make unfortunate mistakes."

We had prayer together and from that time on Campus Crusade began a great effort to expand this ministry to help reach the millions of high school students.

So the High School Ministry, since renamed Student Venture, was launched under the direction of Carl Wilson. The strategy then, as today, calls for the staff to focus on a broad spectrum of students on the campus. It is also a part of the Student Venture strategy to reach out to the campus leaders — the athletes, student council officers, club presidents, cheerleaders, etc. As the staff reach a few of the leaders, other students will follow. One of the biggest things that keeps students from coming to Christ is a fear of rejection. But when a student knows that the peers he respects are taking a stand for Christ, he has the freedom to respond.

Staff members contact students before and after school and, in some cases, minister on campus during the lunch hour. At an all black high school in Atlanta, a staff member had so many students wanting to talk with her after school that she asked Carla, a new Christian, to meet with two of the girls. Carla read the Four Spiritual Laws booklet to them, and they received Christ. Thinking that the students were loitering in the hall, the assistant principal asked them what they were doing. Carla explained that she had shared with the girls a booklet about Jesus Christ and asked if he would like to know what it said. "It wouldn't hurt me to listen," he said, and in the hall outside his office, he asked Christ into his life.

Staff members also often take surveys or hold meetings with entire sports teams or clubs, thereby exposing several students at once to the issue of Jesus Christ.

These staff are seeking to win and disciple students who will be faithful in their walk with God and bold in their witness to their classmates. Mike, a student in Chattanooga, Tennessee, was one such student. He stood before fifty football players and cheerleaders and invited each of them to get together with him personally to discuss their relationship with God. Mike said, "I know a lot of you use God as a good luck charm before every game, and some of you pray to Him when you're in trouble, but I want you to know that knowing God is much more than that. I want to meet with any of you who are interested in developing a personal relationship with Jesus Christ."

Currently, Student Venture's 225 staff and their volunteers are ministering at more than 175 high schools in 18 metropolitan areas across the country, reaching out to more than 100,000 students each year. "Our ultimate goal is to help communicate the message of the love of Christ to every high school student in America," says Chuck Klein, Student Venture's director. By the year 2000 the ministry plans to help field outreaches at 3,800 schools.

Student Venture staff members help build Christian students in their faith through personal follow-up, discipleship groups, retreats and conferences. Conferences, called "Getaways," gather students each summer for a week of challenge, fun and training for action at four regional sites across the country. Some of the Getaways have attracted as many as 1,000 students and their leaders.

Kathy Schmid, a physical-education teacher, brought students to a Getaway for three consecutive years.

"The Getaway offers an environment where students can get to know God beyond a surface level," she says. "The Getaway offers an environment where all the other clutter in their lives — the stereos and other distractions — are gone."

Student Venture's "VITAL People" strategy involves volunteers, interns, teachers, affiliates and lay people in ministry. Student Venture helps these VITAL People assume more and more responsibility in reaching high schoolers with the gospel. Conferences such as the National Convention of High School Discipleship offer the kind of resources and training necessary to equip individuals to minister to high school students.

In 1985 Student Venture staff, working with Youth for Christ staff, sponsored a conference of another kind. Titled Youth Congress '85, the convention brought 20,000 students to the nation's capital to motivate them and equip them for the task of reaching their schools — and their world — for Jesus Christ.

Student Venture is committed to working with other Christian organizations, churches, volunteers, teachers and parents. The commitment is great, but the cause is greater — to reach a generation. Chuck Klein describes high school ministry as "an investment in the future of our culture. We're dealing with people at an age when they're formulating values for all of life. For any movement seeking to change the world, young people have been the main target."

Not only are we finding that we can make a difference in the lives of the young people, but sometimes whole families are influenced. At a March, 1984, program in San Diego, 1,300 students and parents attended a performance by André Kole, one of America's leading illusionists. The performance was sponsored by Student Venture. A total of 258 people turned in comment cards indicating that they had prayed to receive Christ. One of those was Rob, a junior at one of the high schools in the area. When one of the staff came to follow up with Rob, he discovered that Rob's mother and two sisters had also indicated decisions to accept Christ that same night.

Parents notice when their children's lives are transformed by Christ.

"Pete really has begun to live the Spirit-filled life," said one mother.

Kenny's parents were a bit concerned at first that he would "get so involved with Campus Crusade that he wouldn't be faithful to his own church." As it turned out, Kenny and several other students, motivated by a desire to transfer to others the truths they had learned, took on increased responsibilities in their local churches.

One mother remarked, "I have never before seen kids such as these — standing up for what they believe. The high school staff are certainly sending out missionaries for eternity!"

CHAPTER FOURTEEN

"Basic Training" for Military Personnel

We have the prediction of the Bible that we will continue to have wars and rumors of wars. With world conditions as they are, we know that as one hot spot cools off there will be another one to take its place, requiring a constant need for our armed forces personnel. They deserve to hear a clear presentation of the gospel.

The Military Ministry began in 1966, shortly after I was invited to address the congregation of a community church established by a local businessman with investments in real estate. This very gracious southern gentleman was Col. John M. Fain, USAF, Retired. During World War II, he had served on General Douglas MacArthur's 5th Air Force staff in the Pacific, and now he was devoting most of his energies to introducing others to the Savior.

After I had spoken in his church, where a number of people responded by committing their lives to Christ at the invitation, Col. Fain related how in the middle of the night he was awakened and felt strongly impressed of the Lord to ask me to start a new division of Campus Crusade for the military. He added that he would be available in whatever capacity the Lord would have him serve.

Reaching Military Personnel for Christ

This rang a bell with me, for I had long been interested in reaching the military and had on different occasions personally spoken at meetings for military personnel. I had always found servicemen very open to the gospel. Later, I suggested that Col. Fain come to Arrowhead Springs to head up a military division of the expanding ministry of Campus Crusade.

The Military Ministry now has a worldwide outreach. Among other things, it has distributed hundreds of thousands of Van Dusen letters and Four Spiritual Laws booklets in various army bases across the nation and around the world.

Many people who have not been in the service think of the military as uniforms and sophisticated weapons. Our staff see the military installations as very special communities. They are cities in themselves, with their own libraries, recreation areas, police forces, medical facilities and shopping centers. Some even have schools.

The real challenge, though, comes in reaching each individual there with the claims of Christ. The population includes more single men than most civilian communities and has a growing contingent of young, single women. It also includes neighborhoods filled with couples and their children.

Besides living in a diverse and challenging community, Christians in the military have a unique opportunity to reach beyond their bases to the world. The United States has military installations throughout the world which allow a trained man or woman to become an overseas missionary for the Lord at the expense of the government. Also, many countries of the world send their soldiers to the U.S. for special training, giving American soldiers another opportunity to exercise a worldwide influence for Christ.

Because of these factors, the Military Ministry emphasizes training military personnel. When a man leaves a base, we want him to have a vital relationship with Christ. When he arrives at his new base, we want him to be able to formulate his own strategy for winning the men there to Christ and discipling them.

Under the leadership of Col. Glenn Jones, former executive assistant to the chairman of the Joint Chiefs of Staff, our military staff are making an impact on military installations as they take the gospel to America's 2.1 million servicemen.

Our staff work on a specific base with the permission of the chaplain. Most chaplains welcome the assistance, and together with the staff, they develop a strategy to reach their base with the claims of Christ. Bible studies, action groups, prayer, planning and personal witnessing fill the days of the staff members as they work with the already committed Christians to train and build them in their faith.

"I thank the Campus Crusade for Christ staff members for helping us fill in a fundamental and necessary foundation of our chapel program," says Chaplain James Eastland.

Army Chaplain John De Seager explained that the Military Ministry staff work is an extension of his chapel program. "Because of my busy schedule, they often become my eyes and ears and hands and feet."

Evangelistic mass outreaches are also used in this ministry to expose hundreds of men and women to the gospel at one time. Singing groups perform often at military bases, and the Athletes in Action track teams give frequent athletic demonstrations and relate their faith in Christ. After these outreaches, those who receive Christ or express a desire to learn more about Him are contacted for follow-up.

Often, Lay Institutes for Evangelism are held to follow up interested service men and women. Skip Cannevit, a non-commissioned officer, came to a LIFE after attending a Campus Crusade music group's performance: "I was at the concert," Cannevit relates, "when one of the staff members came up to talk to me. I told him that I was a Christian, but that I was frustrated in my faith. He invited me to the LIFE, and there I saw that I hadn't understood what the Christian life was all about. I was trying to walk with the Lord on my own strength and on my own terms." Skip then became active in an action group on his base and reached out to other frustrated Christians and non-Christians.

Weekend Retreats

Weekends on base are times of recreation and intensive training in the Military Ministry, especially if the chaplain and staff members have organized a "Getaway" or retreat. Following one weekend retreat, nine people accepted Christ as their personal Savior, 32 rededicated their lives to Christ and 13 expressed a desire to enter full-time Christian service. Through these and other activities, thousands of servicemen are responding to the claims of Christ.

Military staff also offer assistance to the chaplains in making chapel programs as effective as possible in discipling the congregations and equipping them to be effective in reaching others for Christ. During the Here's Life, America campaigns in 1976, many chapels participated in helping to saturate their bases with the gospel message. This is also being implemented on overseas bases in conjunction with Here's Life movements which are being carried out in the area.

Possibly nothing illustrates the effectiveness of this work so dramatically as the story of one changed life. "All of my life I have searched for adventure," said one man. "Flying jet fighters as a naval officer seemed to be the answer for a while — with the added bonus of prestige and material security. But my craving for real action wasn't filled by combat missions and world travel. So my wife and I began a practical, realistic search for the most effective way to invest our lives for our Lord Jesus Christ. Exposure to Campus Crusade for Christ, to the changed and exciting lives of some staff couples, gave us the answer. We have found the action we sought on the full-time Campus Crusade staff."

CHAPTER FIFTEEN

The Message in Music

Music is a universal language, and tens of thousands are receiving Christ and committing their lives to His Lordship around the world through our music ministry.

The desire to be all things to all people brought about the birth of The New Folk, Campus Crusade's first singing group, and the beginning of the music ministry.

In 1966, 200 of our staff and students convened at Ohio State University for Operation Otherside, which was designed to saturate the campus of some 40,000 students with the claims of Christ. There I heard an outstanding singing group known as the Christian Minstrels, who had come from the University of Minnesota as a part of the Campus Crusade staff and student group under the direction of Ted Martin, then the director of the campus ministry for that area. The members asked me if I thought there might be a place for them in the ministry of Campus Crusade. As we talked and prayed together about such a possibility, I felt impressed to invite the entire group to come to Arrowhead Springs for training that summer.

During the course of that summer, the name was changed to The New Folk. After their training, the members took off for their first year of traveling and visited 125 colleges and university campuses in 27 states, singing before 250,000 people. God blessed their ministry in a remarkable way, and many thousands of students were introduced to the Savior through their concerts.

Overseas Outreach

From that beginning of eight New Folk singers, the music ministry grew to include at one time more than

10 singing groups that performed not only in the United States but also overseas.

The Forerunners, called the most outstanding singing group in Europe by secular and Christian leaders, presented concerts from 1967 to 1974. During one of their tours through Finland, the Forerunners performed before an average of 1,000 to 2,000 people every day. Those in the audience eagerly questioned the group members concerning their faith in Jesus Christ after the concerts. The leader of a large humanistic youth movement confessed that despite all of his attempts to find reality and meaning in working for the betterment of all men, he still found that there was a gaping emptiness within. After he received Christ into his life, he wrote, "You and your music got across to me like nothing has ever done before. It's a wonderful relief to have found the answer."

The Crossroads traveled throughout Asia, presenting evangelistic concerts. In Malaysia they drew 18,000 people to two concerts — making them the largest Christian gatherings in that country in the last 100 years — and performed to a total of 72,500 Asians during a seven-week tour.

After one of the Malaysian concerts, a Muslim girl named Nari asked a Crossroads member to explain to her the difference between Christianity and Islam. They discussed the uniqueness of Jesus, and the next day she talked to another Crossroads member who explained to her why he had become a Christian even though he, too, was from a Muslim nation. After three long talks, Nari received Christ. Later the Crossroads received letters from Nari in which she told them about the changes she noticed in her life since she accepted Christ as the only way to God.

At the same concert, a Buddhist student who was "tired of praying to a wall of stone statues" received Christ with a Crossroads member. Just before the Crossroads left to continue their tour, he expressed his eagerness to share his experience in Christ with his Buddhist parents.

The group's phenomenal impact for our Lord was evident through the results of a 22-month Asian tour. Visiting eight nations, the Crossroads performed 300 concerts, presenting the gospel to 256,000 people and saw 20,413 people indicate decisions to accept Christ as their Savior.

In international thrusts, American music ministry staff have traveled to other countries to give evangelistic and promotional concerts. The promotional concerts are designed to recruit workers who would help saturate a city or a country with the gospel.

On one such trip to the Philippines to assist in the Here's Life, Manila campaign, in personal witnessing after concerts and in random witnessing, music ministry staff talked to more than 900 people. About one-third of these individuals indicated decisions for Christ. In one instance, a staff member began reading aloud the Four Spiritual Laws booklet to a small group after a concert, and eight of the 14 students listening to him asked Christ to be their Savior. A combined total of more than 12,000 attended the 24 concerts, and of these, more than 2,000 signed up for campaign workers' training for Here's Life, Manila during the staff members' 19-day tour.

Hungry for God

Singing groups in the United States also find that people are hungry for God as they see thousands of individuals respond to His claims. At one New Folk presentation in a high school, 260 of the 600 students received Christ, with 125 others wanting to discuss the matter further.

Each of the music groups has developed a different style to communicate with various audiences of laymen, high school and college students, military personnel and prison inmates.

Besides the importance of evangelism in their ministries, stress is also placed on discipleship. Groups travel within specific regions so that performers have opportunities to personally follow up some of the people they lead to Christ during their concerts. Also, to insure discipleship, a follow-up program is set up with the local director of Campus Crusade to be carried out after the concert is over.

Part of the discipleship program also involves teaching others how to use their talents to share Christ. Music Institutes for Evangelism are conducted by staff members who teach individuals interested in music how to share their faith and how to put on an evangelistic music program.

It is the objective of the music ministry to present the ageless love of God and the exciting message of Jesus Christ to individuals through the medium of music. This method of creative expression has an appeal that crosses barriers and communicates throughout the world.

Each music program is designed to present Christ through a sound the audience is accustomed to, whether that be folk, soft rock, contemporary or classical. Communicating the reality of Jesus Christ to each individual in the audience is what the music ministry is all about.

As one student commented after a musical concert, "All the top professional groups have exploded my mind with questions. This group has satisfied me with the answers."

CHAPTER SIXTEEN

When Winning Is Secondary

Athletes have played an important role in the ministry of Campus Crusade since its inception. From the early years, all-Americans Donn Moomaw, Bob Davenport, Don Shinnick, Olympic decathalon champion Rafer Johnson and many others across the nation have been active participants in helping to reach for Christ other athletes and through them an even greater segment of society.

One of the first athletes to receive Christ and to become active in the movement was Donn Moomaw, UCLA's All-American linebacker of 1952. He passed up a promising career in professional football to study for the Presbyterian ministry. In explaining his personal decision, Moomaw said, "I am playing on God's varsity now. The temporary thrills of athletic achievement and the applause of the crowds cannot begin to compare with the challenge and the thrills of sharing Christ with others."

Donn's influence for Christ is worldwide. I met one outstanding young businessman, a member of Donn's church, whose business takes him all over the world. "I was an atheist," he said, "until I met Donn Moomaw. Through his life and ministry I became convinced that Christ is the only way to God."

The December 27, 1954 issue of the Los Angeles Examiner contained a full-page spread with testimonies of nine members of UCLA's great football team, the number one team in the nation that year. These nine first stringers were active in Campus Crusade. Four of them received All-American honors during their college careers.

Warner Award

One of the highlights of my experiences with these athletes was the day that Bob and Barbara Davenport handed me a little gift-wrapped box. Bob was one of UCLA's greatest athletes — a two-year All-American and student chairman of Campus Crusade. Upon opening the box, I discovered a beautiful watch with an alarm on it. I was very pleased, but could not understand why they were giving me such an expensive gift. Then Bob told me to turn the watch over and read the inscription on the back. It read: "Bob Davenport, Warner Award, 1955, to Bill, from Bob and Barbara."

I looked at Bob in amazement because this meant that he was giving me his most coveted award, one of the most prized awards, apart from the Heisman trophy, that an athlete on the West Coast can receive. I said, "Bob, I can't accept it. This is something that you should save for yourself or give it to your son."

But he insisted that because God had used Vonette and me in helping him and Barbara come to know Christ in a vital way, they wanted me to have the watch as an expression of their gratitude and love. You can well imagine how moved I was. In fact, I did what I always do when my heart is filled with joy and gratitude and I have no words to express it: I suggested that we pray. We all knelt together and prayed that, as I traveled around the country, God would use Bob's watch as a means of telling others the good news of our Savior. God has answered that prayer many times.

For example, as I was visiting Michigan State University, I met a junior who was a star football player and who had won All-American honors in both high school and junior college in California. The first thing the young man asked me was, "Do you know Bob Davenport?"

I assured him that I did and asked if he knew Bob.

"No," he replied, "but I have been one of his admirers for many years."

Bob Davenport had once spoken in his high school assembly, he explained, and had given such an inspiring and challenging talk that it had made a lasting impact on the athlete before me. Knowing that Bob never spoke unless he could give his witness for Christ, I asked this young man if Bob had spoken of his faith in Christ, and he said he had. Then I pulled off the watch Bob had given me, and the young man looked at it in wide-eyed amazement. After explaining why Bob had given it to me, I asked him if he had made the wonderful discovery of knowing Christ personally. He said, "No, I have gone to church almost every Sunday since I heard Bob Davenport speak in my high school assembly some years ago, but I have not yet made this decision. I don't know how."

Very quickly I explained how he could know Christ personally, and as we knelt together, he prayed and committed his life to Christ. All of this happened in a matter of minutes because God had already prepared his heart and had used Bob Davenport's watch in answer to our prayer.

Because of the influence that athletes can have, it became increasingly evident that a special emphasis needed to be directed toward athletes. In 1967, I asked Dave Hannah to direct the athletic ministry of Campus Crusade, which later became Athletes in Action. Dave played football for Oklahoma State University, where he led the team in scoring as a kicker. After graduation he tried out for the Los Angeles Rams, but painful leg injuries curtailed his career.

"I had an unquenchable desire to play pro football," Dave said, "but God suddenly took that desire away. Instead, He gave me a vision for challenging athletes to help reach the world for Christ."

A Platform to Share Christ

Dave believed that athletes could be an effective tool

for reaching the world with the gospel. He reasoned that since athletes are some of the most admired people in the country and the world, if they were won to Christ and discipled, they could use their position and fame to share the gospel of Christ with many who might never listen to a pastor, parent or teacher. He felt that an Athletes in Action ministry could establish teams in various sports and compete against colleges and athletic clubs. This would provide ready-made audiences with whom the athletes could talk about their experiences with Christ.

Dave's initial inspiration was a basketball team. By all worldly standards, Dave's idea for an Athletes in Action basketball team had no chance of succeeding. First, he had to get permission from the NCAA to play major colleges and universities as an extra game in their season schedules. Then he had to find schools willing to play an unknown, untried team of former college ballplayers.

Against all odds, permission came from the NCAA, and in 1967 Dave contacted more than 40 major universities who were interested in playing AIA. He ended up with a 29-game schedule for the 1967-68 season. Fortunately, no one ever asked Dave how many players he had or who his coach was. Because at that point, he had only one player. And no coach.

But that one player was the former captain of the number two-ranked University of Michigan team, Larry Tregoning. And by the time the season had opened on December 1, Tregoning had helped recruit nine other players and a coach, Fred Crowell, former head mentor for the University of Alaska.

Opening Games

Dave remembers how they opened their first season on consecutive nights against Utah and Wichita State. "Our scouts reported that while Utah's team was good, Wichita's was tremendous. In our first game, Utah won by more than 20 points.

"As we trailed by 18 points at half-time, I'll never forget the challenge it was for our ballplayers to get up and say, 'Christ is the answer to all the problems of life.'"

After an all-day flight, the new team arrived in Wichita, Kan., dead tired. Their prospects were not promising against the nationally-ranked Shockers. Before 10,000 screaming fans, AIA fell behind 23-5 after the first five minutes. Then a miraculous turnabout took place, and by half-time, AIA was ahead 46-44.

Athletes in Action lost that game, too, but only after a close struggle that went down to the final minute. Coach Fred Crowell recalled his thoughts after the game as the team presented its program. "Standing there lamenting the lost game, I heard Mack [Crenshaw] ask anyone interested in receiving information about how to mature in his relationship with Christ to turn to the back page of the program. Thousands of people responded. God was showing me that winning the basketball game was insignificant compared to our ultimate purpose."

Though winning games is not their ultimate purpose, AIA teams have compiled a fine record over the years. In their first season they finished with a 15-14 record, remarkable when you consider the fact that all of their games were played on their opponents' home courts. Even more important, however, the team spoke to more than 75,000 people about Christ. Dave and I both feel it is important to assemble the best teams possible for AIA. People respect you and listen more attentively to you when you are a winner.

Aiming for the Top

Dave set a very high standard. "If we could put together the best amateur team in the world," he said, "more people would listen to us share our faith in Christ."

Since that first year, the AIA basketball team has defeated many top-flight amateur teams throughout the United States. In 1972, the basketball program expanded to two teams, one located in the eastern section of the United States and one in the west. The teams later became known as the USA team, which played mostly major college competition, and the Challengers, who scheduled their games primarily with small college opponents.

In 1975, AIA began to take steps toward fulfilling Dave's dream about being the best amateur team in the world. During that year, Bill Oates, a successful coach at Santa Ana (Calif.) Junior College, took over the reins of the AIA USA team. Bill prayed often with Dave concerning potential new players.

Big things began to happen. Again and again Oates rushed into Hannah's office with the news that another player had been signed. Eventually, every player the two had prayed for decided to join AIA.

Oates meshed these new players into a unit that brought about a stark reversal of the team's fortunes. From a 30-13 record the year before, the AIA USA squad spurted to a sparkling 37-8 mark. Included in the wins was an 86-61 victory over the tough Cincinnati Bearcats. It was the first loss for Cincinnati on their home court in 33 games. The USA team closed the year by winning the National Amateur Athletic Union championship.

Turning Down Pro Offers

The 1976-77 season marked the arrival of several more talented basketball players. Two of them turned down offers to play in the National Basketball Association, and both are committed to the cause of Christ. UCLA's Ralph Drollinger was one of them. He turned down an offer from the Boston Celtics that year and another offer from the New Jersey Nets a year later for a three-year no-cut contract of $400,000. Ralph turned down these offers because, "I saw that the biggest challenge in my life is to know the character of Jesus Christ — to know Him and the power of His resurrection," he said. "One of my objectives is to help reach the world for Christ, to help fulfill His Great Commission."

Center Bayard Forrest turned down a Seattle Super-Sonics guarantee of $230,000 over two years. "I'm more excited about laying up treasures in heaven," said the former star of Grand Canyon College. With Bayard and Ralph anchoring the center position, the USA team roared to a 54-7 record. Included in those wins were two games that rocketed the team into national prominence.

The first of these games was with the undefeated University of San Francisco Dons, the top-rated team in the country. The game marked the first time in AIA's nine and a half year history that the team would be playing a home game.

They responded to the situation by dominating the powerful Dons, stretching an 11-point half-time lead to a 19-point victory, 104-85. All of a sudden, sports fans across the country began to hear about Athletes in Action. Daily newspapers devoted big coverage to the win, *Sports Illustrated* scheduled a special story and NBC-TV's *Grandstand* carried action spots from the game.

No Fluke

Within two weeks, AIA erased any thoughts that their win had been a fluke. They proved it by demolishing the fifth-ranked team in the country, the University of Nevada at Las Vegas, 104-77. Las Vegas' highly successful coach Jerry Tarkanian expressed his respect for AIA in post-game interviews. "They whipped us in every way . . . they totally dominated us. We got thoroughly whipped by a much better basketball team. They could stick with any team in the country." In addition to the credibility these two wins gave AIA, they also gave the 13,706 fans who attended the two games a chance to hear the gospel through their half-time presentation.

These two games set the stage for the season-ending encounter with the Soviet Union Red Army team, one of the best amateur squads in the world. In a thrilling battle before 10,239 enthusiastic fans, AIA lost 108-106. Clearly, Athletes in Action had made giant strides toward the fulfillment of Dave's dream of putting together the best amateur team in the world. In averaging 95 points per game over the year, AIA had outscored their opponents by an average of 21 points per game, an impressive showing. The team was also able to communicate the claims of Christ to 165,000 people who attended the games during the season.

The team started off the next year by downing the Russian team, 93-84. They went on to defeat Maryland, Michigan, San Francisco, Syracuse, Las Vegas and the coaches' All-American team, a team comprised of some of the year's finest college basketball players. They compiled a 35-game winning streak against college competition stretching over two years. "It's possible that the best non-professional team in the world might be a team of committed Christians who are using the game of basketball to help take the gospel to the world," observed Hannah.

The morning after their final regular season game, the team boarded a plane and flew to South America to join six other Western Hemisphere countries in the Christopher Columbus Cup. Representing the United States in the tournament, AIA defeated Argentina 81-69 in the finals to bring the championship home to this nation. This victory brought the season's record to 37-4, the best ever for the team.

AIA again was honored in the fall of 1978 as they were selected to be a part of the United States team in the World Basketball Championships in the Philippines. We praised God for the chance AIA had to represent the United States. To our knowledge it was the first time in the history of the tournament that a team committed to

Jesus Christ had represented its country.

Although the team struggled hard to win the championship, its efforts fell short. AIA managed to win six games and lose four in the tournament, placing fifth among 14 nations.

AIA's second basketball team, the Challengers, has also had its share of successes over the years. Playing mostly small colleges while the AIA USA team took on major college powers, the Challengers team moved to Canada to set up its headquarters and began playing Canadian colleges and universities. During that year, the Challengers pulled off perhaps the biggest victory in the team's existence by upsetting the Soviet National team, 79-71.

Wrestling Teams

Like our basketball teams, our wrestling squads have been blessed with success. Since the team was launched in 1967 with a tour of Japan, it has rapidly improved to the point where it rates among the top amateur wrestling powers in the United States. In 1971, the team won the Unites States Wrestling Federation Championship, symbolic of being the best amateur wrestling team in the nation.

Several of our wrestlers are former national collegiate champions, and many have been selected to travel overseas as representatives of the United States. Frequently they have had opportunities to share the gospel in foreign countries because of these honors they have received. In the 1976 Olympic Games at Montreal, two of our wrestlers represented the United States and won medals. John Peterson won the gold medal in his weight class, and Gene Davis was awarded a bronze.

Jim Axtell is a living testimony to how the Lord has used the AIA wrestling team to cause people to turn to Christ. During Jim's junior year at the University of Minnesota, he and his teammates wrestled the AIA team.

"After the match the man I wrestled shared with me what Jesus Christ meant to him," Axtell said. "As I talked to him, I could see in him a vital relationship with a living God."

A few days later, Jim decided to give his life to Jesus Christ. He began to see changes in his life over the following weeks and months. After graduating from college, Jim joined the AIA wrestling team so he, too, could use his talent as a means for explaining his faith to others.

Weightlifting

In the fall of 1969, AIA expanded into still another sport, weight- lifting. Russ Knipp, a man who has set nine world records and 30 American lifting records, helped the program get off the ground.

Over the years, the lifters who have made up our weightlifting teams have given exhibitions around the country in high schools, colleges, churches, civic clubs and military bases. During those exhibitions, the weight that they lift often surpasses existing records. Essential to the program is the presentation of the gospel. The lifters share their testimony, telling people how God has changed their lives and how they can allow Him to change theirs.

A track team was added to the list of AIA teams in 1971. Each fall the runners compete in top cross-country meets around the United States. Then they take to the indoor circuit to run against the leaders in amateur track. Several all-Americans and one world record holder have competed for the AIA track team. AIA also has a fine cross-country team, one which has won four national team titles since its inception.

Also touring the country and giving exhibitions at high schools and colleges is the gymnastics team. These athletes, too, take advantage of their exhibitions to present Christ to those in attendance. In addition to exhibitions, the team competes against top college and university teams.

AIA also fields soccer, softball and volleyball teams, has staff who minister to high school and college athletes and coaches, has radio and television programs and ministers to professional athletes.

Part of AIA's ministry to professional athletes has taken the form of training them how to share their faith and helping them to have an impact for Christ through Pro Week, a concentrated evangelistic outreach in one area. In 1973, 20 athletes participated in the first Pro Week in Atlanta, Ga. During that week the players spoke to high school assemblies, college campuses, civic clubs and church groups. As a climax to the week, the pros played an all-star team composed of football players from Georgia and Georgia Tech in a flag football game. When the final tabulation was taken, more than 73,000 people heard the claims of Christ with 10,000 making decisions. Since the Pro Football Week in Atlanta, teams have traveled to many cities and military bases throughout the United States and Canada.

Why AIA?

Much of AIA's incredible success story is told in the lives of the key athletes who make up these winning teams. People often ask the AIA members why they participate in the ministry, especially when there are greater financial rewards to be realized elsewhere. West wrestling coach Gene Davis, who has lost only two dual-meet matches in his 10-year AIA career, explains that he became a member of Athletes in Action "because I saw what a terrific impact AIA and Campus Crusade were having on different people throughout the United States and the world."

One professional football player said he has worked with AIA because of the need people have to hear about Christ. "Somebody was interested enough in me to come and tell me about Christ. And so I feel need to take advantage of the platform God has given me as a football player to tell young people about an answer to their needs."

More than five million people in live audiences have heard individuals on the AIA teams share the gospel through the first decade of the ministry. Millions more have heard the message over radio and television. "There's no way of knowing how many lives have been changed as a result of this ministry," Dave Hannah said. "Numbers can be misleading. But we collect comment cards after many of our appearances so that other Campus Crusade ministries can follow up those who receive Christ." More than 335,000 specified on their decision cards that they received Christ during the ministry's first 10 and a half years.

Through Dave's leadership, the athletic ministry of Campus Crusade has had a worldwide witness for Christ. The joy comes as the athletes hear what happens when they share the love and forgiveness of Christ with audiences. One student wrote after the basketball team played North Carolina State, "I used to be a drug addict and had sex problems. But now I want to live a Christian life. Write and tell me how."

One of the fans who attended an AIA game commented, "What you said tonight needs to be said more often to more people." Toward that end, Athletes in Action teams will continue to travel and compete around the country and the world, telling people about the life-changing promises of Jesus Christ.

CHAPTER SEVENTEEN

Multiplying the Message

Never before in history have we had such unlimited opportunities to reach the world with the good news of God's love and forgiveness. The diversity of the media — radio, television, newspapers, magazines, literature — provides us with the means to communicate to many individuals in the world how they can know Jesus Christ as Savior and Lord.

Bob and Amy George and their family provide a striking example of how the Holy Spirit can use the media to bring people to Christ. One of our earlier films, *Revolution Now*, which showed how God was using college students involved in our movement, was being shown on nationwide television. The Georges, watching the program in their home, were very moved by its conclusion — that Jesus Christ is the world's only hope. They later came to Arrowhead Springs for a personal appointment, and I had the joy of introducing both Bob and Amy to Christ.

Sharing Their Faith

The Georges promptly began to share their faith and joy in Christ with others — family, friends, business associates and employees — and saw many come to Christ. Desiring to know more about effective evangelism, Bob attended three Lay Institutes for Evangelism. Talking with me after one such training session, he asked about the some 2,500 people in the Los Angeles area who, like himself, had responded positively to the television program. I explained that each individual had been put on our mail list for our series of follow-up letters and materials, but due to limited personnel, we were not able to follow up each one personally.

Bob shared his burden for those people with me, stating, "I have felt strongly impressed of the Lord in the last few days that I should be personally responsible for following up all of these other 2,500 people. Would you allow me the privilege?"

I was overwhelmed. Only four months old as a Christian, yet he already desired to build other new Christians and pass on the training and knowledge he had learned. We gave him the assignment, and he immediately began organizing others he had introduced to Christ. Together, they began a program to follow up those in their area who had responded. A few years later, Bob and Amy joined our staff to work full time, and Bob played a major role in the overall success of Here's Life, America as director of the Dallas campaign.

What better way to do so than through the mass media?

The Impact of Mass Media

The communications media — newspapers, radio, motion pictures and television — have made a tremendous impact upon our society. They influence public opinion, keep us better informed than ever before in history, help mold character (usually in a negative way) and touch almost every phase of human existence. I am convinced that we, as Christians, should be utilizing the media for the proclamation of the gospel.

In a sense, proclaiming the gospel is like a military offensive, with the mass media serving as the air force — softening up the objective — so that the ground forces can come in and capture an area. The ground forces are those people making individual presentations of the gospel. The mass media play an important role as they prepare the way for those personal challenges to accept Christ.

Our commitment as a movement to utilize mass media tools to the fullest advantage to communicate Christ acts as a supplement to our commitment to personal evangelism. In many ways, our Mass Media Ministry serves and supports our entire movement, as well as churches across the nation. Our field staff make wide use of our evangelistic publications and materials in their ministries with individuals. Our radio and TV broadcasts reach individuals in areas where we do not have staff. And our staff use our tapes and training films to minister to many people simultaneously, thus increasing the scope and effectiveness of their personal ministries.

Chuck Younkman, who directedof our Mass Media Ministryfor a number of years, explains its importance this way: "Television, radio, films, tapes, audiovisuals and literature provide opportunities to reach millions of people at one time, as well as to increase our effectiveness in one-to-one situations."

Communicating to College Students

Our use of mass media began in response to a scarcity of evangelistic materials to attractively communicate to college students the claims of Christ. We began to publish the *Collegiate Challenge* magazine in 1967 to help meet that need, and since then, our staff and Christian students have used millions of copies across the nation and in other countries.

Thousands of students have made commitments to Christ through the influence of this magazine. One young woman picked up a copy in her sorority house. As she was reading it, a member of our staff dropped by, saw her reading it and began to talk with her about it. Before their conversation ended, she asked Christ into her life. After graduating from college, she joined the Campus Crusade staff and was used to introduce many others to the Savior.

Revolution Now!, a book containing my basic messages and content of our training, was published in July, 1969. The title *Revolution Now!* attracted a rebellious young radical who thought it had something to do with political revolution. As he read, he was surprised but not disappointed, for in the process of reading the book, he received Christ. After several years of exposure to our staff during which he received in-depth training, he made application for staff, was accepted and had a very fruitful ministry for our Lord.

Van Dusen Letter

One of our most popular pieces of evangelistic literature, the Van Dusen letter, came into being when a businessman who had expressed an interest in knowing Christ asked me to discuss the matter. Since he lived in New York and I lived in Los Angeles, it was not possible for me to visit him personally at that time. Instead, I wrote him a letter explaining the basic facts concerning Christ and the Christian life.

After mailing the letter, it occurred to me that this was the kind of letter that I could write to almost anyone whom I wanted to introduce to our Savior. So several thousand copies of the letter were mimeographed with the fictitious name of Van Dusen replacing the name of the friend to whom I had originally written. These mimeographed copies were used by members of the staff with students. The response was so encouraging, in some cases even phenomenal, that we decided to print it. Today, millions of copies of the Van Dusen letter are being used all over the world and are available in most major languages.

A Bible study series, The Ten Basic Steps Toward Christian Maturity, and our series of Transferable Concepts booklets, communicating basic truths of the Christian life, are widely used by all of our ministries. Thousands of local churches and other Christian groups also utilize these materials as they build those who have responded to the gospel and those who have been Christians for many years.

Our *Worldwide Challenge* magazine, sent to more than 100,000 readers each month, is designed to communicate the news about what God is doing worldwide as well as to encourage readers in their relationship with the Lord. Since its beginning in January, 1974, many readers have written that it has helped them to understand our ministry in greater depth in addition to encouraging them spiritually.

Here's Life Publishers

One of our most rapidly growing ministries is Here's Life Publishers. As a publisher, we are now releasing more than thirty new books a year. As a training resource, we are involved in training media staff, writers and other publishing personnel, on an international level. And we are directing translation and international distribution of books and Campus Crusade training materials in 150 countries. Through coordinating the publishing and distribution of these books, audio and video tapes, evangelistic tools and other products, Here's Life Publishers is making a life-changing impact worldwide, fulfilling the goal of moving people to ministry, helping them become active, involved Christians, and equipping these ministering Christians with the tools for evangelism, discipleship and leadership.

Film Ministry

Another branch of the Mass Media Ministry that is having a positive impact is our film department, now called Paragon. Our films are created for one purpose: to communicate the resurrected Christ, thus encouraging individuals to receive Him as Savior and Lord and to commit their lives as His disciples to helping fulfill the Great Commission. These films are shown in a wide variety of places — churches, youth camps, college campuses, reform schools, prisons and military bases. Through film we have communicated the story and miracles of EXPLO '72, ministered to the black community about Christ's relevancy to its needs, exposed the dangers of the occult, and shown Christians how to experience the joyous, fulfilling life Christ offers and how to communicate the good news to others.

One man, writing to tell us how God used *Too Late to Wait*, a film designed to communicate the gospel to minorities, shared with us the excitement of watching God work in his church after they showed the film in a secular high school sociology class. He wrote: "One of the teachers was very moved and thought the film was excellent. . . .As a result of this one film and other evangelical tools used in our congregation, the high school youth group has grown from three to over 30 witnessing Christians."

Other films on the Christian home and the role of the pastor are also available through our film lending library.

Our tape library also makes available hundreds of messages that have been part of our training programs over the years. With the compact, inexpensive, playback equipment now available, many are finding that they can listen to tapes anywhere. Messages available include the ministry of the Holy Spirit, training for evangelism and family living, evangelistic messages and a series of studies of several books of the Bible. In addition to these training tools, our Mass Media Ministry also supplies a variety of visual aids for our training institutes, classes and the School of Theology.

Television broadcasts of selected Athletes in Action basketball games have also reached many people. In addition to being treated to fine sports entertainment, the audiences have been presented with the claims of Christ through half-time programming.

CHAPTER EIGHTEEN

JESUS Film

Beneath a cool, starlit sky, Pakistanis of all ages sauntered out from pitch-dark corridors, finding a place to sit before the movie screen. Women dressed in flowing saris sat on woven mats, several rocking discontented babies slowly to rest. A horde of wide-eyed children squeezed close to the screen, their heads cocked uncomfortably back to look up at the picture. A wall of men stood around the dark perimeter of the gathering.

For most of the people in the small village of Korungi, this would be the first movie they had ever seen. The film was *JESUS*, a portrayal of the life of Christ based entirely on Luke's gospel.

The crowd swelled to about three hundred as the show began in Urdu. As the film unwound through four reels, the people remained hushed and transfixed. During the crucifixion scene, several faces contorted in anguish. Many people sobbed aloud. But when the risen Christ appeared to His disciples, sighs of relief whispered throughout the crowd.

"Tonight I have a new relationship with Jesus," said Mustaq, an 18-year-old street sweeper. "To think that He did all that for us — all that pain He suffered. Now I want to do something for Him."

This scene has been repeated across the globe as more than 250 million people have seen the story of *JESUS* and tens of millions of people — like Mustaq — expressed their desire to receive Christ as their Savior. The film has been translated into more languages than any other movie in history and has been called by some missions leaders "the greatest tool for evangelism in the history of the church."

The completion of this film and its use to present the gospel to so many millions is the fulfillment of a dream for me. Since 1947 I had wanted to be involved in the production of a film about the life of our Lord. At that time I was a young Christian and had a great deal of zeal, but not a lot of knowledge. Still, I approached Cecil B. DeMille, the famous filmmaker, about the project. In the silent era he had made a film about our Lord entitled, *King of Kings*, as well as other masterpieces including *The Ten Commandments*. DeMille was a great inspiration to me. On one occasion I met with him after he spoke at a church service.

DeMille told me that his father had been a Broadway actor who had come to Christ and endeavored to take the gospel to that segment of the entertainment industry. DeMille had come to Hollywood to make Christian films and said he would make nothing but Christian films if he had the money.

Neither did I have the funds to begin such a project. This lack of funding continued to thwart my dream for thirty years. For years after the founding of Campus Crusade for Christ, we discussed the need for a film on the life of Christ as an ideal tool for evangelism. We obtained copies of many of the more than thirty films done on the life of our Lord. Most of the films were not biblically correct. We even seriously considered buying the rights to one of these films and doing the work necessary to make it biblically accurate.

Although we felt that such a film would have incredible potential as an evangelistic tool, we never were able to secure sufficient funds for the production costs.

Then in the fall of 1976, I met a man in my office who had an amazing concept. He wanted to put the entire Bible on film. It was an awesome undertaking, but John Heyman seemed like a person with the background to make such a dream come true. Heyman was an outstanding Jewish movie producer who had produced more than twenty feature length films.

I introduced him to Paul Eshleman, who at that time was the director of our Campus Ministry in the United States. Paul and John formed a solid friendship.

Over the next few months, I had numerous meetings with John. Often when I was in Washington, D.C., he would fly in from his office in New York and we would talk until the wee hours of the morning about Jesus being the Messiah. Paul had even more frequent conversations with John.

Finally the day came when John was ready to make his commitment to Christ and God touched his life in an encouraging way. It was not long after that when John came to Arrowhead Springs for a special meeting. Paul Eshleman was with him, as were Bunker and Caroline Hunt, longtime friends and generous supporters of the ministry.

We chatted about the possibility of a film on the life of Christ which John Heyman would direct. The Hunts volunteered to play a major role in financing the project. In just a few moments, what I had prayed about for more than thirty years became a joyful reality.

Accuracy and authenticity were the watchwords of the film. Painstaking work by a team of researchers produced a 318-page document giving the biblical, theological, historical and archeological background of every scene. The Gospel of Luke provided the foundation of the script. In essence, the film was really a documentary/drama, with the film moving simply from scene to scene with no embellishments to the Scripture.

Jewish actors were used for most roles, but the search for an actor to play the lead role took months. Two hundred sixty-three actors were screen tested, and finally Englishman Brian Deacon was chosen.

Brian memorized whole chapters of Luke and read the Gospel twenty-two times before filming began. He was so convincing as Jesus that bystanders often broke into applause at the end of one of his speeches, and many asked to be healed by him after the healing scenes were filmed.

During the filming, all of which took place in Israel, Heyman demanded excellence, paying meticulous attention to detail. He stopped the filming once when he noticed a ripple-soled tennis shoe print in the dust.

Movies are notoriously difficult to make, and this one was no exception.

"This is absolutely the most difficult film I've ever tried to make," Eshleman remembers John saying. "You have no idea the problems we've faced."

When shooting began for Jesus' baptism and for the calming-of-the-storm scenes, the weather and water were freezing. Deacan caught pneumonia, and two days of filming were lost.

During the filming the message of Christ touched the lives of many involved. On one occasion a college dropout showed up looking for work. He had been drifting through Europe trying to find direction for his life. He wound up in Israel with empty pockets and an empty heart.

After carrying props on the set for a couple of days, he picked up a Gideon Bible in a Tel Aviv hotel room and began reading Luke. As he finished he slid to his knees and received Christ as his Savior. Five months later he was studying at Dallas Bible College to become a minister.

Even before *JESUS* was shown in theaters, it changed lives, often in surprising ways. When Eshleman was meeting with Hollywood executives to work out the film's distribution, he met one Warner Brothers executive who asked, "How would I begin, I mean with a faith in Jesus?"

Later, with a tear-choked voice, he bowed his head and asked Christ to come into his life.

"This is what the *JESUS* film is about," Paul says. "Searching people given new life, new hope and a reason to live."

JESUS opened in America in the fall of 1979. By the end of the commercial run a year later, more than four million people had seen the film.

After one film showing a teacher told her students she would be happy to tell them how to know Christ personally if they would come to her after school. Two days later she had led fourteen students to Christ.

In Birmingham and Jacksonville, theater managers gave their lives to Christ. At a special screening for college students in Sacramento, twenty-one indicated their desire to become followers of Jesus.

From its inception, however, *JESUS* was planned for the world. The very format of *JESUS* — with its simple, straight narrative right out of Luke — makes it easily adaptable for foreign translations. More than $10 million has been raised and spent so far on 100 translations — most of them lip-synchronized. Most versions also include an attached evangelistic closing. Campus Crusade plans to finish translations for 271 major languages by 1990, and another 1,000 dialects by 1995.

When the film opened in Europe's theaters, few expected much response. A theater owner in Zurich, Switzerland, reluctantly agreed to show the film, but only for a few days because he felt it would not be profitable. Six weeks later the film had shown to nearly 4,800 people.

A headline in England, where at one theater 10,000 people saw the film in four weeks, read "*JESUS* outdraws *E.T.*" The greatest theater run was in Singapore, where 200,118 people saw the film in four weeks.

We have seen phenomenal response in developing countries, where oftentimes fishermen and farmers still ply their trade the same way people in Jesus' day did. While hundreds responded to the film in America and Europe, thousands responded in Asia, Africa and Latin America. In these Third World countries, film teams equipped with portable screens and projectors take the film to remote villages. After setting up their equipment and passing out fliers, they often draw crowds of more than 1,500 people. For many it is their first opportunity to view a movie.

Team members sometimes operate at great risk to present the film. They have been attacked, robbed, imprisoned, stoned, poisoned and burned with firebrands.

"Every film team in India has been stoned and beaten," says Charlie Abro, coordinator of the film there. "We don't even think about it anymore. We just expect to have difficulties, and this is one of them."

The sacrifice and persecution is worth the effort. In several villages of Maharashtra, India, people often waited until 3 A.M. for the electricity to come on — and the program didn't conclude until 5:30 A.M. In other areas the people asked the team to show the film again as soon as it ended the first time. In one location it was shown three consecutive times.

The stories seemingly never end. During one week of some of the fiercest fighting in El Salvador, *JESUS* was shown in Santa Telca. Half of the city of 52,000 saw the film with 5,600 indicating salvation decisions. By the end of 1984, the film had been shown to more than 250,000 people in El Salvador.

In Burma the remote people of Hsanguang sent word to a Campus Crusade film team that they wanted to see *JESUS* during their harvest festival. The only way to get there was by helicopter, and the expense of that was prohibitive.

But the villagers did not give up easily. Soon projectors, generator, petrol, screen, cords, follow-up materials and team members were loaded onto elephants to carry them over the mountains to Hsanguang. During the harvest festival on two successive nights, 6,500 saw the film, and of those, 141 professed faith in Christ.

In many cases, some of the best news about the film takes place after it leaves. The village of Pamongan lies in the heart of Indonesia's Muslim stronghold. Still, about 200 villagers gathered in an open area one balmy evening to view *JESUS*. Just as the projector had started, the amplifier blew out. There seemed no choice but to cancel the show. A mullah (Muslim teacher) quickly offered to lend an amplifier from the local mosque.

At the end of the film, a villager named Subawi, his mother, Sunarti, and a brother named Swandini were the first to take a public stand for Christ. Two others, including a 50-year-old laborer named Parti, followed. The other was a mullah.

Campus Crusade staff members came to conduct follow-up sessions with the new believers. The first meeting had eight people present. But by the end of one year, nearly 200 people from the village gathered at Sunarti's house. This young church was then transferred to the care of a Southern Baptist church in Semarang.

"Jesus Christ is amazing," said Parti, the laborer who trusted Christ that first night at the film showing. "In the eyes of people, I am nothing. But because I am a Christian now, I am a son of God. It is a great privilege."

It is my prayer that in the coming years, literally billions of people — many in the Third World — will have the same opportunity Parti had to hear the life-changing message of Jesus Christ through the film, *JESUS*.

CHAPTER NINETEEN

Life at the Nerve Center

For many years, I have spent much of my time living out of a suitcase. Because of this, whenever Vonette and I return to Arrowhead Springs, every day there is almost like Christmas. No place in the world is more attractive to Vonette and me than Arrowhead.

I am not the only one who looks forward to coming to Arrowhead Springs. Often guests visiting Arrowhead comment on the radiant countenances, the cheerful attitude, the overflowing life and the beautiful spirit they see in our staff at Arrowhead Springs. It is the staff at our international headquarters who provide a vital supportive ministry for the worldwide work of Campus Crusade.

Oftentimes I am given credit for the phenomenal ministry of Campus Crusade — credit which I do not deserve or seek. The real credit must go to the Lord. But in His sovereign wisdom and grace, He has called a most unusually gifted and dedicated group of men and women to assist me in the direction and leadership of this ministry. These individuals with whom I am privileged to work are mature, Spirit-filled, able people who for the most part average 10 years of more with the ministry. Together we pray, plan, strategize and work to help fulfill the Great Commission.

Steve Douglass, vice president for administration, gives leadership to all the headquarters ministries which support the worldwide outreach. Steve graduated with honors from MIT and in the upper two percent of his class from Harvard Business School. Loren Lillestrand, our field director for the U.S. Ministries, is also based at

Arrowhead Springs and gives direction to our staff in various ministries.

Board of Directors

A remarkable group of outstanding businessmen serve as the board of directors for Campus Crusade. Their wise counsel has helped me to avoid many mistakes and make better decisions than I could have on my own. These men are:

S. Elliot Belcher, Jr., Chairman of Southern United Life Insurance Co.; Clarence E. Brenneman, Chairman, C.W. Tozer, Ltd.; Claude T. Brown, Chairman, Brown Transport Corporation; Bruce A. Bunner, Partner, Peat, Marwick, Mitchell & Co.; Leroy O. Eger, President, Decent Devices and IXTUS F.A. Costa Rica; Edward L. Johnson, Chairman and President, Financial Federation, Inc.; L. Allen Morris, President of the Allen Morris Co.; Arlis Priest, President, Priest Enterprises. The final member of the board is my beloved wife, Vonette.

I would like to write an entire chapter on each of these people and the others who report to me because of all that they mean to me and to this ministry, but to do so would require another 200 pages at least. Yet, you cannot understand the reason for the remarkable success of this ministry apart from these and thousands of others whom God has called and anointed to make this ministry possible.

Those who are responsible for the headquarters ministry at Arrowhead Springs belong to a team of qualified and successful businessmen who have dedicated their lives to Christ and to helping fulfill the Great Commission through the Campus Crusade ministry. These men serve under the direction of Steve Douglass and assist me in many important management decisions.

Choosing Campus Crusade Over a Secular Position

Typical of these is Jim Schroeder, who, with his wife,

Marti, left a profitable career in management with a telephone company to join He explains his reason for leaving business to join the staff as follows: "I found I was really desirous of living and sharing my faith constantly. And I felt that God had provided me with the skills in business that could be used in the best possible way for Him in full-time Christian work. I am thrilled with being able to share in the miracles God continuously performs through this ministry."

Says one staff member serving in a secretarial position, "I sincerely believe that every single function at Arrowhead Springs helps to reach thousands of people."

"Just knowing that I'm helping someone get information about what God wants him to do in terms of reaching the world for Christ is exciting for me," adds a secretary who works in personnel. She handles up to 40 letters a day from individuals asking how they might serve in the various ministries of Campus Crusade.

"We're all members of the same body," says one administrator, "and I count it a privilege to be serving in my capacity at headquarters. I love what I'm doing, but more important I love the Person I'm serving. Because God has called me to this ministry, I have a worldwide ministry and an excitement for what He can do."

These people, together with many other qualified, dedicated individuals who are totally committed to Jesus Christ and are bearing fruit in His power, are the force that makes Arrowhead Springs the bustling, productive, exciting, *living* place that it is.

Impact on Others

Arrowhead Springs is alive with impact. The 800 staff members, because of their direct involvement with thousands of programs and materials and millions of lives in a worldwide ministry, are influencing for Christ an unbelievable number of people of other lands and cultures. While field staff man the front lines, execute programs and use an increasing amount of materials, they depend on the staff at Arrowhead Springs to provide the supply line — to keep the action going.

Arrowhead Springs is alive with work. The staff at the international headquarters are constantly planning, organizing, corresponding, creating, reviving, reporting, training, teaching, publicizing, studying, rehearsing, praying, writing, reaching. Although Arrowhead Springs was formerly a resort and spa for business tycoons and Hollywood movie stars, it is now definitely a workspace for the Lord.

Arrowhead Springs is alive with multiplication. As an international training center, it is the location for continuous teaching and training of Christians — showing them how to experience the Spirit-filled life, how to share their faith, how to teach others to experience and share the same life of victory and fruitfulness. In other words, they are trained to multiply. This training — whether it is through a Lay Institute for Evangelism, the Institute of Biblical Studies, a high school conference, Pastors' or Executive Seminar, a Church Growth or Management Institute — is also available to all of the headquarters staff.

Fellowship

The entire Campus Crusade staff, including myself, whether at headquarters or on a campus or in a community, are daily challenged to be all that Christ wants us to be — that is, servants living in obedience to His commands under the power of the Holy Spirit. Together we are laboring to help fulfill the Great Commission in this generation. Every ministry, every office, every publication, every policy, every activity and every project revolves around this goal.

A major department within the financial system of the ministry is accounting. This office reports to the director of finance and assists me with the responsibility of caring for God's money; administering all financial policies, bookkeeping, budgeting, payroll, accounts receivable and payable; and administering insurance.

Also under the financial system are computer services, purchasing and the word processing center which handles much of the ministry's typing and correspondence. For greater efficiency and economy of operation and thus greater glory to God, computer services use electronic data processing equipment. Computer operation, key punching, programming and systems analysis are the main responsibilities of this necessary department.

Conference Services

The conference services department seeks to provide warm, efficient Christian hospitality to visiting staff, students, laymen, conferees and dignitaries. This responsibility involves hotel management, guest reception, food services and housekeeping. The Arrowhead Springs campus is considered one of the most beautiful conference centers in America. When not used for our training conferences, the facilities are made available to churches and other Christian organizations.

Technical services is another area vital to the management and upkeep of headquarters. Since the time the Lord first gave Arrowhead Springs to us, we have shown our gratitude and willingness to care for His gifts by assigning a full-time staff to maintain the grounds and buildings and to landscape and plan the development of new facilities. Under the direction of the grounds staff, the Arrowhead Springs campus becomes increasingly more beautiful each year.

With plans and prayerful expectation for 110,000 regular and *Agape* Movement staff, the personnel department is constantly involved in recruiting and placing staff, maintaining personnel files and managing personnel. Its primary aim is to be used of God to place His people in strategic areas of His service.

The Mass Media Ministry serves with the belief that nothing is impossible with God. Through wise use of magazines, newspapers, mail campaigns, radio, films, television programs, evangelistic audiovisual aids and counseling by mail with both Christians and non-Christians, we are helping this generation hear of the love of Jesus Christ and learn how to know Him personally.

Handling the Mail

Within mail systems is the correspondence department. It has the mammoth but rewarding task of corresponding with thousands of new Christians on a regular follow-up schedule, plus maintaining the entire Campus Crusade mailing list.

Separating and making sure that incoming mail gets to the right people is a major function of mail systems. In addition, the department records all contributions made through the mail and relays the information to the accounting department.

Using God-given Skills

Arrowhead Springs is alive. Here is a place where any committed Christian, no matter what his special skill or talent is, can fit in and be used of God in a fruitful and world-changing way. In fact, we are continually praying for more individuals with secretarial, clerical and administrative background and skills — qualifications that one does not normally associate with Christian service but that are actually indispensable to a worldwide evangelistic movement.

The headquarters staff member is in a strategic spot. He is in the heart and nerve center of a movement that is being directed and blessed by God. He is a prayer warrior for missionaries of the whole world; daily he has cause to praise God for specific miracles occurring throughout the world. He is doing the initial, necessary work that results in much more fruit on the field. Every day he is helping to plant and water thousands of seeds of the Word of God and is reaping 30-, 60-, or 100-fold. If you are interested and qualified for one or more openings for headquarters staff, please write for more information.

CHAPTER TWENTY

EXPLO '72

In 1969, I was sitting on the platform of the great City Auditorium in Minneapolis during the U.S. Congress on Evangelism. Together with evangelist Akbar Haqq of India, I was enjoying one of Dr. Billy Graham's messages.

At one point during the message, I leaned over and mentioned briefly to Dr. Haqq that I had felt a strong impression from the Lord that Campus Crusade should sponsor a congress on evangelism — primarily to train young people in how to share their faith.

"Bill," he said, "I think you should do it."

This was the birth of an idea which later became one of the most tremendous events in the history of our movement.

100,000 Delegates

After returning to Arrowhead Springs, I presented the idea to our ministry directors, some of whom were enthusiastic. Others were skeptical that we should undertake such a big task. Finally, after several months, we were in agreement to proceed. So, we began talking and praying about assembling possibly 100,000 students in a major city of America for such a congress. The suggested time was the summer of 1972.

On February 21, 1970, I was speaking at a conference in a Chicago hotel. After my message, I asked Paul Eshleman, then our campus director in Madison, Wis., and his wife, Kathy, if I could meet with them for a few minutes. That was when I told Paul that our regional directors had voted to assign the general management of this gigantic, week-long training session to him. I asked him if he would do it, and after several days of seeking the Lord's guidance, he accepted.

Things started rolling very soon as, in March of that year, Paul visited the two possible locations for EXPLO '72 — Dallas and Chicago. The Texas city turned out to be the one which, we discovered, could best accommodate the number of students and lay people we were going to host.

As Paul met with incredulous officials at the Dallas Convention Bureau and the Chamber of Commerce to discuss our plans, the task became realistically clear: We were going to be moving a city into a city! But the leaders of Dallas gave us the go-ahead.

In May, Paul and Kathy moved to Dallas and then spent the summer at Arrowhead Springs, where we developed the initial plans for EXPLO.

At the end of the summer, 10 "charter staff members" for EXPLO accompanied them back to Dallas to begin the two-year-long preparations.

The responsibilities of the EXPLO staff, which eventually grew to 300 by the time of the Congress arrived, were mammoth: building a national promotional strategy including radio and TV spots, a promotional film, newspaper releases, ads, brochures, church bulletin inserts; inviting Christian leaders from across the U.S. to speak, *and* arranging for rooms, beds, meals, transportation and registration for 100,000.

Prayer Power

They worked long hours, sacrificing personal time and sleep. But even more, they prayed. And around the country, as we prayed with and for them, we saw God supply their needs day by day as they believed Him for big things.

For example, we prayed for 200 promotional film agents who could help build enthusiasm for EXPLO. By the time EXPLO began, there were at least that number, with 1,000 films in circulation — the largest distribution of Christian films ever developed, the producer told us.

Trusting God for office equipment, the staff prayed for an adding machine. A man brought one to them. They prayed for a copier. A man donated the use of his. They asked the Lord for a good entree with hotel sales managers, and before the congress was over we had the largest bookings ever given to any organization for a convention in Dallas.

And, of course, we continued to pray for the delegates who would come. We prayed that the Lord would cause many thousands to see a need in their lives for a closer walk with Him, a desire to share Him with others, and practical, natural ways of doing just that.

85,000 Registered

In February, 1972, only four months before EXPLO was to begin, we had registered only 19 delegations. By opening date, under the dynamic leadership of Mary Banks, a remarkable businesswoman who volunteered her services, we had 1,300 delegations coming from 1,000 cities. The total number of registered delegates grew to approximately 85,000, with representatives from about 70 countries. On June 12 they poured into Dallas by plane, automobile, motorcycle, bus, in campers, on foot and on bicycles. As early as 3 a.m. that morning, buses began arriving at huge Market Hall, just off the Stemmons Freeway, where the delegates would register.

During the long hours of waiting to register that day, amid the heat, the inevitable inconveniences and the transportation complications, many of the conferees sat on suitcases, studied their Bibles, sang or prayed. Their attitude was an inspiration. Most of the delegates adopted the slogan, "You can't make it tough enough for me to complain."

As the staff met for prayer at dawn, Dallas morning papers carried full-page ads with the words: "Something

historic is happening here." The same message flashed
continuously from an electronic sign on the Blue Shield
Building downtown. Mayor Wes Wise repeated the
words on TV spot announcements all morning. Dallas
gave a warm welcome to EXPLO '72.

The congress became historic because it was the
largest week-long Christian training effort in the history
of the world (up to that time). Specialized training was
held in 63 locations throughout the city for collegians,
high school students, lay men and women, pastors, faculty members, military personnel, blacks, business
executives and their wives, athletes and 2,000 international delegates.

Basics of the Christian Life

In morning sessions, presented in workshop and lecture format, conferees heard about the basics of the Christian life: how to walk in the power of the Holy Spirit
daily, how to experience God's love and forgiveness, how
to know His will, and how to communicate His love and
plan to someone else. This was the "meat" of EXPLO.
Many guest Bible teachers like Dr. J. Edwin Orr, Dr.
Harold Ockenga (president of Gordon-Conwell Seminary), and Sam Wolgemuth (president of Youth for Christ
International) gave messages that helped clarify the real
meaning of discipleship.

Students were also assigned to small action groups
of six to eight with a leader. Action groups met several
times during the week so that students could discuss
what they had been learning and receive personal counseling from their group leaders.

Afternoons offered an array of 49 optional seminars
of which delegates could take advantage. Topics ranged
from Christian marriage and dating to using the mass
media for Christ, black rap sessions, self-acceptance and
dealing with the occult.

After hearing a message entitled "How to Live With

Your Parents," one girl, a graduate student at the University of California at Berkeley, said, "I'm going to go home and ask my mother's forgiveness for my rebellion."

Free time in the afternoons found the delegates visiting the Christian Opportunities Exposition, which allowed them to investigate staff possibilities with 206 Christian missionary groups, schools and churches from around the world. We had invited them to come to EXPLO '72 as our guests to promote their ministries. We were told that nothing like this had ever happened before. Many delegates, having come to EXPLO with open hearts, willing to go anywhere for God, found the exposition invaluable.

Intercristo, a Christian computer matching service, provided a personalized computer report on specific job openings in many of the organizations at the fair. For $3, the delegates received lists of five to ten opportunities which matched their own skills and education. With that, they were prepared to investigate the organizations that they knew were looking for someone with their qualifications.

The Wycliffe Bible Translators showed a multimedia presentation of its work in primitive countries. By the end of the week, in addition to 480 requests for more information, four couples had made definite plans to begin training for Wycliffe staff.

We did everything we could to enable the students to spend as much time as they needed at the Exposition, allowing the pavilions to open early and stay open until midnight on some occasions. We were encouraged and overjoyed to hear most of the exhibitors report that the EXPLO exposure was the most profitable they had ever had.

Nightly Meetings in the Cotton Bowl

Each evening of EXPLO week, the Dallas Cotton Bowl literally rang with praise to God as delegates, united in what seemed to be a gigantic family reunion, filled nearly every seat in the stadium. An overflow crowd, made up primarily of enthusiastic high schoolers, settled on the plastic-covered astroturf of the playing field, and still others watched by closed circuit TV in nearby Memorial Auditorium.

The evenings were filled with the blessing of God as Dr. Billy Graham, EXPLO's Honorary Chairman, and Dr. E. V. Hill of the Mt. Zion Baptist Church in the south central area of Los Angeles joined me in speaking to that vast and enthusiastic multitude. Performances by well-known Christian singing groups, on-stage interviews with delegates who were eager to share something that God had done or taught them during the week and reports from international representatives rounded out the mass rallies.

Each night the spirit was spontaneous and full of rejoicing as delegates clapped to the music and sang along with the performers. The stands resounded with the words "Praise the Lord!" and often the response "A-a-a-a-men!" would come from another place in the stadium. Bob Horner, our area director for Colorado-Wyoming, emceed these sessions. "I've never been on a stage where there was so little fear," he said. "It's just like performing at a family reunion."

Governor Reubin Askew of Florida, an EXPLO delegate himself, agreed. "What stands out the most when I see this group of young people, black, white and yellow, in the Cotton Bowl [approximately 60,000 of the delegates were college and high school students] with long hair and short hair — is that they have found a common bond in Christ. They accept each other for what they are — God's children."

Spreading the Good News

But the delegates to EXPLO '72 could not and did not keep the love of Christ just within the "family circle."

His love caused them to take advantage of every opportunity that week to tell Dallas citizens, policemen, shop-
pers, bus drivers and news reporters that God had a
plan — a wonderful, abundant plan — for their lives,
too.

We were praying that EXPLO would serve as an important steppingstone toward the fulfillment of the Great
Commission in the entire United States by 1976 and the
world by 1980. And as we saw 85,000 delegates, supplied
with Four Spiritual Law booklets and Gospels of John,
move throughout the Dallas-Ft. Worth area and willingly
take the good news of our Lord to tens of thousands on
the Tuesday and Wednesday afternoons of witnessing,
we were reassured that the Great Commission truly can
and will be fulfilled.

Although records were incomplete, estimates indicated that at least 25,000 had received Christ by the end
of the week.

Joye Scott, from Rockford, Ill., said the people she
talked to were open and receptive. "They welcomed us
into their homes and were curious to find out what we
really had to say. Most agreed that we did have something to tell the world."

"I've been approached by several [delegates] and they
all seem very sincere," noted Dallas public accountant,
J. M. McDonnel. "The EXPLO movement is the greatest
hope the world has had in decades."

In a spot survey taken by the *Dallas Times Herald*,
the reporters found that "the mood of an overwhelming
majority of businessmen, secretaries and office workers
interviewed on downtown streets Thursday was one of
frank support for the delegates."

Captain John Squier of the traffic division reminded
Dallas citizens of the importance of being patient in the
midst of traffic tie-ups during the week. "When you
consider that these people are here in the spirit of Christ
and brotherhood, I would say that it's a worthwhile traffic
jam were are having."

As did many that week, Dr. Graham commended the hospitable Texans. He praised them for the "wonderful spirit in which you have taken EXPLO delegates to your hearts and into your homes."

Final Rally

A final Cotton Bowl rally was held on Friday evening, ending in a moving candlelighting ceremony which symbolized the spreading of God's love from person to person throughout all the world. Then on Saturday the congress was climaxed by an evangelistic Jesus Music Festival attended by 180,000 — many of whom were not Christians when they came. The festival began at 7:25 a.m., since people had already started settling down in front of the 150-foot wide rolling stage, erected on a huge vacant area downtown where the Woodall Rodgers Freeway would later be built. Christian musicians such as Johnny Cash and his family, the Statler Brothers, Andrae Crouch and the Disciples, Connie Smith, Kate Henley (from "Godspell"), Larry Norman and scores of others made the arena reverberate with songs that uplifted the Savior.

By 3 p.m., after Dr. Graham had given his message, everyone at the festival had heard a clear explanation of how he could receive Jesus Christ if he had not already done so. And afterward, across the long stretch of pavement, EXPLO delegates could be seen sharing God's love through the Four Spiritual Laws with individuals hungry for a new life.

That day, 85,000 trained men and women and students left Dallas with a plan and a desire to capture their communities for Jesus Christ. As a result, I believe that a new emphasis on evangelism was introduced into many churches and Christian youth groups. As newscasters interviewed delegates to ask what the week had meant to them, the most common reply was, "This week I learned how to witness for Christ." Trained people can change communities everywhere.

On the last two evenings in the Cotton Bowl, when I challenged delegates to stand if they were willing to invest their time, talent and treasure for the fulfillment of the Great Commission, the majority of the audience stood.

Also, we praise God for the testimony that EXPLO was to the non-Christian world. Approximately 400 media representatives converged on Dallas from the U.S., Holland, Norway, New Zealand, Israel, Germany, France, India and the Philippines. National media — CBS, NBC, UPI and AP — major Christian and secular magazines and even some radical underground papers were also on hand. Around the world, the news media were saying, "These students are different."

The exposure of the congress was increased even more during the two months that followed, as three hour-long EXPLO '72 specials were broadcast over nationwide television on 235 stations across the U.S. Each program had an estimated audience of 35 million.

And finally, EXPLO '72 served to give us all an increased concern for the nations of the world — that millions would have an opportunity to hear the gospel.

The five days in Dallas were ended, but we believe that the spiritual explosion begun there will continue to have results around the world for generations.

CHAPTER TWENTY-ONE

The Great Commission Prayer Crusade

"There's nothing I can do."

I've heard that statement many times, and yet I am amazed that even Christians believe that to be true of the crises confronting our world.

There is something anyone can do — whether he or she is a business man or woman, a homemaker or a student. Any Christian can pray, and prayer is the greatest power in the world.

One day, when all of the secrets of God are fully understood by the children of men, most Christians will marvel that they never fully appropriated the mighty spiritual resources of God's promises to all who believe in Christ because they never learned how to pray. No privilege known to men compares with the privilege of having fellowship with God — literally talking to Him and experiencing His response.

In 1972, our nation was faced with one of its greatest times of crisis in 200 years. Because of the importance and the urgent need for prayer, my wife, Vonette, felt impressed to launch the Great Commission Prayer Crusade, which was initially designed to organize, mobilize and motivate women to pray. Leading Christian women, including Mrs. Billy Graham; Mrs. Harold Lindsell, wife of the editor of *Christianity Today*; the late Mrs. Howard Davidson, daughter of Abraham Vereide, founder of International Christian Leadership; and Mrs. Fred Dienert, speaker with the Billy Graham Evangelistic Association, joined Vonette in speaking at various city-wide prayer rallies. There was a great response, not only on the part of women but also by men. Their concern for the spiritual and moral climate of our nation became a basis for a movement to inform and unite Christians from all denominations and organizations to pray, in groups of two to 20, for a spiritual awakening throughout the world.

Encouraging Christians to Prayer

As the name Great Commission Prayer Crusade suggests, it is the purpose of this ministry to encourage millions of Christians to unite in praying for world revival and the fulfillment of the Great Commission. God has impressed us throughout the years to continue to give the highest priority to prayer. I believe that is one of the major reasons why He has consistently poured out His blessings on Campus Crusade ministries.

The ministry began in 1951 with a 24-hour prayer chain. The 24 hours were divided into 96 15-minute periods, and around the clock people were praying that God would speak to the students on campus. There were dramatic conversions; people who hated God and who were enemies of God had fantastic transformations. There is no way to account for what happened apart from the supernatural intervention of God in answer to prayer.

I think of a young man who was a big man on campus, socially and athletically. He hated God and was very critical of the Christians on campus and in his fraternity. He drank heavily and was on the verge of becoming an alcoholic.

I was invited by some of the men who had received the Lord through our ministry to speak in the fraternity house where he was president. When they approached him to extend to me a formal invitation to speak in their fraternity, he said, "I don't want any of those religious fanatics in this house. If Bill Bright comes, it will be over my dead body." I didn't know about this at the time, but later these men, several of whom were husky athletes, told me that they replied that was all right with them — over his dead body. So, over his objection, I was asked to speak.

As I spoke that night and gave an invitation for those who wanted to receive the Lord to come and talk to me, this fraternity president was one of the first to approach me. I invited him to have lunch with me later in the week.

"I Need God"

As we sat over lunch, he told me that everyone thought he was happy because he was always the life of the party, a big athlete, a big fraternity man and always living it up. "But," he said, "I'm probably the most miserable fellow on this campus, and I need God." In the car as I drove him back to his fraternity, he received Christ into his heart.

That afternoon he began to read his Bible. His roommate inquired, "What did you do, get religion?" He said, "Today I received Christ." The roommate answered, "I know you. You are just boning up for a debate." The next morning he stood before all his fraternity brothers, many of whom were also Christians, and announced, "Yesterday I received Christ. You know what kind of a fellow I've been, and I know I'm going to have a rough time living the Christian life; I want you to pray for me." God used him to make an impact on the entire campus; I believe this was a result of prayer.

Year after year we have witnessed miracle after miracle, I believe, as a result of prayer. In December of 1971, many groups of Christians in neighborhoods, businesses, churches and on campuses began to pray for EXPLO '72. There were many problems, and the registration was very small. The future looked bleak indeed. It was only as thousands of Christians around the country began to pray with a deep sense of urgency and faith, largely because of Vonette's influence through the Great Commission Prayer Crusade, that God met many of the logistical needs of the gathering, and registrations began to pour into Dallas. Through prayer, God brought more than 85,000 people to EXPLO '72.

Around the Clock Prayer

In the wake of the mighty outpouring of God's Spirit at EXPLO '72, we decided to broaden our prayer base even further by establishing an ongoing 24-hour prayer ministry at the Guy F. Atkinson Memorial Chapel at Arrowhead Springs. We have seen some dramatic answers from that prayer chain and the others that have sprung up on campuses and in communities around the United States and the world.

On one occasion, I was to speak to more than 1,350 leaders at a governor's and mayor's prayer breakfast. I had to fly all night to arrive in time for the meeting. In spite of my weariness, 369 people indicated that they received Christ that morning. Certainly one important reason was prayer. While I was speaking, there were 30 staff members on their knees in the chapel at Arrowhead Springs where it was 5:30 a.m. I believe that this was a dramatic demonstration of the power of their prayers, and those of others, including my own.

In an effort to unite individuals and groups to pray, we discovered that people are relatively easy to marshal together for urgent crises or emergency issues. After a few meetings, however, the interest for many people wanes because persistent prayer seems mechanical and repetitious. Even though prayer is the Christian's most powerful weapon against wickedness and the powers of darkness, it is perhaps the most neglected facet of Christian worship — probably because people don't know how to pray. Realizing this, the Great Commission Prayer Crusade developed the Dynamics of Prayer workshop to teach people how to pray. Trained representatives teach these workshops through a concept that is transferable.

Prayer/Care Ministry

Another ministry, the Prayer/Care Ministry, blossomed in 1977 when Vonette posed the question, "If prayer is so important, so vital to any ministry, then why aren't there full-time ministers of prayer?" Senior staff were recruited for this ministry. Assessing the implications of Vonette's question, staff member Paul Utley responded by giving his full time to prayer and encouraging other staff who joined Prayer/Care. "I thought about that over and over again," he said. "Then I found a scriptural precedent in the life of the prophetess Anna. She spent every day in the temple in intercessory prayer."

Contrasting Anna's vibrant example with the prayerlessness of most American Christians, Utley agreed with Vonette that combining a telephone prayer and counseling ministry with round-the-clock intercession for a host of prayer requests could have a significant impact. September 16, 1977, was inauguration day for Prayer/Care.

That day, the first caller was an 18-year-old girl, a victim of leukemia. One of our staff members listened as the girl told how doctors had given her but three months to live. Soon the staff member led her in prayer as she indicated her willingness to trust Christ as her Savior.

Her story, however, doesn't end here. Intercessory prayer will attend her far beyond the first phone call and those infant steps as a new believer. Such follow-up is the goal of Prayer/Care's request monitoring system.

Neighborhood and Church Prayer Groups

A number of cities have adopted the strategy of choosing a prayer coordinator with a steering committee of individual church prayer coordinators who divide the city in areas, encouraging neighborhood churches and church prayer groups. A monthly praise and prayer bulletin is distributed to inform individuals, churches and groups about local and national concerns for which to pray. This effort supports the various Christian out-reaches in the city. The bulletin locally is a supplement to the Praise and Prayer Sheet that is mailed monthly by Campus Crusade to thousands throughout the United States and other parts of the world. This mailing encour-ages Christians to pray for many different projects and organizations.

The Great Commission Prayer Crusade is a vital part of the prayer movement for Here's Life around the world. As a result, city-wide 24-hour prayer chains in many churches have continued.

"Calling the world to prayer" is the slogan of the Great Commission Prayer Crusade. It is the goal of this ministry that every major city around the world initiate an established prayer ministry, uniting and informing Christians of issues for which to pray, with a prayer center similar to that of the present Prayer/Care Ministry at Arrowhead Springs. This goal can be realized by churches committing themselves to praying within a specified number of hours one day a month. It is possible for as few as 31 churches to support such a ministry if one church is responsible for 24 hours only once a month.

To unite and aid individuals in specific prayer, a per-sonal prayer diary was developed in 1978 encouraging Christian people to pray for specific concerns Sunday through Saturday. It also includes a map and listing of countries of the world, encouraging prayer for world concerns. There are also included many prayer helps allowing the individual to adapt the diary to his personal use.

Calling Thousands to Prayer

In recent years, since our sons have gone away to college, Vonette has called thousands to prayer as she has traveled with me. She has helped to launch the Great

Commission Prayer Crusade in scores of countries.

Prayer has steadily been an integral part of our work in Latin America, too. At the Latin American Training Center in Cuernavaca, Mexico, a beautiful Great Commission Prayer Chapel has been built almost entirely by Latin American Christians. In this center, two 24-hour prayer chains operate. One chain prays for Latin American concerns, while the other concentrates on world needs. At 3 p.m. daily, Latin American Christians are encouraged to pause for prayer for their country. This hour was chosen because of *siesta* time, and also because of the accepted hour that is attributed to Jesus' death on the cross. Many churches which were formerly locked are opening their doors for people also to come to early morning prayer meetings.

Prayer in the Middle East

Iqbal Massey, the wife of our director of affairs for the Middle East, Kundan Massey, has traveled throughout this part of the world speaking to thousands promoting united prayer. In Morocco, where there are only a few more than 150 Christians, there are seven prayer chains in existence — one chain for every day.

There have been many faith-building experiences in regard to specific prayer. In Egypt, where Vonette traveled with a group of staff women, she met with church leaders from around that nation. This meeting took place at the same time as the first summit meetings to agree on peace terms for Israel and Egypt were being held with Sadat, Begin and Carter in Washington. The women went to their knees numbers of times, praying for these leaders. At the same time, they were planning a prayer strategy to help fulfill the Great Commission in Egypt.

In the summer of 1984, Vonette was one of the leaders in gathering together 3,200 people from 68 countries for the International Prayer Assembly in Seoul, Korea.

Christian leaders from all over the world have referred to that week of meetings as a second Pentecost. Most of us who participated would never again be the same because of what happened that week.

One reason for such a blessing was our opportunity to see the commitment of the Korean Christians to prayer. The church in Korea is more like the first-century church than that of any other nation in the world. Each week hundreds of thousands of people spend all night in prayer. The church there has grown from three million to seven million in the last 10 years. I believe the reason for this growth is largely due to prayer. Dr. Joon Gon Kim, our director for Korea and for all of Eastern Asia, has played a large part in this commitment.

I am grateful to God for Vonette's leadership in the prayer assembly and in so many other prayer movements in our country and around the world. We are committed to prayer because we know that no matter how effective the strategies, plans, techniques, materials and leadership, unless the Holy Spirit of God empowers, little spiritual fruit will be harvested for the glory of God.

CHAPTER TWENTY-TWO

To Reach the World

Can you imagine the impact of 100,000 lay men and women going to the cities and villages of the world to practice their vocations and make Christ known? God gave me the vision for such a movement shortly after EXPLO '72. He assured me that if He could bring almost 100,000 to that historic conference, He could certainly raise up 100,000 men and women to invest two years or more of their lives to help take the gospel to the ends of the earth. As I prayed, God confirmed in my heart that this was indeed His will, and the leaders of the movement responded very favorably to the idea.

In the next few months we put together the basic structure of what would soon become The *Agape* Movement. (*Agape* is the Greek New Testament word for God's love.) In January, 1973, we invited the leaders of several missionary organizations to consult with us. Those who came were Dr. Clyde Taylor, general director of the National Association of Evangelicals; Dr. Edward Frizen of the Interdenominational Foreign Missions Association; Dr. Donald McGavran of the Fuller School of World Mission; and Cliff Barrows and Walter Smyth from the Billy Graham Evangelistic Association.

We shared with these men as fully as possible the shape which we wanted the new movement to take. After we had told them everything that we knew at that point, I asked these men, whose judgment I greatly respect, whether they thought we should proceed with the idea. There was a breathless pause for a moment around the table.

Encouragement From Christian Leaders

Dr. Taylor broke the silence: "If you had asked me this a year ago, I would have said, 'No, you have no business attempting anything so large.' But EXPLO '72 changed my answer. When I saw how God used this organization to bring nearly 100,000 people together and solved the unbelievable logistical problems, not only do I think you should do it, I also think you are the only organization in North America which ought to attempt it."

Dr. Frizen spoke next: "I too feel you ought to proceed. My reason is not because of the magnitude of EXPLO '72, but because of the spirit of EXPLO '72. When I saw that you had brought 200 Christian groups together to present opportunities within their organizations, I knew that this is the kind of spirit it is going to take if we are ever going to see the world reached for Christ."

(Campus Crusade had invited these Christian organizations to come to EXPLO as our guests to promote their ministries, as an expression of our love and desire to help create a spirit of unity among different Christian groups.)

Dr. McGavran shared: "Twenty years ago, when I was inaugurated as the dean of the School of World Mission at Fuller, I said in my address, 'If we're really serious about the Great Commission, we've got to ask God to raise up at least 100,000 missionaries to reach the world.' I've sat here today and heard that God has impressed you with the same vision and, not only that, but He has also given you the wherewithal to make it possible."

The next around the table was Cliff Barrows: "You don't have to convince me of the merit of this kind of a program. My father, who is a retired farmer, actually served in this kind of a program, and it changed his life."

All that was left for Walter Smyth to say was, "I want to pledge all the resources and influence of the Billy Graham Evangelistic Association to support the pursuit of this vision."

Seeking a Director

Assured that we were headed in the right direction, we needed to find a director for this new venture. In December, 1972, God had impressed me that Dr. Larry Poland, president of Miami Christian College, was the man for the job. But when I asked him to assume this position, his response was, "No, I'd like to, but I am already committed to an expansion program here." However, he did agree to consult with us as we constructed the basic framework for the movement.

It became almost humorous as I periodically asked Larry if God was yet speaking to him as He was to me. Of course, I made it clear that I would not want Larry to come unless God called him, but in my heart, I had the assurance that he was God's man for the task of helping us achieve the vision that God had given me. God never gave me a peace about any other man for the position, though Larry continued to say "No." Finally, in March, 1973, through a series of remarkable circumstances, God's timing was complete, and He called Larry to come to assist us as director of this new venture.

First of all, The *Agape* Movement is designed for laymen, many of whom have little formal theological background. Bible college and seminary training are important, but there simply are not enough people with this kind of training to do the job. If the Great Commission is going to be fulfilled, we must mobilize masses of laymen to do their part.

Staff From Around the World

Not all of the *Agape* staff are North Americans. Already European *Agape* staff have gone to other countries to meet needs. Training centers are being planned for each continent and in several countries to prepare the nationals to help others on their continent and in other parts of the world. Our Chinese staff are praying specifically that God will raise up 10,000 Chinese to be involved in this way.

Before reporting overseas, the *Agape* staff attend both the regular staff training for Campus Crusade staff and a special three and a half month program called *Agape*-International Training. In addition to the basic Campus Crusade training in how to live a Spirit-filled life and how to share Christ more effectively with others, much attention is given to helping the trainees feed themselves through Bible study and understand scriptural principles. Emphasis is also placed on cross-cultural communication and interpersonal relationships. Practical lessons for living overseas include how to learn the language once you arrive and precautionary health measures.

The *Agape* staff have found that what they learn in their training sessions is invaluable. One young teacher who was on her way to Africa commented, "I've seen my deepest weaknesses become my strengths. I'm a totally different person."

The *Agape* Movement involves strategic placement. Doctors, nurses, teachers, agricultural workers, engineers and financiers can go so many places that missionaries cannot. The need for trained people like this is so great that they are allowed into many countries where missionaries are banned, even though the authorities know that they will be sharing their faith in Christ while doing their assigned tasks.

A good example of strategic placement is the case of an *Agape* staff member sent to a West African nation. Since he is an athlete and coach, he was placed in the national sports commission to help the country develop national competitive teams. Athletes are so highly regarded in this country that this man will likely have a far greater impact for Christ than would almost anyone in a purely missionary capacity.

Another unique aspect of this movement is the combination of the vocational with the spiritual in the staff member's work. A large portion of the staff member's time is involved in discipleship and evangelism, and as he uses his unique skills, he will be communicating something about the gospel through His Christ-centered lifestyle.

Team Concepts

The *Agape* Movement utilizes a team concept. Often missionaries are sent into an area by themselves or with only one other person. *Agape* staff, however, are always placed with their team members nearby and at least one other staff person with them. A strong witness is produced as the nationals watch these team members relate to one another. As they see Christ at the center of this miniature community, they begin to grasp what He can do within their own society.

"We were living in a fishbowl," said one *Agape* staff member who taught school in Swaziland. "Every moment we asked the Lord to help us reflect His character. I think it is understandable that people accept as credible what you say if your life shows it. One of the happiest moments for my roommate and me was when one of the students said she had seen Jesus Christ in our relationship."

The *Agape* staff members agree to spend two years in the country to which they are assigned, though they often choose to continue on a permanent basis after the experience of being used of God in such a wonderful way. Since they know their stay may only be temporary, their minds can be focused on what they can do to help prepare the nationals to reach their own country for Christ.

The multiplication of nationals, vocationally and spiritually, is the key to The *Agape* Movement. When the staff member returns home, he expects to leave behind nationals who are trained in his vocation and to leave behind more believers who are trained and discipled to reach their nation for Christ.

Medical Clinic in Korea

A team of *Agape* staff in Korea demonstrated this principle of multiplication vocationally and spiritually when they established a medical clinic in one of the poorer sections of Seoul. Working alongside Korean nationals, the team treated approximately 20,000 patients and saw more than 3,700 decisions for Christ in little more than a year. When they left the clinic to return to the United States, they left behind a Korean doctor and nurses to continue the ministry.

The spirit of The *Agape* Movement is that of having a servant's heart. No matter how skilled the staff may be, it is of no use if they do not go in the fullness of the Holy Spirit, with humble hearts. In many cases they will be serving under national staff members and must be willing to do so with the attitude of a servant.

Aiding National Christians

In addition to the trained lay men and women who travel overseas using their vocational skills as a platform for sharing the good news of Jesus Christ, some 375 North Americans are currently overseas providing training, specialized skills and administrative expertise to help the national Christians in reaching their countries with the gospel.

Dr. Al Rhea is an example of staff who serve in this capacity. A successful dentist in Jacksonville, Fla., Dr. Rhea left his practice to join our staff and subsequently moved his family some 8,000 miles to Nairobi, Kenya, where he works closely with individuals from various African nations in the East Africa Great Commission Training Center. Dr. Rhea supervises three to four men during each training period, schooling them in the principles of evangelism and discipleship and aids them as they put what they have learned into practice by developing their own ministries.

"It's very rewarding to build relationships with the trainees, knowing that these leaders will return to their own countries and put the training into their own languages and situations," said Dr. Rhea. "They go places that we never will. If we did go to their area, it would take us years to understand their culture."

In the fall of 1976, The *Agape* Movement convened the first World Thrust conference in Birmingham, Ala. The conference was the first of many such gatherings held for the purpose of showing practical ways for believers to be involved in the world evangelization effort.

Assisting Missions Agencies

During the conferences, delegates were encouraged to talk with representatives from dozens of world missions sending agencies, including denominational and interdenominational missions boards such as OMS International, Gospel Recordings, Mission Aviation Fellowship, Wycliffe Bible Translators, Christian and Missionary Alliance and the Conservative Baptist Foreign Mission Society. In all, 145 agencies exhibited at one or more conferences.

"We have been able to share with people about our ministry and how they can become more involved even if they can't go personally," said Alison Boyer of Language Institute for Evangelism. "Already we have had some people from past World Thrust conferences apply to our mission as missionaries. "These experiences have been shared by many of the missions agencies represented at World Thrust.

The first 18 World Thrust conferences were attended by 18,406 people. Of these, 2,150 made decisions to go to other lands with the gospel, 3,677 committed themselves to pray for a specific group of unreached people, and 979 made decisions to support world evangelization through financial investment.

I personally believe that preaching the gospel of the Lord Jesus Christ involves a concern for the widows, orphans, prisoners, the poor, the sick, the illiterate and the aged. One cannot say "I love God" and not demonstrate love for those in need. Genuine concern results in specific action. But I also believe that the greatest thing one can do to help other people, whether young or old, sick or well, in prison or free, is to tell them about the love and forgiveness of Jesus Christ and help them receive Him as their Savior. As servants of the Lord, we need to emphasize caring for the poor and the downtrodden. But we need even more to give a strong emphasis to preaching the gospel. In that way, every person on the face of the earth will have a chance to say "Yes" to Jesus Christ and to know the liberating joy that comes from following Him in faith and obedience.

Barrio of Thieves

One beautiful example of the combination of social concern coupled with evangelism occurred in the Philippines. A young Filipina doctor together with some American *Agape* staff formed a medical team to work in a village known as "the barrio of thieves." Within one year, more than half of the population of 2,000 had been converted to Christ, and many Bible studies were being held in the village.

When I arrived in Baguio City, I asked that an interview be arranged for members of our team with the mayor of the barrio, who was a teacher. He shared that few if any of the villagers worked; most stole for a living. Then the medical team came into the village and set up the clinic. It was open certain hours of the day with the rest of the day set aside for door-to-door witnessing and Bible studies. As a result of more than 1,000 people receiving Christ, crime was reduced 80%. No longer is the village known as "the barrio of thieves"; the citizens renamed it Easter Village.

This is what can happen when individuals decide to invest at least two years of their lives with The *Agape* Movement, serving others. We are praying that God will use our *Agape* staff, currently under the direction of Paul McKean, to produce similar results in hundreds of thousands of other villages and cities throughout the world.

May I suggest that you pause right now and ask the Lord if He wants you to be a part of this remarkable witness for Him. Write today for more information.

CHAPTER TWENTY-THREE

God's Speciality: The Impossible

Now that we talked about our ministry overseas through The *Agape* Movement, I would like to go back to EXPLO '74 and share with you the tremendous vision for reaching the world that the experience in Seoul gave to tens of thousands who attended.

That week was truly an example of how God's supernatural blessings have been on the life of one man — Dr. Joon Gon Kim, our ministry's national director in Korea. God has brought Dr. Kim along a unique path in making him the great man of God that he is today.

One of the difficult steps along that path took place when he was enjoying one evening with his family. It was springtime, and the rain was falling gently as the family was sharing the events of the day. Suddenly, an angry band of Communist guerillas invaded the village, killing everyone in their path. The family of Dr. Kim was not exempt. In their trail of blood, the guerillas left behind the dead bodies of Dr. Kim's wife and his father; he himself was beaten and left for dead. In the cool rain of the night, Dr. Kim revived and fled to safety in the mountains with his young daughter. They were the sole survivors.

Loving His Enemies

Dr. Kim is a man of God, and he had learned from Scripture to love his enemies and pray for those who persecuted him. What was he to do? What was to be his attitude concerning those who had snatched his dear ones from his side — his beloved wife and honored father? The Spirit of God impressed upon Dr. Kim that he was to return to the village, seek out the Communist chief who led the guerilla attack and tell him that he loved him. then he was to tell the man of God's love in Christ and seek to win him for the Savior. This he did, and God honored his obedience. Dumbfounded, the Communist chief knelt in prayer with Dr. Kim and committed his life to Christ. Within a short time, a number of other Communists were converted to Christ, and Dr. Kim helped to build a church for these and other Communist converts.

The name of Dr. Kim became known throughout South Korea, but this humble servant of God wanted to help evangelize his whole nation for the Savior. Indeed, his vision reached far beyond Korea to the whole of Asia, and he believed that his people, the Koreans, could help evangelize the Orient. Though he was a pastor of a large church, one of the largest in Korea, and had finished his theological studies in Korea, he came to the United States for further graduate study, working toward an advanced degree at Fuller Theological Seminary.

Campus Crusade in Korea

Upon meeting Dr. Kim at Fuller in 1958, I was challenged by his dedication to Christ, his humility and his vision. Together we covenented with God that we would seek to help evangelize Korea. This was in keeping with the original vision that God had given me for Campus Crusade. When I laid before Dr. Kim my strategy for the world, he responded by agreeing to launch the ministry of Campus Crusade in Korea and to be our first national director overseas.

From the beginning, Campus Crusade has believed that the national can do a better job of reaching his own people than can the missionary. The national does not have the problems of language and culture that confront the missionary. However, we strongly believe in the importance of the missionary, so long as he is willing to serve the national. Dr. Kim and all overseas directors who have joined us since 1958 have been indigenous leaders. They have been trained and instructed in the philosophy, techniques and strategy of Campus Crusade, and we stand ready at all times to assist them in reaching their own people. Therefore, it was with joy that we saw Dr. Kim become a staff member.

Within a relatively short period of time, he was established in the ministry and was recruiting and training other nationals to join with him to help reach students of Korea for Christ. His has been one of the most remarkable ministries in the history of Korea.

Holy Ground

The culmination of this ministry was EXPLO '74. During that entire week, I felt as if I were on holy ground. Day after day I observed the supernatural, miraculous work of God. Night after night as I stood to speak from the elevated platform and looked out over the sea of faces, I was filled with awe and reverence. I could sense the presence of God in a very real way.

Every time I think about what God did at EXPLO '74, I want to sing praises to Him, for truly all of the honor, praise and glory are due to Him alone.

I have already shared with you some of the "firsts" of that unprecedented gathering. The most meaningful to me was the information Dr. Kim gave me on the phone — that 80% of the first-night audience of 1.3 million people indicated that they had accepted Christ or received assurance of their salvation by faith as a result of my message. The essence of that message is recorded in the appendix of this book.

No number of human beings nor group of organizations could ever have accomplished what happened at EXPLO '74. All the glory, honor and praise must go to God. Nils Becker, coordinator of the international delegations (more than 3,000 came for the week from 78 countries), said that in the early planning fo EXPLO everything was just too big for them to even comprehend, much less accomplish. But miracle after miracle occurred because, as he explained, "People were praying and God answered."

Importance of Prayer

No doubt prayer, more than anything else, prompting the moving of God's Spirit, can explain EXPLO '74 and the spiritual revival that has been going on in Korea for many years. The road has not been an easy one. Since the gospel first reached that country if 1876, the Korean church has survived difficulties. During a bitter 35-year occupation, the Japanese tried to force Shintoism on the people. Then the land was cut in two by Communism. Indeed, two-thirds of the Christians formerly lived in what is now North Korea. During the Communist takeover, many thousands were slaughtered and many fled south, leaving behind their possessions and, in many cases, their families.

Still the Christians' dedication to prayer and commitment to evangelism have caused the church in South Korea to double in size each decade since 1940 and to grow at a rate presently four times that of the population. For years, believers have gathered in the pre-dawn darkness in churches to pray for their country. At least 30 prayed and fasted for 40 days and nights specifically for EXPLO. The night before EXPLO '74 officially began, an estimated 300,000 Koreans held a spontaneous prayer meeting. And each night after that, hundreds of thousands stayed on the Yoido Plaza to pray until daybreak. "Christians have been praying for three decades for a spiritual awakening in our country," said Dr. Kim. "EXPLO '74 was part of God's answer to their prayers."

Sacrifice

Such commitment to prayer exemplified EXPLO.

Hundreds of families tithed their rice the months before to help provide food for the delegates. Some families sacrificed one meal a day for several months to help provide scholarships. Twenty college students sold their blood to pay for the registration. During the week of EXPLO, some 44,000 Koreans lived in a tent city of Yoido Island, where they endured two days of rain and, later in the week, hot sun and winds. Another 176,000 slept on the floors of 2,944 primary, middle and high school classrooms. Most of the remaining 100,000 delegates stayed at their homes or in the homes of friends and relatives in Seoul.

To feed such a group took 7,000 sacks of rice and 20 mammoth rice steamers designed by Dr. Joon Gon Kim. A staff of 320 men and 60 women worked from 5 o'clock in the morning until late each evening supplying the EXPLO delegates with food. They supplemented the rice diet with *duk kwang*, a yellow radish-type vegetable; *saewoo*, a type of fish; and bread. A total of 600 tons of rice, 150 tons of *duk kwang* and *saewoo*, and 3.6 million pieces of bread were consumed by the Koreans during EXPLO week.

The more than 3,000 "international" delegates lived in more comfortable conditions. Half stayed in 12 Seoul hotels and the other half in dorms of Ewha Women's University (the largest women's university in the world), the 18-story Korean Campus Crusade building and in U.S. military housing for the more than 200 service personnel who came in for the training. A fleet of 50 buses transported these foreign delegates to Yoido Plaza each evening. The rally messages were then translated for them into English, Japanese, Cantonese, Mandarin, Spanish and German which could be picked up by special transistor radios provided for each international delegate.

The delegates came to Seoul by almost every means possible. Approximately 1,000 young Koreans came in a bicycle caravan. Each night most of the Koreans walked many miles to attend the mass rallies. Some even jogged, chanting "Jesus Revolution! Explosion of the Holy Spirit" as they ran.

High school students in Hartford, Conn., raised $3,750 in four weeks through bake sales, car washes and church donations to send five representatives. One American girl was so determined to go that she joined the U.S. Air Force a year before in order to attend as part of the military delegation. Gideon Umandap missed the Philippines charter flight when he was denied an exit permit due to his record of communist activity before becoming a Christian. Meeting the next day with an army general, Gideon explained his "new life in Christ." The general not only gave him the exit permit but also had him driven to the airport in time to catch a plane.

Vital Training

Each morning the various conferences met at locations throughout Seoul. But regardless of whether the delegates met in a tent, classroom, or hotel, each received training in how to live a meaningful Christian life, how to appropriate the fullness of the Holy Spirit and how to communicate his faith in Christ with others through the Four Spiritual Laws. Special Four Laws booklets for EXPLO were printed with one side in Korean and the other side in English, Japanese or Chinese.

The afternoons were free for delegates to attend optional seminars which made up what was called the Institute of World Missions. These featured such men as Dr. Peter Beyerhaus, professor of missions at the University of Tubingen in West Germany; and Dr. Samuel Moffett, president of the Presbyterian Theological Seminary in Seoul.

On Saturday afternoon, August 17, the delegates spread out through the streets of Seoul, the world's ninth largest city with 6.5 million people. They talked to

420,000 people and saw 272,000 indicate decisions for
Christ with another 120,000 expressing a desire to know
more about how they could become Christians.

One American serviceman, who had been stationed
in Korea for two months, witnessed to a wealthy contractor that afternoon. Not only did the man receive Christ,
but he also eagerly asked God to control every area of
his life with the power of the Holy Spirit. The soldier
commented, "This man was hungry for all the material
I gave him. I gave him everything I could, and he would
have wanted more if I had had it."

A Canadian businessman and Campus Crusade
board member, Peter Dueck, stated, "I had heard of the
openness of the Korean people to the gospel but didn't
think we would be able to share with people who didn't
know the language." He proved himself wrong. During
dinner one evening, Peter shared Christ with a couple
from the university and then invited them to the meeting
on Yoido Island. They were there at 7 p.m. sharp, and
the young man received Christ.

Counting the Crowds

As you have been reading about the large crowds
who attended EXPLO '74, you may be asking, "How can
one determine to any degree of accuracy the number of
people attending such a large gathering?" The Rev. David
J. Cho, one of Korea's most prominent Christian leaders,
who served as arrangement chairman for EXPLO as well
as for the 1973 Billy Graham Crusade in Seoul, explained
the process: "According to official measurements, Yoido
Plaza is 1,400 meters or 4,714 feet long and 480 meters
or 1,901 feet wide. If 3,000 people are seated at 50-cen-
timeter or 20-inch intervals along the width, a total of
2,100,000 can be accommodated at one time. At each
meeting, under my direction, the planning coordinator
with six assistants used a map and the above figures to
estimate the crowd. This estimate was then given to Dr.

Kim who examined the figures so that they were as conservative as possible and that they were consistent with police estimates. The official estimate was then released to the public."

One amazing fact of EXPLO was that 600,000 people (by police estimate) turned out for the Thursday night meeting despite all-day rains and the tragic death of President Chung Hee Park's wife in the assassination attempt on the President's life. Even with the rain that night and the fact that a Japanese citizen had been arrested in connection with the assassination, Dr. Akira Hatori, noted Japanese evangelist, spoke as scheduled.

Asking Forgiveness

Everyone was visibly moved as Dr. Hatori asked the many Japanese delegates to stand and then told the Koreans, "We stand here with broken hearts for the sins we Japanese have committed against you. We ask for your forgiveness in Jesus Christ, and we long to be like you Christians in Korea, sacrificing ourselves."

Mrs. Georgalyn Wilkinson, who heads the Far East Broadcasting Company in Japan, well remembers that night. "I opened the door to the booth where the Japanese men were translating the invitation to receive Christ," she said. "Tears were streaming down their faces as they spoke, and they prayed silently that their own people would respond to the invitation."

Though Dr. Kim asked me to bring the major messages during the week of meetings, a number of internationally-known Christian leaders also addressed the evening meeting. Other speakers in the evening rallies were Dr. Kyung Chik Han, pastor emeritus of the Young Nak Presbyterian Church, the world's largest Presbyterian church; Dr. Chandu Ray, executive director of the Coordinating Office for Asian Evangelism; and Dr. Philip Teng, pastor of the North Point Alliance Church and professor at Alliance Bible Seminary in Hong Kong.

Worldwide Broadcast

Each mass rally was aired worldwide by the Far East Broadcasting Company. One station beamed the address across Latin America while another reached the Philippines, Southeast Asia, Australia, New Zealand and Indonesia. FEBC's Carl Lawrence and Dave Hudson worked with the taping and editing of all major talks. Mrs. Wilkinson, who had the difficult task of arranging all the interpreters for us, remarked, "The Lord gave us the best people we could have found." How grateful we were for the invaluable help of the Far East Broadcasting Company.

EXPLO '74 was a time most of all for discipleship and training. As Dr. Kim told the crowd, "Each of you must become a spiritual fireseed — a spark that will in turn set fire to your local church." No doubt most of the delegates became such "fireseeds."

Dr. Hatori told me, "We have had some big spiritual conventions in the past where people received blessings, but nothing like EXPLO '74. This convention was characterized by training and by total dependence upon the Holy Spirit and a holy, biblical strategy."

Dr. Chandu Ray said, "I am excited about the training of more than 300,000 lay people. I believe this is a new phase that will revolutionize and explode all over Asia. This brings tremendous encouragement to me."

Chinese Delegation

When one considers that two-thirds of the world lives in Asia, the importance of such training becomes even more obvious and urgent. I was thrilled about the more than 450 Chinese delegates who came to EXPLO from Hong Kong, the Republic of China and other Asian countries. One afternoon many of them met together to discuss strategies to help reach the then 800 million people in mainland China. These delegates were excited about the EXPLO training and wanted more training. On the day of witnessing, they saw 419 of the 963 people with whom they had shared the Four Spiritual Laws indicate that they received Christ.

Chi Young Min, one of the 1,200 delegates from Cheju, a small island off South Korea, said, "After EXPLO '74, we want to go back and begin evangelizing the whole island."

Pastors Participate

Campus Crusade has always sought to serve the local church, and this was another key goal of EXPLO. Some 13,000 Korean pastors, assistant pastors and evangelists, representing nearly all of Korea's 12,000 protestant churches, attended the pastors' conference. For five days they crossed denominational and doctrinal lines to study, pray and spend time together. Including personal devotions, lectures, optional afternoon seminars and the nightly mass rallies, their schedule ran from 5:30 a.m. to 11 each night. Then the schedule read "all night prayer." Sleep was optional! But as one pastor put it, "When these pastors return to their rural or city churches, we'll begin to see throughout Korea a preaching of the gospel like that in the book of Acts."

Many other pastors and laymen attended the Ministry of Management course, designed to teach Christians to be the best stewards of their time and talents. One of the speakers, Dr. Howard Hendricks of Dallas Theological Seminary, pointed out, "If you don't plan your time, other people will plan it for you. And they will be the ones who do not have your interests or your commitment to Jesus." Korean evangelist Joseph Toh and Chinese theological student Chiu Pei-Chi said they increased their understanding of how leadership principles and goal-setting related to their full-time ministries. Hexel Hernando, one of the 80 students from the University of the

Philippines, spoke for his classmates, many of whom attended management seminars: "There is a real excitement in us about going back to school this fall and applying the things we're learning about management." Dr. Hendricks concluded his last message with, "The effect of EXPLO '74 will not be determined by what happens this week here in Seoul. . .but by what you do as a result."

And the results have truly been miraculous! Eisuke Kanda, our director in Japan, stated, "As a result of this week, most of the 1,000 Japanese delegates are now convinced that the saturation of our country with the gospel is a real possibility." A woman from Idaho said, "God really opened my life to believe Him for things I never could believe Him for before. This has resulted as I've seen the people in Korea and have been impressed by their hard work and singlemindedness." A Korean layman stated convincingly, "Our nation will be altered, changed, transformed because we now know how to take evangelism home. By taking these skills home, we can Christianize the whole nation. In that way, Korea will be changed." A government report published in 1978 showed one of the long-lasting effects EXPLO '74 helped to contribute to Korea. The report revealed that the Korean church grew from three million in 1974 to seven million in 1978. In the four short years following EXPLO, the church of Korea more than doubled, and the miracle continues. To God be all of the praise!

CHAPTER TWENTY-FOUR

Here's Life, America: Saturating the Nation City by City

I remember sitting with several of my fellow staff leaders one day in 1973, discussing the challenge of reaching our nation for Christ. As we discussed the problems of our society — crime, poverty, divorce, alcoholism, drugs, etc. — we were all increasingly aware of the only solution: a spiritual and moral rebirth in our land. And yet, we realized that this solution in Jesus Christ would come about only as every person in the United States had the opportunity to respond to His invitation, "Come to Me, all who are weary and heavy-laden, and I will give you rest" (Matthew 11:28). Then, as these people were trained and discipled, change would occur in the moral fiber of our country. We discussed and prayed about the answers to this question for several months. During this planning period, eight principles emerged that seemed to provide the foundation for a plan which could actually help us achieve our goal.

First, we recognized that if we were talking about reaching our entire nation, we must go where most of the people are — in the cities.

Second, we recognized that the resources for accomplishing what we had talked about were already available in and through the local churches.

Third, we determined that local leaders were needed in each metropolitan area — pastors and laymen who would be willing to commit their time and resources toward accomplishing the task.

Fourth, we realized that Christians must pray and believe God for a plan to reach their cities for Christ.

185

Fifth, we anticipated that Christians would need to be trained in order to release their full potential for our Lord.

Sixth, we determined that at some point we needed to get the attention of an entire city. That can be done only through mass media — TV, radio, newspapers, etc.

Seventh, we reasoned that the city must be broken down into small, "bite-size" pieces so that each trained Christian could have his personal part in reaching the city for Christ.

Eighth, we felt that churches should be assisted in developing ongoing discipleship and evangelism programs within their own congregations.

Considering these eight points and praying much, we launched a movement which was ultimately to be called Here's Life, America and later, Here's Life, World — a movement which would help to introduce many millions of people to Christ.

We were convinced that the principles were sound. But in the fall of 1973, the real question had to be answered — would it work?

To verify the principles in a real life situation, I asked three men to launch this plan in three cities. Bruce Cook, my special assistant at the time, was asked to go to Atlanta, Ga., to try out the plan. I sent an outstanding businessman who had joined our lay staff, Bob George, to Dallas, Tex., and Sid Bruce, our Military Ministry director, to Nashville, Tenn.

For the following year, we learned lessons in each city which began to point toward a workable "city saturation" strategy. From Bob George, the Dallas coordinator, and his work at the First Baptist Church, emerged the concept of neighborhood church outreach groups. From Sid Bruce, the Nashville coordinator, and Tom Cummings, a Nashville businessman, came the idea of using a computer to divide the city into workable units and track the progress in calling every household.

Initial Testing Ground

It was in Atlanta that our staff team first had an opportunity to bring all the pieces of the plan together to see a city begin to be saturated with the gospel message. Every step of the way was marked by a pattern of prayer, plan, work, problem, more prayer and miracle!

Bruce Cook, whom I later asked to co-coordinate the nationwide Here's Life movement with Paul Eshleman, shared some of the highlights of what happened in Atlanta: "The first step in the plan was to organize a local committee of pastors and laymen who would provide leadership for the effort. Then, as a result, we in Campus Crusade felt that we would be in a position to do what we do best — assist, train and serve in a resource role.

"But after three months of meeting with various laymen and pastors, no leadership seemed to surface. Then as Cobby Ware, the Atlanta city director for Campus Crusade, and our staff prayed, a man came to our minds — Jerry Nims, president of a newly-formed business in Atlanta. On presenting to Jerry our vision and challenge for the movement, we witnessed our first miracle in his response, "I've been praying that God would give me something in which I would really be involved in serving Him," he said. "This is it. Tell me what to do.'"

Nims, chairman of the board of Dimensional Development, Inc., crowded an already overloaded schedule with countless meetings and telephone calls for the movement, often beginning the day with pre-dawn breakfast sessions.

"I'd been praying for a long time for a chance to really get involved for the Lord — to climb right into the trenches," Nims later told us. "When this opportunity came along, I have to admit that it was more than I expected. But God reassured me that He would enable me to do a good job."

Prayer Coordinator Chosen

One month later, in February of 1974, we saw our second miracle. Mrs. Joyce Hopping, when approached to lead a city-wide prayer effort, replied, "Now I know why God has been teaching me about prayer in my own life over these last two years." Within one month, more than 1,000 women had committed themselves to a 24-hour prayer chain to undergird *Agape* Atlanta, as the movement was then called in Atlanta. What an answer to our prayers!

That spring we saw various lay people and staff begin ministries in various areas of the city. Bob Reinhart, a stock broker, organized an outreach in the "singles" community; Rusty Wright, one of our staff, organized classroom speaking teams to present Christ in relevant terms in the 23 colleges in the Atlanta area; Martha Ozmit, an Atlanta homemaker, began training women in how to conduct evangelistic coffees and teas in their neighborhoods; Harold Thompson, an ex-convict, spearheaded a prison ministry, not only in Atlanta but also throughout Georgia — with the approval and endorsement of then Governor Jimmy Carter.

With so much to be excited about, we still had to recognize that the key to reaching Atlanta was church members. Unless a significant number of churches came together for a concentrated campaign in the city, Atlanta would not really feel the impact.

The spring of 1975 seemed to be the obvious time for such a campaign, so Bruce and his staff began to plan. Throughout the summer and fall of 1974, a saturation campaign strategy began to take shape.

In this strategy, the city would be divided into various neighborhoods. A single participating church would be responsible for each neighborhood. Each neighborhood would then be subdivided by a computer into street blocks of 50 homes each. So, only 8,000 trained workers from the churches would be needed — each to reach one block. With this plan, a pastor could show people how they could have a specific part in reaching an entire city for Christ.

At the same time, a city-wide media campaign would be launched using every form of media — TV, radio, newspaper, billboards, lapel buttons and bumper stickers — to make Jesus Christ a relevant issue in the lives of all the people in the city.

Problems Encountered

After developing this plan and beginning to work toward its implementation, the inevitable happened. We ran into problems. On November 15, 1974, the Atlanta staff found themselves with no money, no computer system, no media plan and worst of all, no committed pastors to lead the campaign which was scheduled to begin in just five months!

Bruce, Cobby and the rest of the staff went back to their knees, and God began to work miracles. First, He provided leaders. Dr. Charles Stanley, pastor of the First Baptist Church, agreed to head up a pastors steering committee to direct the campaign. Second, I invited Bob Screen, an advertising consultant, to meet with us for a number of creative sessions that gave birth to a campaign theme — "I found it! New life in Christ." Third, a computer system took shape that divided the city into blocks with names and phone numbers for each block assignment. But the money was a little slower in coming.

By March 30, 90 churches were involved with 4,000 trained workers. Enough money had come in to pay the early expenses for the campaign, including 122 billboards strategically located in various parts of the city.

But April 1 was the deadline for the money needed for the television and newspaper advertising — $50,000. On April 1, at 2 p.m., the staff received a phone call. King Grant, one of Atlanta's leading businessmen, agreed to take the responsibility of raising the $50,000 over the next few months and arranged for a personal note which he signed for the money to enable them to go ahead with the campaign.

10,000 Decisions

During the three-week saturation campaign, more than 140,000 households were contacted, and 25,000 phone calls were received from interested people, with more than 10,000 decisions for Jesus Christ. That was just the beginning of a week-by-week continuous effort by church members to reach the city.

How would I describe what happened in Atlanta? Only in miraculous terms. It reminds me of what Nehemiah said in the Old Testament when the Jerusalem wall was rebuilt in 52 days: "They recognized that this work had been accomplished with the help of God" (Nehemiah 6:16).

Those few weeks were exciting beyond words to express. The phenomenal success of the campaign in Atlanta and the launching of Here's Life, America in other cities, with its potential for introducing millions to Christ, were all added blessings to the reports of what God was doing through the lives of our staff.

What started in Atlanta was only a beginning. In the next two years, Here's Life, America reached 246 major cities and thousands of smaller communities. Through the media campaign, our marketing consultants assured us that at least 179 million Americans were exposed to the "I found it!" campaign. A total of some 7.7 million people were contacted personally and exposed to the claims of Christ through the witness of 325,000 trained workers from 15,000 cooperating churches. More than 532,000 people indicated salvation decisions during the campaigns.

Impact on Millions

I believe that these figures represent only the tip of the iceberg because it is completely impossible to record all that God has done and is doing through so many trained workers and cooperating churches. It is my conviction that millions of people made decisions to invite Christ into their lives during the Here's Life movement and many thousands of trained Christians have continued to live Spirit-controlled lives and to witness for Christ.

During those two years that the Here's Life movement was being planned and implemented, I lived out of a suitcase. When I was traveling, which was most of the time, I spoke in a different city almost every day, sometimes three cities a day — working with students, laymen and pastors, trying to encourage Christians to pray and work for a worldwide spiritual revival. I wouldn't have done that for a million dollars, but I was glad to do it for my Lord.

I attempted to devote every waking moment of that time to helping to accelerate Here's Life, America and to raising the necessary funds to help saturate the United States with the gospel by the end of 1976. I said "No" to everything that did not directly contribute to the total saturation of this country and to help bring the United States back to God.

That was an exciting time in the history of our nation as we saw God work miracles across the land through the Here's Life, America campaigns.

"One of the highlights of the campaign was the unity of the churches from different denominations all working together," said Tim Calahan, a lawyer who worked with the movement in the Washington, D.C., area. "People from different racial groups and different economic levels were all working together."

Two high school students in the Washington area, Pam and Scott Cox, decided, as part of the campaign, to phone the members of the school band in which they played. Twelve of the 17 students Scott called and 18 of the 23 his sister called accepted Christ as their Savior. All 30 of the new Christians began meeting with more mature Christians to learn about their new life in Christ. More than 9,000 people in the area made decisions to receive Christ.

Warm Response in Inner-city

In Philadelphia, a total of 430 churches cooperated in reaching that city of nearly five million people for Christ. Approximately 100 black churches were involved in the campaign, and some of the most outstanding results occurred in predominantly black areas.

The Rev. Nathaniel Winslow's church, New Testament Baptist, is one of many black churches that participated. In addition to his 30 members, Rev. Winslow found 10 more people to take the Here's Life training. These trained workers then contacted people in their neighborhoods. Some 130 individuals received Christ with the workers, and 206 enrolled in follow-up Bible studies.

"In the inner-city, it's unusual for people, for any reason, to let a stranger into their house at night," said Woody Parker, pastor of another small black church involved in the campaign. "Usually they think that you're going to try to mug them. But they've been open to the members of our church, and 50% of the people we contacted received Christ."

In the western United States, the Lord also brought about great results. "One of the highlights was the cooperation of the churches," said Jim Burke, city coordinator in Portland, where 230 churches worked together during the campaign. "Many pastors and laymen commented about how so many churches of all denominations were working together to reach the city."

A crisis occurred during the Portland campaign when 80% of the "I found it!" TV schedule was canceled and the TV station personnel made it clear that nothing would change their minds. The people in Portland and several other cities began to pray. Later on that day, the man who had flatly refused to allow any broadcast time to be purchased asked them to hurry over so they could figure out a new schedule to air the spots.

In the greater Los Angeles area, 950 churches cooperated in the campaign, including 35 Oriental, 67 Hispanic and 73 black churches. A total of 27,600 people received Christ as their Savior during the campaign.

Chain Reaction

Two of the workers in the campaign saw some unexpected results when they went to follow up a man they had made an appointment to see. When they arrived at his house, they found that the man had been called to work, but his teenage son was at home, so they asked if they could talk with him.

As the two workers presented the gospel, the boy received Christ and asked Him to take control of his life. He asked the workers to wait while he called some of his friends to come over.

Soon five more boys arrived. Again the workers went through the Four Spiritual Laws, and all five boys received Christ. One of the boys called his parents, and they said, "We want to see what is happening over there. We'll be right over."

When that boy's parents arrived, the two workers again shared the claims of Christ and the parents chose to receive Christ.

Seeing what had happened, three of the other boys contacted their parents. Soon after arriving, the parents of these boys received Christ. The final outcome of the one follow-up appointment was 14 people coming to Christ.

In the Phoenix area, some 5,800 people indicated that they invited Christ into their lives. A crippled woman who lived in the area and was confined to a wheelchair took advantage of her C.B. radio during the campaign. As truck drivers came through town, she told them to come by and see her if they wanted to know what "I found it!" meant. Five truckers responded to her invitation and asked Christ to come into their hearts through her witness.

The same type of miraculous results that occurred in the East and West also happened in the South and Midwest. "I resolved doubts about assurance of my salvation," said one Here's Life worker in the Chicago area. "And for the first time I shared my faith and that person received Christ." This worker's story was multiplied innumerable times across the country as thousands of those who were trained were assured of their salvation and thousands more were used of God to lead their first person to Christ.

Negative Story Brings Positive Results

"I believe our greatest strength has been our weakness," said Col. Nimrod McNair, one of the leaders of the Chicago campaign. "Our media effort was weak due to lack of funds, plus the fact we could not get on the major TV networks. However, on November 19, the *Chicago Tribune* hit the streets with a critical story on the Chicago Here's Life campaign. Negative, yes; but the results were positive." In the wake of the *Tribune* article came more objective interviews with NBC, ABC and CBS/TV news and an article in Chicago's *Sun-Times*. As a result of the publicity from these sources, the awareness of Chicagoans about the campaign leaped from 20% of the population to 70%. Thousands recorded decisions for Christ.

The South, where the Here's Life campaigns began, had similar experiences to those in the other sections of the country. "Here's Life, Dallas, has revolutionized our church," said the Rev. Joe Masterson of Kenwood Baptist Church. In another Dallas church, 17 of its members introduced someone to Christ for the first time in their lives during the first week of the campaign.

Roger Vann, Houston city coordinator, pointed to God's dealing with the media as an interesting development in their campaign. "One network station had a policy against paid religious advertising," he said. "God changed their hearts and gave us $20,000 of prime-time TV spots. It was better coverage than both of the other stations which were paid for."

"We placed quite a bit of emphasis on follow-up," said Dick Burr, who coordinated the outreach in Miami. As a result, 34% of those who invited Christ into their lives enrolled in follow-up Bible studies. This total of 2,240 people signing up for the Bible studies was one of the highest in the nation.

Praise Rallies

At the conclusion of the campaigns in most of the 246 cities, praise rallies were held to give glory to God for what He had accomplished. As I visited city after city to participate in these rallies, I was intoxicated with joy and gratitude to God for the thousands who were introduced to Christ in each city.

In Chicago, Vonette and I attended the National Association of Evangelicals convention. Scores of pastors stopped us every few feet in the halls between sessions and in display areas to tell us how God had used Here's Life, America and a particular staff member or members to bless them and their church.

I would say that the Here's Life movement was phenomenally successful. So far as I have any knowledge, it was the most remarkable movement of its kind in history. During a single time span, more people in our country heard the gospel of Jesus Christ and made commitments to Him as Savior and Lord than at any time since the birth of our nation, and more people became involved in discipleship and evangelism training than ever before in the history of this country.

Also, one of the most important aspects of the movement, according to the pastors and laymen whom I meet, is the feeling of brotherhood that exists between denominations and in other local churches. They worked together, witnessed together, prayed together and demonstrated the love of Christ together.

Dr. Billy Graham frequently states that the real success of his city-wide crusades cannot be determined for at least five years; authorities say that same principle applies to Here's Life America. Only God knows what the results will be as thousands of laymen have learned to share their faith, as tens of millions have heard the gospel and as churches have learned to work together toward the common goal of reaching the world for the Lord Jesus Christ.

CHAPTER TWENTY-FIVE

Here's Life, World

God has truly accomplished miracles in bringing people to Himself through our staff and volunteers in the 150 countries where we have ministries. But there are still so many people who do not yet know Him. Authorities tell us that in 1984 the world's population was 4.7 billion people, with the total expected to reach 6.25 billion by the turn of the century. From the human perspective, our goal of helping to reach every one of these people with the gospel seems ludicrous and impossible. But so was the parting of the Red Sea and the feeding of the five thousand with a few loaves and fishes.

When Jesus commanded us to go into all the world and preach the gospel, making disciples of all nations, He promised to go with us. Because all authority in heaven and earth is His, we can go to each of the 210 countries and protectorates of the world with the absolute confidence that the One in whom dwelleth all the fullness of the Godhead will go with us and supply our needs. Thus, the very thing He came into the world to accomplish — to seek and to save the lost and to communicate His love and forgiveness to all men — will be fulfilled.

Proven Strategy

God has been enabling us to take great strides toward helping to fulfill His Great Commission through Here's Life, World. This movement incorporates much of the same strategy and many of the concepts that proved so successful in the Here's Life, America campaigns. These strategies are received by other nations with even more enthusiasm and success than they were in the United States, if that is possible.

During 1977, Bailey Marks, then our director for Asia, invited me to help launch Here's Life in a number of countries throughout the continent. Again and again I heard the expression, "Nothing like this has ever happened in the history of our country." There seemed to be an unprecedented moving of God's Spirit, calling Christians from various organizations and denominations which did not normally cooperate to work in harmony and love.

When I arrived in Pakistan to help initiate the Here's Life movement in that country, Pakistan was in a state of political turmoil. Even though riots were raging all around us, with buses and trains being burned and people being killed, the Christians still came to the meetings. Sessions were held each morning and afternoon with as many as 1,200 present in a single meeting. Many of the Christian leaders of Lahore and Karachi, Pakistan's two largest cities, met together for prayer, fellowship and strategy sessions, with a view toward launching Here's Life in those key cities.

The media campaigns in Manila and Baguio City in the Philippines started in March that same year, and God blessed in a mighty way with many thousands receiving Christ. Early returns on the campaign encouraged me and the other staff greatly as we heard what God was doing. Statistics showed that 1,971 workers and 102 churches participated in the outreach; and 209,830 responses were received from the various forms of media advertisements. In the first 13,000 times the gospel was presented as a part of the campaign, 9,242 persons indicated decisions to trust Christ, an incredible 70% positive response. More than half of these individuals who accepted Christ as their Savior enrolled in Bible studies to be trained in the basics of the Christian faith.

Cultural Adaptations

Although many of the strategies were the same as those used in Here's Life, America, cultural differences made alterations in the Asian campaigns a necessity. For example, the outdoor "I found it!" advertising was more prevalent in Manila and Baguio City than in American cities. Shop owners were much more willing to have banners and posters displayed in their windows. Thousands of taxis — which dominate the streets in both cities — carried bumper stickers. "Sometimes you couldn't look anywhere without seeing 'I found it!'" noted Bailey Marks.

Also, in Manila and Baguio City, there was only a small systematic telephone calling campaign, which was the main thrust in America. This was true in many of our subsequent campaigns conducted in areas where only a few people have telephones. So the main emphasis of the media campaign was to urge people who wanted more information about Christ to respond either by telephone or by filling out a coupon and dropping it into one of the 800 "I found it!" boxes located throughout the two cities. The strategy worked: more than 180,000 of the 210,000 responses were retrieved from the boxes.

One couple in Manila spent 40% of their time contacting people who had responded during the media campaign. All of the employees in the five offices this couple own found new life in Christ.

Eager to Hear

The campaign held in Tijuana, Mexico, in November of that same year was also highly successful. On the first day of the "message revealed" phase of the campaign, when people could respond by calling the Here's Life number or returning a coupon, residents of a village suburb of Tijuana were so eager to find out how they could find new life in Christ that they waited in line to deposit their coupons in a box outside a local super-market.

One woman in another part of the city not only listed her name and address on the coupon, but on the back she also explained exactly how to arrive at her house, which bus to take, where to get off and how to go from there. "She was so anxious for someone to visit her home that she did everything but enclose bus fare," com-mented one worker.

Many of the people who came to Christ during the campaign showed an intense desire to grow in their faith. Of those who made decisions for Christ, 89% enrolled in the follow-up Bible studies.

Another Latin American campaign occurred in the Caribbean city of San Cristobal, the Dominican Republic. Located near the country's capital, Santo Domingo, San Cristobal is a city of about 44,000 of whom 2,000 are evangelical Christians. There are 18 Protestant churches, 17 of which took part in the campaign, creating a corps of 640 trained workers. That many volunteers were defi-nitely needed, because more than one-third of the city's total population requested the "You Can Find It, Too," booklet, an explanation of the gospel.

90% Response

As workers began to follow up the requests, they encountered a level of receptiveness unprecedented even for campaigns in gospel-responsive Latin America, where an overall average of 50% of the people who hear a personal presentation of how to receive Christ ask Him into their lives. Yet in San Cristobal, the average was an incredible 90% — 10,260 recorded decisions from among the 11,400 people who personally heard the gospel.

The campaign in Singapore faced special problems. This tiny island republic of about two million people is composed of large international populations including Chinese, Malays, Indians and westerners. Not only is it multi-racial, but it is also multi-lingual and multi-religious, and many people wanted it to stay that way. Because the task of reaching this city seemed so overwhelming, leaders of the Here's Life movement there asked God to raise up enough prayer warriors to have at least 10 Christians praying at all times for the saturation strategy. By February, 1977, five 24-hour prayer chains had been formed. By the beginning of the media campaign, the remaining five chains had been formed. Almost 8,000 Christians were involved in these two prayer chains.

Churches Working Together

The campaign was well supported by the churches as 100 of the approximately 180 churches in Singapore were represented by campaign workers. "The training I received has turned me from a convert into a disciple with fire and zeal in my heart," said one young man from Jurong Christian Church.

Nine of the individuals in the city's main telephone center were blind. As they telephoned people, they used Braille copies of the Four Spiritual Laws in their sharing with people. Reports indicated that they were leading people to Christ with the same effectiveness as other campaign workers.

The Here's Life campaign in Malaysia was the first effort of its kind to be launched in a Muslim nation. The law in Malaysia is clear: Christians are not allowed to approach Malays with the gospel. Therefore, Here's Life, Malaysia represented a united effort to reach the 48% of the population which is Chinese.

Although threatening telephone calls were received every day, and vehicles bearing "I found it!" bumper stickers were maliciously damaged, campaign workers remained undaunted. George Lee, a member of the Here's Life, Malaysia executive committee, returned to his car one afternoon to find that the "I found it!" stickers had been scraped off with a knife, along with much of the car's paint. He responded to the situation by saying, "Automobile paint is still being manufactured. When Here's Life, Malaysia is over, we will repaint the car. In the meantime, we will simply cover the scratches with more 'I found it!' stickers."

Hong Kong Campaign

Another remarkable campaign was held in Hong Kong, a city of some 4.5 million people. I remember how thrilled I was to receive the initial report from Andrew Ho, the director of the outreach there. A total of 359 churches were involved in the campaign, and 300 of these churches held evangelistic, revival campaigns simultaneously with the Here's Life media campaign. Trained campaign workers numbered 15,000 while another 85,000 people participated in other ways. These 100,000 believers represented about half of the colony's Protestant population.

By the close of the campaign, 28,174 people had indicated decisions for Christ. One exciting aspect of the campaign was the number of new believers who became involved in local churches. One month after the campaign, 200 churches reported growth in attendance of between 30 and 150 persons each. Several congregations started branch churches.

Prior to the media campaign, a missionary guest speaker in a church began by endorsing Here's Life, Hong Kong. He explained that he wasn't sure what the church was doing with the movement but encouraged them to participate. In response, the pastor tapped the guest on the shoulder and explained that, as a result of the Here's Life training, 70 new members had been added to the church. The pastor asked everyone who was present as a result of the campaign to raise his hand. "Hands went up all over the congregation," recalls the astonished missionary.

The campaign in Nairobi, Kenya, was another one that saw churches benefit immensely. Following the campaign which recorded some 15,000 decisions for Christ, six Baptist churches baptized a total of 2,600 new members as a direct result of the outreach.

Cities on the European continent also successfully implemented Here's Life campaigns. In Barcelona, Spain, 35 churches took part in the campaign, representing 75% of the city's evangelical population. The Tolra Church is an example of those who participated. Although it became involved late, Tolra's members were still able to participate in all aspects of the training. They made 119 home visits and shared their faith in 109. Twenty-four people accepted Christ, and 31 signed up to be in Bible studies.

Tripled Attendance

Tampere, Finland, saw church attendance triple in the first three Sundays following the start of its campaign. One church in the suburbs, with a seating capacity of 350, had a regular attendance of 150. But during these three weeks, there were more than 600 trying to sit in the 350 seats. Our director of affairs for Europe, Kalevi Lehtinen, who is a native of Finland, has expressed great enthusiasm about these two campaigns and others that are scheduled. He feels, as I do, that the campaigns in Europe can help spark a great revival that could very well sweep the continent.

Lahore, Pakistan, was the site of our first campaign conducted in the Middle East. Our national director for Pakistan, professor Daniel Bakhsh, said that Jesus Christ was the talk of the town for probably the first time in history.

With such a large majority of the population being Muslims, the campaign faced opposition on every side.

Yet, through it all, God blessed in a unique way. Professor Bakhsh reports that the 1,000 decisions for Christ are unprecedented in Pakistan.

A campaign volunteer working among non-Christians where he was employed said that for the first time his fellow workers were coming to him to learn more about Christ. He said hundreds of students were asking him what "I found it!" meant.

The success of these campaigns in reaching cities around the world filled me with praise and gratitude to our wonderful Lord. But, it has been a sobering thought to realize that an estimated 62% of the world's population doesn't live in cities at all, but in villages and rural areas. That's why I became so excited about what happened in the Kilungu hills, a rural area of Kenya.

Like much of the world's rural areas, the majority of the people in Kilungu (75%) were non-literate. Therefore, a tape recording was used to train pastors and laymen in evangelizing the area. A booklet of photographs illustrating how to receive Christ was used in conjunction with the tape training.

Material Memorized

Since learning through hearing is the norm in most African countries, and memorization often replaces written notes, the training tool proved very effective. Thus, trained pastors and laymen could equip their own churches, using the same tape packages they had learned from. The successful development of this vital training is a tribute to the prayer and hard work of our African staff and the outstanding leadership of our director of affairs in Africa, Don Myers.

Once the training was completed, four cars and a motorcycle — equipped with loud speakers — began sounding the local language's equivalent of "I found it!" — "*Niniwonete*" — through the 100-square mile section of the Kamba tribal lands. Soon the cars couldn't go anywhere in the area without being met by children singing the *Niniwonete* jingle.

During those first days, the drivers helped churches set up bright yellow banners to aid interested people in locating the places where they could find the new life in Jesus Christ that the cars "sang" of. These same banners also showed where follow-up Bible studies were being held.

People frequently walked miles — often up steep hills — to find out about the new life that Jesus Christ offers. An average of 50 % of those who came to the information centers indicated decisions to accept Christ. In some places, where the climb was most difficult, 75% of those who came accepted Christ as their Savior.

Other types of rural campaigns have been used in Mexico and the Philippines to circulate the life-changing message of Jesus Christ. The potential of these campaigns thrills me as I think of the hundreds of millions of people living in villages that can be reached in this manner.

Saturation Campaign in India

One of the most spectacular results of the saturation strategies occurred in the Indian state of Kerala. Our national director in India, Thomas Abraham, chose to believe God for the total saturation of this state of 22 million people by the end of 1976. From the busiest streets of sprawling coastal cities to remote mountainous tea plantations, trained workers went house to house communicating the good news of Jesus Christ. At the end of the campaign, 99% of the homes had been contacted.

During the last three months of the campaign, large evangelistic meetings were held in all 11 districts of Kerala. This was done to insure that those people who were at work or school during the day and had missed the visits of the workers going house to house would still have a chance to hear the gospel.

The program at these public meetings was structured so that individuals had three opportunities to receive Christ: through a short, evangelistic message given by a Campus Crusade staff member; in Andre Kole's film, "World of Illusion"; and through another film, "Life Is Where I'm Going."

On one occasion, a church which had given permission to use its property for a public meeting withdrew permission. "As we were praying about what to do, someone suggested we use the compound in front of a mosque," said Thomas Abraham. "It is inconceivable that Muslims would provide a place with electricity free of charge for a gospel meeting, but that's exactly what happened. It is probably the first time a Christian meeting was held in a temple yard. Many came to know the Lord in a personal way that evening." A total of 380,028 people invited Christ into their lives through meetings such as this one, making a grand total of 1,850,982 individuals who accepted Christ as their Savior during the campaign.

"It began as an impossible dream in 1969," said Thomas. "But by the grace of God, on December 31, 1976, almost every home in Kerala had been contacted. The staff of India Campus Crusade and I are praising God for the completed task of saturating our Jerusalem with the good news."

Reaching Colombia

We saw God do a similar mighty work in Colombia. I had the opportunity of joining Sergio Gargia, director of affairs for Latin America, and Nestor Chamorro, our director in Colombia, for three fantastic days of witnessing firsthand the saturation campaign in this Latin American nation. During 1978, an estimated 65-86% of Colombia's 27 million people heard how they could have a personal relationship with Jesus Christ. Many were approached on a personal basis, others heard through radio announcements, television, newspaper ads and fliers.

During the first half of that year, the emphasis was on house-to-house evangelism. Cities were sectioned off geographically, and thousands of associate staff members of Campus Crusade and volunteers were given the responsibility to saturate specific blocks.

There were also mass outreaches. At least 750,000 people were exposed to the gospel during Easter week alone. By July 1, Nestor estimated that 45% of the population had heard the gospel.

On August 1, nine groups of students and single staff embarked on the "sacrificial mission." These teams traveled throughout Colombia's villages and rural areas, saturating them with the gospel and establishing prayer groups. Another group, the "mission impossible" team, developed a ministry among government officials in Bogota. In December, media campaigns, mass rallies and other projects completed the task of saturating the nation.

Reports indicate that nearly 18 million people were directly contacted through personal presentations or in group meetings. They and millions of others were also touched through the mass media. Only God knows the true extent of their response, but more than 2.6 million decisions to accept Christ as Savior and Lord have been recorded.

Fund-raising Campaign

Undergirding much of the efforts to reach people around the world is a massive fund-raising campaign. Helping to coordinate this project are our Office of Development staff members. These dedicated people are in regular contact with many individuals, ministering to them spiritually as well as informing them how their finances can be used to help fulfill the Great Commission.

The campaign has been designed to supply badly needed funds for the Here's Life movements in various cities overseas. The goal is to raise one billion dollars to help finance these efforts in order to help reach at least one billion people for Christ by 1990.

Wallace E. Johnson, co-founder of Holiday Inns, Inc., is the honorary international chairman of Here's Life, World; Joe Foss, former governor of South Dakota, is the international chairman; Roy Rogers, actor and business-man, is vice-chairman; Nelson Bunker Hunt, oil executive and investor, is the chairman of the international executive committee; and Ed Johnson, chairman and president of Financial Federation, one of America's leading financial institutions, is the campaign chairman for the United States.

Wallace Johnson's words at the initial stages of the campaign to raise the funds set the tone for the entire effort: "We must dedicate ourselves to this program which is so vital, so big, that it will set fire to the minds and imaginations of others for decades to come," he said. He also emphasized that the fund-raising campaign was to be targeted at potential funds not now being channeled into other Christian organizations or churches. "It is not our desire to compete with any other religious group for money or projects," he said.

As God continues to work through the Here's Life, World movement, I have never felt more optimistic or more confident. Never have I felt more assured that God is going to do something incredibly great to demonstrate His love and forgiveness to all men and nations throughout the world by the end of 1980.

CHAPTER TWENTY-SIX

"P.S." Ministries

Campus Crusade's prison outreach, "P.S." Ministries (a Personal Savior is the only solution to a Penal Situation), had a unique beginning. It started with a phone call to staff member Larry Benton who was later to become the director of the ministry. "Larry, this is your neighbor, Pat," the voice over the phone said. "A man broke into your home, assaulted your wife and stole your car. Can you make it home?"

Larry Benton quickly hung up the phone and headed for home. He began to pray, "Dear God, I know You are in charge of all things and that You either cause or allow things to happen in our lives. I know You didn't cause this, but You did have to allow it. Why? You have promised to work all things together for good, but how can You do it in a case like this? I know You have commanded us to give thanks in everything, and although I don't feel like it, I thank You by faith. Please, God, use this to Your glory."

When Larry arrived at his driveway, the first thing he noticed was an empty garage. The front door gaped open; knotted belts strung the hallway welcoming him home. The house was teeming with policemen.

Larry's wife, Beverly, was at the neighbors, crying convulsively; her face was badly bruised. Soon, the ambulance came, and she was gone, giving Larry time to study the situation as he traveled from room to room. The evidence was clear — a fight in the kitchen, Beverly dragged to the living room and then to the bedroom. A dirty razor was lying in the sink where her assailant had taken a leisurely shave.

At the hospital Beverly related more. "He said he was going to keep on committing one crime after another 'because the world is in such a mess.' I told him that was not the answer, but Christ in the hearts of men was the answer to peace in the world. Before he left he said, 'I had planned to kill you, but you can thank your God that I didn't.'"

32-year Prison Record

This man was caught and extradited to the county jail; he had a 32-year long record of crime. As a result of Larry and Beverly's letter of forgiveness and personal witness, he came to know Christ. A happy ending to an otherwise traumatic incident!

Instead of an ending, this event was to be the beginning of a whole new chapter in the lives of Larry and Beverly Benton. It became a launching pad for the "P.S." Ministries, an outreach of evangelism and discipleship to inmates in a variety of penal institutions.

A year after the break-in at their home, Beverly began teaching craft classes in the San Bernardino County jail. The classes expanded to Sunday evening services; eventually 150 women prisoners received Christ as a result of her jail ministry.

From the city jail, the ministry moved to the California Institute for Women at Frontera, Calif. There, Beverly began to teach the Ten Basic Steps Toward Christian Maturity and the Transferable Concepts. Also, she began to show a series of films entitled "The Christian Home," featuring Dr. Henry Brandt, a noted Christian psychologist and lecturer.

Because of the success of these films, the Bentons arranged for them to be shown in 18 California prisons and prisons in Texas, Idaho and Pennsylvania. In the process of distributing the film series, the Bentons were able to visit chaplains in each of the major penal institutions in California and hold Lay Institutes for Evangelism at these prisons.

Overworked Chaplains

Most of these chaplains had more work than they could possibly handle. For example, one exhausted chaplain was in charge of 3,000 men. Because of the shortage of staff, the men had to sign up three weeks in advance to attend chapel. Shortly thereafter Larry and Beverly began to lay plans to train "para-chaplains" to help lighten the load of chaplains in ministering to the spiritual needs of the inmates. In the summer of 1975, the training of the first para-chaplains was begun.

Most discipleship takes place as Campus Crusade staff meet together with the inmates one-to-one or in small groups. Antha Avril, formerly an inmate in the California Institute for Women, is one of the many individuals Larry and Beverly have discipled.

"One evening a friend invited me to come to a meeting sponsored by 'P.S.' Ministries," says Antha. "At the meeting, these people didn't condemn me for my mistake in life as so many others had; they were telling me of God's love and plan for my life — my ruined, hopeless life. I knew I had to find out more about this love and plan. So, I invited Christ into my heart. Six people have become Christians through my singing in the shower. 'Why are you singing in prison?' they ask. 'How can anyone be happy here?' Then I share with them about Christ."

"P.S." Ministries' work with inmates once they are out of prison includes special Bible studies led by laymen trained by "P.S." staff. They are set up to help the inmate readjust to society. "We found that one of the hardest things for them is re-entry," says Larry. "I realized one day that there was as much cultural difference between the inside of a prison and the outside as there is between any two countries. The networkd Bible study serves as a bridge between the inmate and his family and the institutional church."

The man who assaulted Beverly was a recipient of the Prison Ministries' follow-up and discipleship program. When he had served his prison term, he left to take his place in society. After some time passed, he wrote to the Bentons, sharing that for the first time since he was a boy he was off parole and supervision by the law. He also expressed his gratitude to the Bentons for their influence in leading him to the new life he had found in a personal relationship with Jesus Christ.

The change in the life-style of inmates working with "P.S." Ministries presents an interesting contrast to crime studies. Robert Martinson, a sociologist from the City College of New York, conducted a major study and concluded that "the prison which makes every effort at rehabilitation succeeds no better than the prison which leaves its inmates to rot." In spite of this, "P.S." Ministries has had success in turning the lives of inmates in a new direction. Larry Benton believes this has happened because the para-chaplains and volunteers in "P.S." Ministries help to deal with the root causes of crime instead of the surface symptoms. "Crime is simply the outward manifestation of sin," he says. "The real problem is with men's hearts. A personal relationship with Jesus Christ and learning to apply the Word of God on a daily basis is the only solution."

CHAPTER TWENTY-SEVEN

Family Ministry

She had lost all hope for her marriage, her family and her life. She had decided to commit suicide. Divorce was the only other option. The pain in her relationship with her husband was unbearable, and her days were filled with total despair. She never dreamed such misery could exist. She felt like a complete failure as a w͡ˊ ˋ, mother and businesswoman.

Friday, April 27, was the first day of the Family Life Conference sponsored by Campus Crusade for Christ's Family Ministry. This woman's husband, who was not a Christian, called her to invite her to go to the conference. She told him no and said she would meet him Monday at the courthouse to start divorce proceedings.

But something rare and wonderful began to happen. This woman's husband somehow convinced her to go with him to the conference. During the weekend, the husband committed his life and his future to the Lord. For the first time the couple found hope they could cling to and a plan for their lives.

On the last day of the conference, the wife came up to one of the speakers in tears and hugged him. She then explained how she and her husband were starting afresh with a new life, a new marriage and a new hope. They also agreed to follow up with professional counseling in the weeks and months ahead.

The American family is indeed in a time of great conflict. For the past several years, a million couples each year have been dissolving their marriages. Statistics tell us that 59 percent of America's children under the age of eighteen will spend part of their lives living with just

one parent. The single parent family is the fastest growing family unit in America.

Against this backdrop of families in crisis, our Family
Ministry has risen to answer the cry of the distressed.
During 1984 this ministry experienced another year of
incredible growth, with a 60 percent increase in attendance at its conferences. At 19 conferences, 17,000 people
attended, as conferences in Denver, San Francisco, Dallas, New York and Minneapolis each drew more than
1,000 people, with the gathering in Chicago attracting
1,550. Without question, people are hungry to find answers to the family problems they are experiencing.

They are finding answers. One couple who attended
the conference in New York City had been married for
about thirty years. One of the application projects had
been to write a love letter to your spouse. As this couple
began the project, they both began to cry and continued
to cry for more than an hour as they poured out their
hearts to one another. The wife said later that it was the
first time her husband had really communicated with
her in all of their years of marriage. She said that Saturday
night was when their honeymoon finally began. A year
later she shared that their marriage had grown into an
intimate, joyful and fulfilling relationship.

The Family Ministry was initially formed to aid the
staff members of the Campus Crusade ministry. At first,
the emphasis was to help prepare engaged staff members
for marriage, but gradually it shifted to add marriage
enrichment. The idea was to help couples be strong in
their marriages so they could be more effective in ministering to others and help to fulfill the Great Commission.

"We seek to show in our seminars what has happened
to the American marriage today, and how the Bible gives
us a plan for action," says Dennis Rainey, the director
of the Family Ministry. As Dennis and other conference
speakers present God's plan for marriage, they are able
to help couples come to grips with the pressures of life

by showing why marriages are failing in our society today. Then, from this emphasis the conference goes on to teach practical aspects such as communication, sexuality, handling conflicts, etc.

But the conferences are not all lecture. The subject material is spread out over a three-day period, with evenings free for the conferees to discuss with their mates what they have been learning.

This ministry fits beautifully with the evangelistic and disciple- building emphasis of Campus Crusade. The purpose of the Family Ministry is to help churches equip families so they can be healthy to go to the world with the good news in this and in the next generation.

Healthier Christian families will help produce more missionaries to send to the world. And unless something happens to improve the health of American families during the next two decades, we're going to be needing missionaries ourselves.

The great need in American families for a biblical perspective on marriage has caused explosive growth in the Family Ministry. A cassette tape series, "Foundations for Family Living," and a conference notebook enables conferees to take the material home for personal study and use in churches, as well as for small group studies.

In 1983 Here's Life America staff members organized a New York City conference and saw 700 people attend — more than twice what they expected. The next year saw even more astonishing results. About 1,325 people attended, which at that time was the largest conference in the Family Ministry's history. It was so large, in fact, that 200 people had to watch the speakers on a video screen in an overflow room. As a result of the conference's success, gatherings were later scheduled in Philadelphia, attended by 900 people, and Boston, attended by 800. This draws a striking picture of spiritual warmth in an area that is usually thought of as cold to spiritual matters, Dennis says.

A pastor who attended the New York City meeting approached one of the speakers. Though he and his attractive wife looked like they had a good marriage, such was not the case. As he held his wife's hand, he told the speaker that his marriage was near divorce. The following Monday he was prepared to tell his congregation that he and his wife were going to divorce. But God had dealt with this couple that weekend and had healed many of their wounds. The conference had given them a sound biblical blueprint for their marriage and family. He said that they were not going to get a divorce, but that their marriage had new hope.

Changing lives for the glory of God is what the Family Ministry's 61 full-time staff and team of 20 speakers are trusting God to do. And it continues to happen at conference after conference.

"We came to this conference with some serious marital difficulties, discouraged and questioning our commitment to working on our relationship," said a Kansas City housewife who had been married for fourteen years. "But the practical methods and application of biblical principles has helped us to renew our commitment to each other and to our family. I praise the Lord for this weekend as it took us from despair to delight with our marriage and each other."

"This has revolutionized me as a Christian, a husband and as a father," said a Dallas insurance agent and real estate broker. "Setting aside two and a half days with my wife alone and *working through* the projects, has helped me get my role and priorities together as a Christian, husband and father. This is the most practical experience for marriage and guidance I have had."

CHAPTER TWENTY-EIGHT

Reaching the Nation's Leaders

Through the centuries, world history has been shaped by men of vision, faith and dedication. For example, those who gave birth to America were men who possessed these qualities. They were willing to pay a great price for their freedom and ours. Consider the bitter winter of 1777-1778 when Gen. George Washington knelt in the snows of Vally Forge. It seemed that the battle for independence was lost. He cried out to God for help and that battle for freedom was won.

Consider that critical meeting of the Continental Congress when the representatives from various colonies had reached an impasse. When there seemed to be no hope for reaching an agreement, Benjamin Franklin stood to his feet. "Gentlemen," he said, "I have lived long enough to know that God rules in the affairs of men and nations, and if a sparrow cannot fall to the ground without His knowledge, neither can a nation rise without His benediction. I move that we adjourn for prayer." History records that following that prayer meeting, the representatives came to a happy and immediate solution of their differences.

In a very real sense, we are a free people today, living in the most spiritually blessed country of history because God answered the prayers of multitudes of Christians.

Righteousness Important

It is vitally important that our nation have righteous leaders making the decisions that guide our country. The Bible tells us, "With good men in authority, the people rejoice; but with the wicked in power, they groan"

(Proverbs 29:2, Living), and "Righteousness exalts a nation" (Proverbs 14:34a). Because of this great need for righteous people in positions of authority, we began the Christian Embassy to minister to leaders in the various branches of government in Washington, D.C. By sharing the good news of Jesus Christ with these individuals, they could have the opportunity to know Him and lean on His wisdom and strength for the great responsibilities of their jobs.

Though Campus Crusade staff had worked in Washington for a couple of years before, and staff member Eleanor Page had had a fruitful ministry with several congressional wives, the Christian Embassy ministry was officially launched on February 23, 1976, in a gathering that included a number of leaders in Washington as well as Swede Anderson, the director of our ministry there, and our Embassy staff. From the beginning of this work, God has repeatedly shown us the spiritual hunger of the men and women in positions of leadership.

I saw this hunger demonstrated one day when I walked into the office of a senator whom I had never met. A mutual friend had said, "Drop by to see him." Within a few moments it seemed as if we had known each other for a lifetime. I asked him if he was a Christian and shared the gospel with him through the Four Spiritual Laws. Within 10 to 15 minutes after I had entered his office, he said he would like to receive Christ.

On another occasion, I spoke at a congressman's home to several congressmen and their wives. After the meeting, several individuals came up to me and asked me to come see them.

I went by the office of the first man the next day and asked him, "Did what I said last night make sense to you?" "It sure did," he replied. "Would you like to receive Christ?" I asked. He said that he would and knelt beside his couch to pray.

Down the hall I shared Christ with another congressman who had been present the night before. He too, said he would like to receive Christ.

Interested in Training

Not only are these individuals interested in receiving Christ, but they also are interested in being trained in how to live a more effective Christian life. At one meeting, I asked a leading senator to attend a 14-hour mediated Christian training session. I told him that I recognized that his busy schedule might not permit him to attend all of the training. He responded by saying, "Bill, if I'm too busy to take this training, I'm too busy. There is nothing more important. When can I begin?"

The Christian Embassy staff involve leadership of all branches of our government and the military in dinner meetings and luncheons, both large and small, to share Christ with them. Those who respond are invited to study the Bible with their colleagues (over 20 such groups are in action now) and to attend special seminars designed to equip them to grow in their Christian life and introduce others to the Lord.

Washington for Jesus

The highlight of our ministry in Washington, D.C., was a huge rally of an estimated 500,000 people. They came to spend April 29, 1980, in prayer for our nation. I believe this event, entitled "Washington for Jesus," was a great turning point in our nation's history.

Emotions welled up within me as I sat on the platform on the mall a couple of hundred yards from the Capitol Building. Indescribable feelings of worship, praise and joy vibrated through my heart as I looked out on the vast crowd of men and women who had come from across our country.

I had joined Pat Robertson of the Christian Broad-casting Network as the co-progam chairman of the event. In that capacity it was one of my responsibilities to encourage evangelical leaders to participate in the event and lend their efforts to making it a success. The group which attended represented a broad spectrum of the body of Christ. Greek Orthodox, Roman Catholics, Protestants, charismatics and non-charismatics all came together for one purpose: to repent, to turn back to God on behalf of our nation, and to express sorrow for our sins.

The day was filled not only with powerful, anointed preaching, but also with prayer and musical reminders of our dependence on God. I joined in prayer with my brothers and sisters in Christ, together claiming the promise of 2 Chronicles 7:14: "[If] My people who are called by My name humble themselves and pray, and seek My face and turn from their wicked ways, then I will hear from heaven, will forgive their sin, and will heal their land."

It occurred to me that surely this great host of men and women — and our sincerity — had touched the heart of God. Following the rally, Adrian Rogers, Ben Haden, Pat Robertson and many other Christian leaders agreed that this was one of the most important days in our nation's history.

U.N. Outreach

About half of the Christian Embassy staff come from fruitful ministry experience on other continents and concentrate their ministry efforts among the diplomats who people the embassies in Washington and the United Nations in New York. This ministry was begun in 1978.

Most nations send their most outstanding leaders to represent them in Washington and New York. Few of these people develop close relationships with American Christians. Christian Embassy staff spend time with them personally, entertain them in their homes and hold special dinners and receptions for them.

A Latin American couple who received Christ antici-
pate sharing their new- found faith with their friends in
the leadership of their nation when they return home,
and the same is happening among Africans, Europeans,
Asians and Middle Eastern diplomats.

Twelve staff led by Frank Obien and Glen Kleinknecht
talked with delegates and U.N. staff about a personal
relationship with Christ and invited them to a reception.
Included among the 70 who attended the reception heard
a short gospel presentation were a minister of foreign
affairs, more than six ambassadors, vice consuls, under-
secretaries, U.N. delegates and their staff.

Influential Contacts

Swede Anderson feels that this work in the U.N. and
embassies in Washington can help expand our
worldwide movement. "One of the most important facets
of the Christian Embassy, we believe, is that through
leadership persons introduced to Christ (those who work
at the U.N., World Bank or in embassies), the lives of
leaders on each continent will be changed and doors of
opportunity for spreading the gospel in many nations
will open."

We find that, when these people recognize their need
for Christ and as He enters their lives, He begins to
satisfy the deepest concerns of the person and of his
family life. Christ also gives him confidence that He can
guide him in the midst of the pressures of his professional
responsibilities. Restored families and new hope are
among the results seen in this vital international outreach.

With the Christian Embassy ministry established in
these two cities, a foundation is now laid for launching
embassies in all the major capitol cities of the world.

Another vital outreach that is designed to work with
the leaders of the world is the Executive Ministries of

Campus Crusade. Reaching business and professional leaders, the Executive Ministries is making a powerful impact on these influential people.

Executive Seminars

One of the key elements of the strategy is the Executive Seminars, held several times each year at Arrowhead Springs and other locations across the country and around the world. Through large meetings, small group seminars and one-to-one interaction, the executives and their wives learn how to maximize their talents and resources for Jesus Christ. They learn that they are important in helping to fulfill the Great Commission. And, just as important, they discover that they have personal needs that only God can meet.

Throughout the week of a seminar, men and women respond personally to God's love and to the challenge of beginning or renewing their relationship with Him. When executives who have reached the top of the financial, business and professional ladder come to Christ, they frequently become as excited as any other group, including students.

Joyful Experience

On one occasion, one of the executives with whom I had prayed the second day of the seminar (his wife had received Christ only the day before) spoke across the table during lunch to another businessman with whom I had prayed only 20 minutes before. The first man, although very dignified and reserved normally, was bubbling over with great joy. "My wife is four days old," he said, "and I am three days old." (He was referring, of course, to his age as a Christian.) "How old are you?"

The second man paused for a few moments and then replied, "I am 20 minutes old." Many others scattered across the dining room at Arrowhead Springs were only a few minutes, hours or days old. Great rejoicing was taking place among us and in heaven as well!

The desire to lead a changed life ultimately infects nearly everyone who attends the seminar, and the contrast between the arrival and departure atmospheres is evident in the radiant faces, warm interaction and joyful singing at the close of each seminar. But the difference is most evident when they return to the "old routine" with new perspectives and priorities.

One woman wrote, "The seminar was so organized and so exciting! I really desire to go back to Oklahoma and come alive with what I've heard and felt. I am asking God to show me exactly what He wants me to do in my community for Him. I want to be totally His woman!"

Another executive commented this way: "My wife and I wish to thank you for the many God-given benefits we have received from the recent Executive Seminar. We have both rededicated ourselves to a Christ-centered life — to seek God's will for us!"

"I liked the evident love and friendliness of everyone," wrote another executive. "The program was worthwhile and most influencing. All of this has made for a week that has changed both my wife's life and mine."

Similar seminars have been conducted with great success overseas, as executives and professionals in Asia, Latin America, Africa and Europe have responded warmly to the invitations to make their lives count for the cause of Christ.

American executives frequently participate in these seminars in other countries as a part of a vision tour. These tours take them overseas where they observe the Campus Crusade international ministry in action. In addition to having their vision stretched as they see what God is accomplishing, they also have the opportunity to minister to executives from other nations.

Ministering Through Dinner Parties

Another aspect of the Executive Ministries outreach is that of evangelistic dinner parties. For 13 years, Art De Moss, who was a member of our board of directors, and his wife, Nancy, hosted dinner parties where the guests had the opportunity to hear the claims of Christ. Art has gone to be with the Lord, but Nancy has continued the ministry.

About every six weeks, the couple hosted a dinner party for 150-700 people at their home. After dinner, the guests heard from such nationally-known figures as Charles Colson, Pat Boone, author Joni Eareckson, Senator Bill Armstrong, Roy Rogers and Dale Evans, and several professional athletes, all of whom shared their faith in Christ.

Those who trusted in Christ during the presentation were invited back for a smaller dinner party which could lead to their involvement in Bible studies to foster their spiritual growth. Approximately 600 men and women participated in these studies led by Campus Crusade staff.

An individual who became involved in one of the Bible study groups said, "My decision to join the group was only part of a larger decision to let the Lord guide me practically instead of just in theory. Life is suddenly more meaningful when I ask Christ what I should do and let Him guide me in doing it."

Many Christian couples from around the country attend dinner parties now given by Nancy, and then they participate in two-day seminars on how they can hold their own evangelistic parties. Using these principles in their own communities, these individuals also see gratifying results, and have had as many as 54 people indicate decisions to receive Christ at a single dinner.

Art saw the spiritual hunger of the socially prominent as one cause for the success of this ministry. "But the most significant factor," he emphasized, "is that God is in this, and people who seemed unreachable are being reached for Christ."

Reaching people who can have a wide influence for Christ not only in their community but also throughout the world is what the Executive Ministries is all about. And it is a ministry that God is using greatly. To Him be all the honor, glory and praise!

CHAPTER TWENTY-NINE

Training Centers

Several years ago I had the privilege of addressing a unique group of people. It was another hot, humid day in Manila, the capital city of the Philippines, when I stood in a simple classroom, bare of all but the most necessary essentials. The students had a plain desk with hard wooden chairs. A blackboard was the only other adornment in the room.

Gathered from many countries across Asia, these students had come to be trained to be more effective in their service to our Lord. I spoke to them that day on the qualifications for spiritual revolution. My message was a simple one. I challenged them to crown Christ as Lord of their lives, be filled with the Holy Spirit, maintain their first love for Christ and keep fresh their vision for the task of reaching the world for Christ. Finally, I urged them to be committed to God's Word and to prayer and to tell everyone who would listen about Christ (Colossians 1:28).

I emphasized that they could do this only through the power of the Holy Spirit and not in the energy of the flesh. I reminded them that God does not call us to do anything for which He does not supply the power, the wisdom and the grace. After my message the students were excited about what I had to say and we all had a great time of fellowship together.

In the days and weeks following my visit, the individuals continued an intensive time of evangelizing and discipling of new believers in preparation for their ministry in their home countries. I'm sure some of the students were somewhat apprehensive at first about their time at the training center. They were unsure of how this time was going to benefit them as they prepared for the ministry they felt God wanted them to have back in their home country.

But as the weeks went by, they continued to receive instruction on many of the essentials of the Christian life — how to be filled with the Spirit, how to live a holy life, how to witness, how to help fulfill the Great Commission, and many others. Not only did they hear lectures, but they actually put the instruction into practice by leading Bible studies at local campuses and witnessing for their faith as they went about their daily activities.

The results were that when they returned to their home countries, they had not only knowledge, but experience. They then launched successful ministries that in some cases greatly affected the cause of Christ among their people.

One of the graduates of the training center came to Bailey Marks, who was then the director of affairs for our ministry in Asia, saying, "If I go back to my country and do what I have been taught to do, I will end up in jail or dead, because in my country it is against the law for someone to change his religion."

Bailey assured him, "You just do what God tells you to do. You won't be under any pressure from us."

When the recent graduate of the training center returned to his home country, he began translating Campus Crusade's materials into his native language. At that time only a few hundred believers lived in this isolated nation.

As important as the translation work was, our director became increasingly exasperated at his lack of witnessing experiences. Finally, he told his wife, "I am going out to witness, no matter what happens."

That afternoon the first three people he spoke to about Christ trusted Him as their Savior. The next day they all came for Bible study and our director began passing on to them what he had learned at our training center in Manila.

Today it is a matter of history that a great explosion of ministry has taken place. More than 25,000 people have been baptized and at least that many people have embraced Christ, but not yet been baptized. And our director, with the emphasis on evangelism and discipleship that he learned at the training center, provided the spark for this revival.

But these great advances have not come without significant cost. Our director has been imprisoned, along with other believers, on a number of occasions. And yet he and his family have maintained a joyful, radiant spirit in spite of this roadblock. I asked his wife how she felt about her husband being imprisoned. She replied, "I'm jealous. I wanted to be in prison for our Lord."

Their teenage daughter responded in like manner. When she learned that her father had been imprisoned for his witness, she said with tears, "Mother, why does Daddy get all the privileges?" Certainly it was a reminder of how the early Christians responded to suffering.

It is my prayer that people like our director and his wife will be raised up in every country and trained through our training centers so they can be as effective as possible in helping to change their communities and nations.

Training centers like the one in Manila have been extremely effective in training staff members around the world. Lasting from nine months to one year, these vital centers provide the foundation our staff need upon which to build dynamic evangelistic and disciple-building ministries.

Similar training centers have been established for laymen. Varying in duration from several weeks to three months, these training centers are an abbreviated version of the instruction which has enabled our staff to plant dynamic ministries in various parts of the world. It has been my prayer for years that we would be able to plant a training center of this type in every city in the free world with a population of more than 50,000. Our present plans call for 5,000 such training centers before 1995.

In this manner, those who come to Christ through showings of the film *JESUS* and evangelistic radio programming will have a place nurturing their faith.

Some of the training centers have been positioned in remote rural areas because of the critical needs there. Dale Robertson, a veteran Campus Crusade staff member from Vista, California, coordinated the training center near Davao, Philippines. He and his staff team regularly made trips to a training center located far from urban life.

The trip began by taking a ride to the end of the bus route. Dale and his co-workers then boarded a jeepney, a small, open mini-bus, for a two- hour ride on which they forded a river and trundled over mountains into the Arkann Valley. The trip was tiring and frequently left their boots and clothes splattered with mud. Once they arrived, however, they found trainees with hungry hearts.

One group of 16 trainees included 12 pastors, representing virtually every church in the valley. "Basically these people are untrained, uneducated farmers who are serving as pastors," Dale said. "It's so exciting to see how teachable they are."

Isobello Bamunya put his training at the Davao training center to good use by leading 50 people to Christ during one two-week period the center was in session. Many of these people responded to the gospel after he showed the *JESUS* film in his home village. On another occasion Bamunya walked nearly 25 miles to another village where he preached and shared the Four Spiritual Laws with local residents. As a result of the trip, the people in that area decided to build their own church.

The Here's Life Training Centers work with local

churches, which benefit from the training and from increased attendance. In some cases, when there are no churches for new believers to join, home Bible fellowships are started so Christians can meet on a regular basis.

In northern Thailand, as a result of the Here's Life Training Centers evangelism strategies, which include showing the *JESUS* film in rural villages, there are thousands of new Christians. Many of them are from villages where there is no church.

Now there are more than 520 home Bible fellowships with at least 15 members each in that part of Thailand. Of those fellowships, 400 are in areas where there were no known Christians before.

The same results are being seen elsewhere:

— During 1984, 280 village evangelists, lay leaders and pastors were trained at the Madhya Pradesh HLTC in India. From that group 60 home Bible fellowships were started and many new believers were baptized.

— In Pakistan, the Lahore training center has trained 1,500 students, 150 pastors and 1,200 laymen since its inception. The *JESUS* film has been shown to 930,000 people by the trainees and trainers, with 139,000 of those people indicating their desire to receive Christ.

— In Indonesia, two training centers were held in 1984 in Kelet, training 95 individuals. Using various methods, trainees shared the gospel with 7,920 individuals, with more than one-fourth indicating their desire to receive Christ. A total of 70 home Bible fellowships were started, and nine branch churches have been formed out of the Kelet church. Most of the training is done by the church leaders.

Under the leadership of Curt Mackey, the director of the Here's Life Training Centers around the world, this strategy is providing a growing base of trained lay people who are equipped to be spiritual leaders. And they are even improving on their own training as graduates of the program return to staff future training center sessions. These lay volunteers often prove extremely effective in discipling their peers.

But what of the countries which cannot be reached through the *JESUS* film, and where converts cannot enroll in training centers or home Bible fellowships? Although at first glance many counties would seem to fall into this category, it is my belief that one day every country will have home Bible fellowships. I am praying for 25 million home Bible fellowships to be operating worldwide.

I believe many of these fellowships will come into being as a result of a worldwide network of radio which will leapfrog the seemingly impregnable barriers which exist in our world today. In the People's Republic of China those barriers are political; in the Middle East, religious; and in India, logistical.

Since 1979, Campus Crusade for Christ has attempted to hurdle these barriers through Christian radio broadcasting. With the help of Christian radio broadcasting facilities such as Trans World Radio and Far Eastern Broadcasting Company, programs of Christian teaching and discipleship have been broadcast into China, India, the Middle East and Indonesia.

Our ministry has received 1,200 letters each month from India, 500 per month from the Arab world and 200 letters per month from China as a result of the broadcasts.

The broadcasts continue to leave their mark on listeners. One listener wrote: "I am an old-time Trans World Radio listener in China. I have been using your programs in encouraging other brothers and sisters. It has also been very helpful to me in my own spiritual growth. Your program is like a rich, spiritual feast to me."

In many parts of Asia programs are used as follow-up for the *JESUS* film. People attending showings of the movie are encouraged to tune in their radios to a Christian station which carries the Campus Crusade training.

By listening to the station they can begin to grow in their faith by hearing the basics of the Christian faith clearly explained.

In India's Quilon district, many people had been listening regularly to Campus Crusade's series of 90 training programs which were being broadcast over the radio. Listeners to the programs were invited to attend a one-day conference at Quilon Mar Thoma Student Center. A total of 107 listeners attended, and 45 invited Christ into their lives. Individuals from 29 localities expressed an interest in establishing New Life Radio Clubs in their area.

Similar conferences have been held in other parts of the country, and now 63 Bible clubs are meeting weekly, with 919 people attending.

By beaming these programs from transmitters located in Guam, Sri Lanka and Cyprus, our ministry has a potential listening audience of one billion people. We're praying that we will continue to receive responses like the letter one Turkish listener sent us.

"I am following your radio lessons, and I will continue," he wrote. "I know very little about Christianity. I will go to the city and search on this subject. I know I will have to seek and struggle hard, but whatever it may cost, I am determined to do this."

Without question, Jesus' observation to His disciples is still true today: "Behold, I say to you, lift up your eyes, and look on the fields, that they are white for harvest" (John 4:35). Through the use of the *JESUS* film, training centers, home Bible fellowships and a worldwide radio ministry, we are seeking to help those who are the results of this harvest become established in a joyful, dynamic walk with Christ.

It is our prayerful objective to establish 5,000 training centers, one in every major community in every country of the free world by 1995. We hope to train millions of Christians of every denomination to help evangelize their own communities and countries. These trained Christians will help to show the *JESUS* film to more than 5 billion people by 2000 A.D., at which time experts estimate there will be approximately 6.5 billion people in the world. From these film showings and other means we hope to see one billion people come to Christ. The trained Christians will also help to lead the 25 million home Bible fellowships designed to teach and disciple the billion or more new believers in their Christian faith.

You and your church can be a part of this magnificent plan to help fulfill the Great Commission by financing a Here's Life Training Center for $25,000 and supporting it for a couple of years until it becomes self- supporting. You can also help support a *JESUS* film team of approximately six people for an entire year for $25,000, which includes their salary, travel, films, projector, etc.

Through your involvement in the Here's Life Training Centers and the *JESUS* film, you can help change the world.

CHAPTER THIRTY

International Christian Graduate University

Looking at today's university community, the fountainhead of secular humanism and a cauldron of conflicting moralities, it is intriguing to note that more than 100 of the first and foremost institutions of learning in this country were founded on Christian principles.

Consider the example of Harvard University, founded in 1636. The school seal reads, "In Cristi Gloriam," which is Latin for "In Christ we glory." Although the Puritans who founded Harvard did not intend it as a theological institution, one of the college's 19 laws did state that every student should consider "the mayne end of his life studyes to know God and Jesus Christ. . .and therefore to lay Christ in the bottome, as the only foundation of all sound knowledge and learning." One early authority estimated that 52 percent of the school's 17th century graduates went into Christian service.

Columbia University was originally known as King's College and its charter was specific in its emphasis on spiritual pursuits. Advertisements at the time stated as much: "The chief thing that is aimed at in this college is to teach and engage [students] to know God in Jesus Christ, and to love and serve Him, in all sobriety, godliness, and righteousness of life, with a perfect heart and a willing mind. . . to lead them from the study of nature to the knowledge of themselves and of the God of nature, and their duty to Him, themselves, and one another, and everything that can contribute to their happiness, both here and hereafter."

Scores of other universities like Princeton, Dartmouth, William and Mary and others were established as Christian schools.

Obviously, the university community has strayed far from its moorings. Leading educators are expressing their concern, even alarm, over the growing bankruptcy of instruction in the classrooms of our country. Even high school graduates in some areas are functionally illiterate.

What is the problem? For the most part, higher education has abandoned the true and living God to worship the god of secular humanism. Today, humanism has become the dominant emphasis in the classrooms of America. For decades, biblical Christianity has been ridiculed in the classrooms, and outspoken Christians have been frequently intimidated or discouraged from seeking advanced degrees or have even been denied them after years of faithful study.

Since the university influences every facet of society and since Christian ethic is the very basis of our culture, this dramatic trend away from the scriptural basis of our school curriculum has striken our nation with a moral cancer. Is it any wonder that our nation is fast becoming morally and spiritually bankrupt, resulting in all kinds of social, economic and political problems?

It is for this reason that I believe God has led us to start the International Christian Graduate University. This university must be of such high and uncompromising standards, both spiritually and academically, that the finest and most highly-qualified Christian professors and students in the world will seek the opportunity to become associated with it.

This university represents the beginnings of the fulfillment of a dream, a vision which God gave to me many years ago. The dream was to help establish an international graduate university for Christians on the level of Oxford, Harvard or Stanford. I do not minimize the importance of the several very fine Christian schools that presently offer some graduate degrees in selected fields. We strongly support and encourage such schools that honor the Lord and His Word. But at the risk of sounding presumptuous, our graduate university is designed to compare with the very finest graduate schools in the world.

I believe that one of the greatest needs of our time is a university with academic excellence and a biblical world view which honors and exalts God instead of the world view of secular humanism which enthrones man. By training graduate students in the fields of theology, communication, government, education, medicine, law, humanities, athletics, business, and labor, leaders will be developed who can make a great impact on our world for the cause of Christ.

I well remember the day in my office, while in prayer, when the Lord first impressed on me the need to build the International Christian Graduate University.

"Lord, how are we going to build this university?" I asked. "Such a university with extension campuses all over the world will cost hundreds of millions, if not billions of dollars."

During the history of this ministry, since 1951, Campus Crusade has not ended a single day with an extra dollar beyond our immediate needs, so there was no money to build the university. But even if we had the money, I couldn't have ethically used it for the university, because it had not been given for that specific purpose.

One day as I was praying in my office, the Lord gave me a specific plan of action. We were to find 5,000 acres of land, set aside 1,000 acres for the university campus and permit the rest to be subdivided for industrial, commercial and residential use on an endowment basis to provide both short- and long-term financing. This program would provide enough money to build the university and the satellite campuses around the world.

I called some of our key men together and shared the vision with them. "The Lord wants us to build a great world-class university, with satellite campuses in all of the major countries of the world," I said. Anticipating their questions, I explained that the financing of this gargantuan undertaking would come from revenues generated from 5,000 acres of land.

"We don't have any money, but even so, we are to look for 5,000 acres. The Lord will provide the funds to pay for them since this project is His idea, not mine," I explained. I am sure that some of the real estate people with whom we talked about purchasing the 5,000 acres must have laughed and shaken their heads in amazement when they discovered that we had no money. Like Abraham, we didn't know where to go, but we were convinced that we were to trust and obey God.

As we began looking for some of the choicest land in all the world for our purpose, we heard about a large farm in the Washington, D.C., area. It turned out that it wasn't 5,000 acres, and it wasn't what we were seeking.

A friend of the ministry bought approximately 2,500 acres near our headquarters and offered to lease 1,000 acres to build the university at $1 dollar a year for 100 years. This was a most generous offer, but could not generate sufficient funds to build and endow the university. The plan which God gave me called for 5,000 acres. We needed the profit from the 4,000 acres to build and endow the university. So I said, "I appreciate your generosity, but it won't help us. God has impressed us to secure 5,000 acres, so we will keep looking and praying."

Another friend heard about our plans and offered to give us a 5,000-acre ranch.

"It's all yours," he said. "Come and build your university."

That, too, was a very generous offer. Although very valuable, the land was not suited to our needs.

As we continued to look, I heard about 5,045 undeveloped acres within San Diego's city limits. We asked the man who did the land planning for the University of California at Irvine to prepare a special presentation for us to give to the mayor and other city officials in San Diego. I shared with them our vision for the International Christian Graduate University and our desire to build it on this choice property. They were very positive about the idea of the university and the economic benefits to the city that would accompany such a project. They encouraged us to proceed with our plans.

Assured of the support of the city officials, we began to negotiate for the purchase of the land and continued to do so for more than a year. I am sure that there was considerable skepticism and probably some laughter going on behind the scenes when we kept negotiating for the purchase of the property without any money. The asking price was $5,500 an acre, which was very reasonable for that area. Similar land right next to the property we sought to purchase was selling for as much as $45,000 an acre. The Lord had impressed us to find 5,000 acres. He had led us to one of the most desirable pieces of property in the entire country. Now it was His responsibility to enable us to secure the finances to purchase this valuable property.

Since Campus Crusade for Christ could not help financially, I shared the vision of the university with some friends. I also outlined the need for funds to buy three 30-day options on the property at $50,000 each. The money for the first option was made available by a friend to whom we explained that he could lose his investment, but if we purchased the property, he would make a profit of $50,000. The same offer was made to a second friend who provided the funds for the second 30-day option. A third friend put up the money for the third 30-day option under similar conditions.

Ninety days passed quickly, and we still did not have the money to buy the property. As it came down to the last day, I had to leave for some very important meetings in Europe, including our European staff conference.

The owners refused to extend our option, so I told our men to place the property in escrow, even though we didn't have the money to close the purchase. We stood to lose the entire $150,000 we had put down for options as well as $20,000 or so in expenses. But God had obviously brought us this far. I knew of no other place in the entire world where we could find 5,000 acres so perfectly fitted for our needs. Furthermore, it seemed the Lord was saying, "Trust Me. I will supply the finances."

Our flight was late in arriving in London, and we were unable to catch the flight to Vienna, so the airline put us up for the night in a London hotel. For the next eight hours I was in touch by phone with different potential investors in America and was much in prayer. At 4:30 in the morning (London time) the final call was made, and we were able to purchase the property. Truly this was a gift from God, a miracle of miracles! We were able to purchase the property on a joint venture arrangement because of a bank loan guaranteed by two friends. But because the property is worth so much more than we paid for it, another bank refinanced the purchase without any signatures of guarantee.

Many characteristics made this property valuable including the cultural and academic atmosphere and an ideal climate within the city limits of one of the larger cities in the United States.

In the ensuing months, we faced many financial cliffhangers as we sought to retain and develop this valuable property, some of the most valuable in the world, according to knowledgeable land developers. It was ideal for our purposes. We were convinced that thousands of couples would move to our La Jolla Valley property on a lease or life-estate arrangement to help us build and endow this great University for the glory of God.

One of the most critical barriers to us retaining the property occurred September 11, 1984, when San Diego's

City Council met to consider our request to develop part of the LaJolla Valley Property which we had purchased. Under the proposal which we submitted, we would be allowed to develop the 1,000 acres for the university itself and 750 acres for a university high tech industrial park. The remaining 3,300 acres, designated for residential, commercial and recreational uses, would not be developed until later.

From a human perspective, there seemed to be little hope that the university project would be approved. And if our request had been denied, the future of the university itself would have been in jeopardy. For without the income we would receive from the development of the high tech industrial park, we would not have sufficient funds to take the steps necessary to build the university.

The project was strongly supported by many top San Diego businessmen and professional leaders, the San Diego Evangelical Association, and others. But intense opposition had come from a new mayor who had taken office and was supported by the homosexuals and some environmental groups.

After four hours of pro and con presentation among the members of council, they voted — a half hour before midnight. The 5-4 vote in our favor was greeted with an instant of what seemed to be stunned silence, followed quickly by an exuberant, sustained burst of applause from the supporters of the project.

After the council gave us its decision, I was so intoxicated with joy and praise that I went back to my hotel room and spent much of the night praising the Lord. I could hardly sleep at all. In fact, even when I did get to sleep, it was but for a brief time and I soon awakened to praise the Lord again.

Finally, about 5 A.M. I felt it was time to get up and prepare for an early-morning breakfast, where I met with a group of pastors and laymen who had joined with us in this effort to give thanks and praise to our Lord together.

Many times I have been asked, "Why is Campus Crusade establishing a university?" I answer these queries by giving a number of reasons. First, the university's philosophy is compatible with the original vision which God gave in 1951 to help reach the world for Christ in our generation through a continuing process of discipleship and evangelism.

Second, Campus Crusade's more than 30 years of experience in developing educational and training programs provides us with a rich background in educational development.

Third, since our ministry originated on the college campus, we have worked with millions of students on campuses throughout the nation and the world. The *Agape* Movement, in which people with vocational skills use their occupations as a platform to present the gospel, provides a unique vocation-missions outlet for graduates. Leaders trained in the university will be able, through their professions, to disciple influential people in many nations of the world.

In addition, Campus Crusade has had broad experience in seminar development which will be used in organizing business, communications, law and other seminar courses. We are committed to the principle of transferability in all teaching methods; therefore, the university's graduates will be equipped to teach the same principles to others in their field.

We believe that God is leading us to fill the gap of badly-needed graduate level Christian education in major academic disciplines, with the School of Theology, established in 1979, providing the unifying principles and ethical foundation for the entire university.

Since its inception, the goal of Campus Crusade has been to help change the world. In order to do this, men and women are needed who are highly- qualified leaders in their professions and whose ethical base is the Word of God. The International Christian Graduate University will provide leaders who will be trained with a biblical world view to share God's love with others, disciple those who respond and demonstrate the validity of a biblically-based lifestyle.

One of the university's key areas is its curriculum. To prepare the curriculum, the graduate university task force, in conjunction with leading educators, is drawing upon the best of 200 years of American educational development in addition to formulating fresh educational concepts. This combination of proven methods with new thought will provide high-quality education from the beginning of the university. The curriculum is planned to exceed the usual academic standards without being bound by traditionally designed systems of training. Since the University will reach out around the world from the mother campus in San Diego, we will employ the finest technology available, including satellites, worldwide radio, TV and computers.

Strong, godly and academically qualified leaders are vital in order to make this program a success. We are especially fortunate to have such leaders in the School of Theology in Dr. Ron Jenson and Dr. Ted Cole.

Before accepting his position as president, Dr. Jenson was on the staff of Philadelphia Church of the Savior, where in seven years he and the church staff saw it grow from 14 couples to an average Sunday attendance of 1,300. He also served as the dean of the Christian Leadership Training Center — a School of Theology extension in Philadelphia — where he directed the weekly training of 75 pastors from 22 denominations in evangelism, discipleship, management and church growth.

Dr. Jenson received his doctorate at Western Conservative Baptist Seminary where he initiated, taught and directed a discipleship and evangelism program. He first became active in Campus Crusade as a college freshman in Oregon.

"We want to be known as a school that knows the most about, and can, in fact, develop a healthy pastor and church, and trained Christian leaders for inter-denominational and para-church organizations," Ron says. "For this reason we are developing a new model among schools for training students."

The new model to which Ron referred is a method of apportioning half of the student's education to academics and half to on-the-field application. For the School of Theology students, this means they are directly involved in a local church body, putting to use what they have learned in the classroom. By the time the student graduates, he has experience in many phases of church work and is prepared to step into a leadership role in the church. This same pattern of half classroom training and half application will hold true in the other academic disciplines as well.

Dr. Ted Cole, the executive vice-president of the school, was one of America's leading pastors for twenty-eight years with a church of 6,500 members. He has several earned degrees, including his doctorate from Eastern Baptist Seminary. He is a model of eloquent preaching, dedicated soul-winning and a loving, compassionate heart. He gives leadership to the School of Theology on a day-to-day basis, aided by several godly, scholarly professors and staff.

I believe that the real battle for the minds and wills of men is being fought in our schools, where we have lost every major engagement for more than fifty years. This is largely because of our lethargy and lack of awareness of what is happening. As the famous British political philosopher and statesman Edmund Burke once said, "All that is needed for evil to triumph is that good men do nothing!"

Many good people have done nothing, and as a result we have lost our universities. Dr. Charles Malik, one of the great statesmen of our day and a former president of the United Nations General Assembly, feels we must recapture this vital institution.

"Nothing compares with the urgency of seeking to recapture universities for Jesus Christ," he says. "Christ is not welcome in the university. In fact, He is ignored, if not declared the enemy. To reach the world in which we live, this secularizing of the universities, this estrangement, if not downright enmity, between Christ and the great universities cannot continue without disastrous results upon the whole of western civilization."

We are trusting God that the International Christian Graduate University will produce the kind of leaders who will help turn this situation around. We believe this university will produce men and women with a global vision for the honor and glory of Christ that will have far-reaching results.

CHAPTER THIRTY-ONE

EXPLO '85

In the summer of 1984 I met with about 30 directors of the worldwide movement of Campus Crusade for Christ at a beautiful mountainside retreat in Austria. Outside, the sunlight filtered through the clouds and glinted off the rocky mountainside. But we were not there to admire the scenery, as beautiful as it was. Instead we were discussing a project which would accelerate this worldwide movement more than anything we had undertaken since this ministry began in 1951.

Today the details of this project — now known as EXPLO '85 — are falling into place. But at that time it was only an idea.

Our idea was to hold a worldwide congress that would light a spark of spiritual revolution on every continent. In years past we had seen the value of such conferences.

In 1972, EXPLO '72 had drawn 85,000 students and laymen for the largest conference of its kind. These individuals returned to their homes with a determination to make an impact for Christ. They did, and many still are.

Two years later a similar conference was held. This time the site was Seoul, South Korea. More than 323,000 attended the daily training sessions in effective Christian living, and crowds in excess of one million participated in a single evening inspirational session.

In 1976 this life-changing training was made available to 325,000 Christians, representing 15,000 churches of nearly every denomination, as part of a coordinated effort to take the message of Christ to the maximum number of people in the United States. Known as Here's

246 COME HELP CHANGE THE WORLD

Life, America, this campaign resulted in 532,000 people registering decisions for Christ. I am convinced that this number represented just the tip of the iceberg as literally millions of lives were changed across the country as a result of Here's Life, America.

Here's Life campaigns similar to the ones held in the United States began to take place in other countries. Christians in many cities across the world banded together to reach their communities. And God blessed in phenomenal ways. One of the most spectacular examples occurred in Seoul when the campaign culminated in a one-week gathering called Here's Life, Korea/World Evangelization Crusade. Crowds in excess of 2 million people attended some of the nightly sessions, with a total of more than 10.5 million participating in the five nightly gatherings.

Truly God had greatly blessed our efforts as we sought to trust and obey Him in His leading to help fulfill the Great Commission. But we were not satisfied. I felt that if we were committed to reaching the world, in obedience to our Lord's command, we needed to organize a gigantic worldwide congress to bring together approximately 40,000-50,000 people who are student and lay Christian leaders in their countries. In this way we could equip, encourage and motivate these people for dynamic ministry in their home countries.

I discussed the idea of the conference at great length with Bailey Marks, who for years had been the director of affairs for our ministry in Asia. Now he was serving as the vice-president for international ministries. As Bailey began to research the feasibility of holding such a conference, he made a startling discovery. The cost of holding such a conference and transporting delegates from around the world to a single location would be astronomical — far more than we could hope to afford.

"For a few days, I lost my enthusiasm for the conference," Bailey said. "However, the Lord would not let me forget about it, and I continued to pray."

One morning after a time of prayer about the situation, Bailey went to his bathroom sink and began to shave. As he was performing this daily ritual, the Lord gave him some remarkable solutions to the apparently impassable barriers we faced.

It was these solutions that he stood to share with our group that day. As I looked around the room before Bailey began to speak to the group, I saw men representing every continent — men of all sizes and colors, from rangy light-haired Europeans to slender, dark-haired Orientals. Americans, Africans, Asians and Latin Americans all gathered around the tables, all one in Christ, all filled with the urgency of taking the good news of God's love and forgiveness around the globe.

As Bailey spoke, God gave us a unity of spirit. Several times we paused to pray for wisdom in dealing with the problems we faced. The difficulty of bringing so many people together did not overwhelm us, because the One who created the heavens and the earth was working through us, as He had so many times in the past.

As we listened, Bailey outlined some ideas that God had given him for making EXPLO '85 a reality. Instead of bringing people from all over the world to a central location, why not hold separate meetings and link them by satellite broadcasts? In this manner as many as 100 conferences could be conducted, and inspiration and training could be beamed to each location. Hundreds of thousands of people could be trained without leaving their own countries.

At first, not every director was enthusiastic about the concept. It was so radically new, and many wondered if it could take place in various parts of the developing world. Yet as these men of God began to pray, think and plan, they began to see how this conference could help them realize their own dreams for their areas of responsibility. They began to see how EXPLO '85 could accelerate their ministry in reaching their countrymen with the message of Jesus Christ. After a few hours of discussion, each of our directors agreed that the plan was God's will and felt we should proceed.

Soon the plans began to gather momentum. Bailey and his assistant, Jerry Sharpless, began to tackle the mammoth tasks of confirming conference locations, preparing satellite broadcasts and trusting God for the finances for the massive conference. A sizable portion of the funds was reserved for scholarships, so that people from the Third World nations would be able to attend who would otherwise be prevented because of a lack of finances.

I continue to be excited by the potential of EXPLO '85. I believe it will be an event of unprecedented significance. At each conference site delegates will be trained in the basics of the Christian life and will be motivated and inspired as they learn through the satellite reports about what God is doing around the world. It will be a worldwide call to spiritual revolution, equipping and motivating people to take the love and forgiveness of God through Jesus Christ to every person in every community in every country of the world.

Satellite broadcasts will be transmitted simultaneously for two hours each day for four days from one of six sites around the world — New York City, Mexico City, Seoul, Berlin, West Germany; and Nairobi, Kenya. These broadcasts will give an international flavor to the event.

Imagine the effect of such a conference on a group of believers in Sri Lanka, where less than one percent of the people are Christians, or in a predominantly Muslim nation. Instead of feeling like a tiny minority, they will see the satellite reports of what God is doing and recognize that they are part of the worldwide body of Christ. They will learn that they too can witness the great and mighty things God has promised to accomplish on their behalf in their own country. Not only will they be inspired, but they will receive the training they need to enable them, through the power of the Holy Spirit, to trust God for great things in their part of the world as well.

My heart leaps with praise to God as I think of what can be accomplished for His glory through such a worldwide gathering as EXPLO '85. I believe the days of December 27-31, 1985, will be remembered in history as this conference sparks explosions of revival across the globe. With conference sites in a hundred locations around the world and hundreds of thousands attending, it is truly an event that can help change the world. It can help change the world as millions of lives are directly and indirectly revolutionized through the living Christ working through this great conference.

CONCLUSION

The greatest challenge ever given to man was given by the greatest person who ever lived — Jesus Christ. This challenge, the Great Commission, was given when our Lord said, "All authority has been given to Me in heaven and on earth. Go therefore and make disciples of all the nations, baptizing them in the name of the Father and the Son and the Holy Spirit, teaching them to observe all that I commanded you; and lo, I am with you always, even to the end of the age" (Matthew 28:18-20).

In Romans, the tenth chapter we read: "Anyone who calls upon the name of the Lord will be saved. But how shall they ask Him to save them unless they believe in Him? And how can they believe in Him if they have never heard about Him? And how can they hear about Him unless someone tells them? And how will anyone go and tell them unless someone sends him?" (Living Bible).

There are 4.7 billion people in 210 countries and protectorates around the world who are waiting to hear the good news of our wonderful Savior. The greatest challenge man can ever begin to comprehend is the privilege of taking the message of God's love, forgiveness, peace and grace through our Lord Jesus Christ to each one of these people.

Continual Challenge

This challenge captivates me day and night. I try to weigh everything I do in the light of the Great Commission. I evaluate and prioritize each hour of every day and try to eliminate those things which have no real significance to the accomplishment of this goal. It consumes me day and night.

I do this not because I am interested in a strategy just for strategy's sake, but because I love my Lord and want to obey Him. He is more important to me than my life. I travel the world day and night making disciples and sharing the "most joyful news" with everyone who will listen because I love Him. We are not to go to the world just to be a part of a strategy, but we go because the Lord commissioned us. This commission is not just for the missionaries or the evangelists or pastors. It is for each one of us in whom Jesus Christ has come to dwell. If we love our Lord, we will take seriously His command.

We must not quietly fold our hands, shake our heads at the evil that surrounds us in our world and do nothing but await Christ's return. It is true that our Lord could return tomorrow, If so, I am ready and would greatly rejoice to see Him whom I have loved and served so long. But, the Scripture tells us that no man knows the day or the hour of His return and that when He does come, it will be when people least expect it, like "a thief in the night."

I applaud every effort to warn Christians and non-believers to be ready for our Lord's return. However, we dare not wrongly interpret the Scriptures as so many in previous generations have done, resulting in a lack of concern for the souls of men and a failure to correct the evil of society. God expects us as His children to be His representatives here on earth. We are to love with His love and meet the needs of widows, orphans and prisoners in His name.

Social Reforms

True believers in previous generations have always been at the forefront of moral and social reforms. For example, child labor laws, women's suffrage, abolition of slavery and other social reforms grew out of a mighty spiritual awakening that swept England through the ministry of John Wesley, George Whitefield and their colleagues. We in our generation must be no less concerned about injustice wherever we find it.

However, the most important way to solve our social ills is to change the hearts of men by introducing them to our Lord Jesus Christ. Our priority commitment as Christians must be to disciple and evangelize in obedience to our Lord's command and then instruct the new believer that "loving our neighbors as ourselves" includes helping them where they hurt. But remember, the Lord cares more about the soul than the body. The sick body when healed will become sick again and die. The soul lives for eternity.

In II Peter 3:9 we read, "The Lord is not willing that any should perish, but that all should come to repentance" (King James). He is giving more time for sinners to repent. In fact, He has even delayed His return in order to give us more time to get His message of salvation to others.

We have this further motivation from Matthew 24:14, "And the Good News about the Kingdom will be preached throughout the whole world, so that all nations will hear it, and then, finally, the end will come" (LB).

As servants of our living God and Savior, let us continue to give ourselves in all diligence, as an expression of our love for Him, to hasten the day of His return. Because "Night cometh, when no man can work" (John 9:4, KJ).

Miracles must happen for the Great Commission to be fulfilled. Nothing short of a supernatural visit of God's power will be enough. But we need to fulfill certain responsibilities, too. I believe we need to do at least four things to see the Great Commission fulfilled.

Supernatural Thoughts

First, we must think supernaturally. Do you remember the spies who went into the promised land? After 40 days they came back with two reports —majority and minority. The 10 spies reported. "It is indeed a magnificent country, but there are giants in the land. They will crush us. We felt like grasshoppers in our own sight. We dare not go."

But Joshua and Caleb said, "God is with us. God will fight for us. He has given us the land." The Israelites cried and said, "Don't lead us into the promised land. We would rather go back to Egypt." So all those above the age of 20 died in the wilderness. Later God gave Caleb and Joshua the opportunity to go into the promised land because they had obeyed Him. The 10 spies were destroyed because they were disobedient. They had a grasshopper mentality. And most Christians of today do also.

The thinking of people with tremendous executive ability is often an amazing thing to me. They think of empires, building great estates, but when it comes to the kingdom of God, they don't even think beyond their little church. They may usher, sing in the choir, go once or twice a week to church and feel that their religious duty is fulfilled. Then when problems arise in their community they say, "Why doesn't somebody do something about that?" Some 125 million Americans profess to be followers of Christ. And yet we have allowed this great nation to disintegrate morally and spiritually.

We need to begin to think with the mind of God. "For as he thinketh in his heart, so is he" (Proverbs 23:7, KJ). We become like we think. If we think of ourselves as weak and insignificant, we become that. Instead, we need to see ourselves as able to accomplish great things for our Lord. We become the kind of person who says, "I can do all things through Christ which strengtheneth me" (Philippians 4:13, KJ).

Supernatural Prayers

Second, we must begin to pray supernatural prayers and believe God for mighty things. Soon after the Supreme Court decision in 1963, which most interpreted as meaning that prayer and Bible study in the schools was illegal, God began to chasten us. It was as though the plug was pulled, and evil came upon us like a plague of locusts. Within a brief period of time, President John F. Kennedy was assassinated in Dallas, the drug culture swept up millions of our choice young people, the black and white racial controversy bordered on civil was in city after city, the campuses were aflame with riots, violence and revolution and the war in Vietnam divided our country.

But something wonderful happened in 1968. God's children began to pray for a great spiritual awakening to come to our land. They claimed God's promises. They interceded, they cried out in obedience to II Chronicles 7:14. And across the nation there were prayer rallies, pastors began to give more attention to prayer, prayer chains became a common thing across the nation until millions of Americans were praying. The tide began to turn.

God raised up an army of people like Rex Humbard, Jerry Falwell, Pat Robertson, Kathryn Kuhlman, Robert Schuller and many others on radio and television, until 125 million people were hearing the gospel every week. Some 85 million people were attending church. The Gallup poll did a survey and discovered that more than 50 million people over the age of 18 said that they were born again. God honored supernatural praying.

Supernatural Plans

The third thing that we must do if we are to see the Great Commission fulfilled is that we must plan supernatural plans. I have shared with you earlier about Dr. Joon Gon Kim and EXPLO '74, but you can imagine his presumption when he stood before 85,000 people assembled in Dallas for EXPLO '72 and said, "In 1974, we're going to have 300,000 people come to EXPLO '74 in Seoul,

Korea, and we want you to come." Never in history had 300,000 Christians been trained at one time.

Dr. Kim, a humble servant of God, predicted something that was impossible. As a matter of fact, his staff gave him more than 70 reasons why it couldn't happen. He cancelled them all by saying, "Jesus said, 'The things that I do shall you do also, and greater than these shall you do because I go to My Father. If you ask anything in My name I will do it.'"

A total of 323,419 people from 78 countries came for training. In the four years following EXPLO '74, the church in South Korea grew from three million to seven million. This man of God, Dr. Kim, had planned supernaturally and God had used him to touch the entire nation.

Expect Great Things

Finally, we must expect God to do something great. "According to your faith be it unto you" (Matthew 9:29, KJ). Some time ago I was in Nazareth and had the opportunity to pray with a man who was one of the leading officials of the city. We were sitting in the hotel in the dining room, and after we prayed together, he was radiantly happy. He turned to me and said, "Mr. Bright, will you send someone back to Nazareth to help us share this new truth with others?" Jesus spent 30 years in Nazareth, and this man was saying, "Send someone to help us share this new truth."

Suddenly, it occurred to me that it was said of our Lord when He walked those dusty, winding streets of Nazareth, "And He did not do many miracles there because of their unbelief" (Matthew 13:58). Then it struck me, this is the tragedy of the whole Christian world — our Lord is hindered because of the spirit of Nazareth — the spirit of unbelief — which has placed much of the Body of Christ in bondage. God honors faith, and apart from faith it is impossible to please Him.

Committed to Christ

Before you can genuinely be involved in helping to fulfill the Great Commission and help change our world, you must first turn over your life completely to God. Jesus said, "But seek first His kingdom, and His righteousness; and all these things shall be added to you" (Matthew 6:33).

Our finances also must be turned over to the Lord. There is nothing wrong with making money. Thank God for people who have the ability to make money, who acknowledge that it all belongs to the Lord and it is not theirs to hoard, but it is theirs to pass on for the kingdom's sake.

Some time ago it occurred to me that there are many Christians who are building estates and putting their money into foundations. When they die, those foundations will be under the control of other people, who ultimately will no longer be faithful to the Christian convictions of the one who built the estate.

If I understand Scripture correctly, God expects us to care for our families. But beyond that, Christians are never to hoard. They are to invest in the kingdom. The very process of hoarding causes souring, just like the manna in the wilderness. God gave the manna for one day, and if it was kept for another day, it soured. As you study the lives of Christians who hoard, you find that their money has cursed them, and it has cursed their children because they have disobeyed God. The money did not belong to them. They were only stewards of it.

Reaching People Around You

Once we have turned our lives and finances over to the Lord, we need to go forth with the gospel. Go to the people in your community where you live. Reach your loved ones, your neighbors, your friends, the people in your peer group.

This is the only way that the entire world can be saturated with the good news of Jesus Christ — if Christians take seriously our Lord's command to proclaim the "most joyful news ever announced" to people everywhere.

Are you willing to turn your life over completely to Jesus Christ right now? Are you willing to give over your time, talent and treasure to be used by Him to help fulfill the Great Commission? If you are, please join me in this prayer:

> O Lord, my God, I bow to acknowledge Your Lordship over my life. I will follow You wherever You want me to go. With Your help, Lord, I'll do anything You want me to do, whatever it costs me. Now, I give You my time, talents and treasures — all that I am and possess — that I may be used by Your Spirit to help change our world and help fulfill the Great Commission in this generation. In Jesus' name, Amen.

If you offered this prayer sincerely, God has heard you and promises to direct your steps. May I encourage you to give special time to fellowship with the Lord in prayer, Bible study and witnessing and to become active in a local church fellowship if you are not already involved. If I or the staff of Campus Crusade can be of any help to you, please grant us this privilege. We shall also be happy to send you additional materials for study designed to assist you in your spiritual growth.

If you feel that God would have you serve Him through the ministry of Campus Crusade, opportunities are many and varied. Please contact our Personnel Department for more information. You can write them at Arrowhead Springs, San Bernardino, CA 92414. They will be glad to assist you.

One final thought to take with you. The life of a true disciple of Christ is not an easy one, though it is a life filled with adventure and excitement. Actually, I have thought of life like this: whether Christian or not, we are going to have problems in this life. Christian or not, we will die one day. If I am to suffer at all and one day die, why not suffer and die for the highest and best — for the Lord Jesus Christ and His most worthy cause! I invite you to join with us:

COME HELP CHANGE THE WORLD!

How to Be Sure You Are a Christian

My experience in counseling students and laymen through the years since I met Christ personally has convinced me that there are millions of good, faithful churchgoers who have "received" Christ but who are not sure of their salvation. Regardless of how hard they try and how disciplined are their efforts to please God, they are still uncertain of their relationship with Him.

Misinformation

Why does this heartbreaking uncertainty exist among so many who genuinely want to know God and have sought Him for years? I am persuaded personally that for many people this lack of assurance is due simply to misinformation regarding who God is, the true meaning of the crucifixion and the resurrection and what is involved in receiving Jesus Christ as Savior.

Could it be that you are still unsure of your relationship with God even though you may have been reared in a Christian environment and have "believed" in Him and in His Son for years?

If you were to die this very moment, do you *know* for sure where you would spend eternity?

Do you have the assurance right now that the Lord Jesus is in your life, that you are a child of God, your sins have been forgiven, and that you have eternal life?

Or perhaps you have only recently received Christ and are still not sure that anything has really happened — you have no assurance of your salvation and have serious misgivings about where you will go when you die.

If you are among the vast multitude who are still looking for God, I am praying that your quest will be realized this very day as you continue to read.

The Greatest Gift

Becoming a Christian involves receiving by faith the greatest gift ever offered to man — God's gift of His only begotten Son — through whom we can experience God's love and forgiveness. Receiving Jesus Christ as Savior and following Him as Lord involves one's *intellect, emotions* and *will.*

In order to become a Christian, or to be sure that you are a Christian, you must have a clear intellectual understanding of what is involved. Christianity is not "a blind leap of faith." It is built upon historical fact, documented by centuries of scholarship and research. Many leading scholars have dedicated their lives to investigating the life, teachings, death, resurrection and influence of Jesus of Nazareth.

Jesus Christ claimed to be God. He said, "I and the Father are one" (John 10:30). "He who has seen Me has seen the Father" (John 14:9). "I am the way, the truth, and the life; no one comes to the Father, but through Me" (John 14:6). To become a Christian, you must honestly face these claims and believe intellectually that Jesus is God, that He died for your sins and was buried, that He rose again and that He wants to come into your life and be your Savior and Lord.

Emotions

Being sure that you are a Christian also involves the emotions. An emotion is a feeling or reaction to a specific act, event or experience. The failure to distinguish between different types of emotions has caused many people to be confused in their relationship with God. Probably no one thing has caused more people to lack the assurance of a vital relationship with God through Jesus Christ than a wrong emphasis on emotions.

One person may be aggressively extroverted and highly emotional, while another may be calm, reserved and introspective. Viewing the same act or participating in the same experience, these two may respond quite differently — one with great joy and the other calmly.

Each person who receives Jesus Christ as his Savior and Lord will have a different kind of emotional experience. Paul met Christ through a dramatic encounter on the road to Damascus. Timothy, on the other hand, was raised in a Christian home where he came to know Christ at an early age and gradually grew in his faith. The fact that your experience with God may not be as highly emotional as that of someone else does not make it any less real. We must not depend on our emotions, for they can be deceiving.

How, then, can one be sure that he is a Christian? Is there not some confirmation that God gives to the man who sincerely receives Christ? Scripture assures us of a three-fold confirmation that Jesus Christ is in our lives, that we are children of God and have eternal life.

God's Word

First, we have the external witness of the Word of God. Assurance is based on the authority of God's Word. When you meet God's conditions, as revealed in His Word, you can be assured that you are a child of God. Second, there is the internal witness of the Holy Spirit who "speaks to us deep in our hearts, and tells us that we really are God's children" (Romans 8:16, LB). Our changed lives are a third witness to the fact that we are Christians. "When someone becomes a Christian he becomes a brand new person inside. He is not the same anymore. A new life has begun!" (2 Corinthians 5:17, LB). This change may be sudden or gradual, according to the personality of the individual.

There is a place for emotions in the Christian experience, though we should not seek them nor attempt to recapture them from the past.

We are not to ignore the value of legitimate emotions. It is more important, however, to remember that we are to live by faith — in God and in His promises — and not be seeking an emotional experience. The very act of seeking an emotional experience contradicts the concept of faith, which is the only way to please God.

Will

In addition to the intellect and the emotions, becoming a Christian involves the will. Our relationship with Christ can well be illustrated by the requirements for a marriage relationship, which ideally must contain these same three ingredients — intellect, emotions and will.

For example, a man may be convinced intellectually that the woman who is his intended bride is the "right" one for him. He may be involved emotionally and love her with all his heart, but marriage requires more than the intellect and the emotions. It also involves the will.

It is not until the man and woman, as an act of the will, commit themselves to each other before a minister or another person of authority that they become husband and wife. The two words "I do" make the difference. So it is in our relationship with Jesus Christ. It is not enough to believe intellectually that Jesus Christ is the Son of God and Savior of men, nor is it enough to have an emotional, spiritual experience. Though both are valid, one does not become a Christian until, as an act of the will, he receives Christ into his life as Savior and Lord.

There may be a difference, however, between the marriage relationship and the Christian experience. In marriage the sequence of commitment is often intellect, then emotion and, finally, will. But in commitment to Christ, the sequence is usually: first, intellect; then will; and, finally, as a by-product or result, emotions or feelings.

Basic Truths

To be sure that you are a Christian, you must be aware intellectually of certain basic scriptural truths.

First, God loves you and offers a wonderful plan for your life.

Second, man is sinful and separated from God; thus he cannot know and experience God's love and plan.

Third, Jesus Christ is God's only provision for man's sin. Through Him you can know and experience God's love and plan.

And fourth, we must individually receive Jesus Christ as Savior and Lord; then we can know and experience God's love and plan.

Does this make sense to you? Have you ever personally received the Lord Jesus Christ as your Savior? If you have received Him, do you have the assurance of your salvation? Are you sure that, if you died right now, you would spend eternity with God in heaven?

If you cannot answer "Yes" to these questions, may I suggest that you find a quiet place where you can be alone and receive the Lord Jesus as your Savior right now.

If you have never received Christ by a definite, deliberate act of your will, you can do so now in prayer. And if you are not sure you are a Christian, you can make sure now. In either case, may I suggest that you pray this prayer, making it your very own:

> "Lord Jesus, I need You. I thank You for dying for my sins. I open the door of my life and receive You as my Lord and Savior. Thank You for forgiving my sins. Take control of the throne of my life. Change my life and make me the kind of person You want me to be. Amen."

Recently a businessman approached me at one of our Executive Seminars. He had been active in his church for more than 50 years. He had always assumed that he was a Christian though he had never "received" Christ as a deliberate act of his will by faith.

He had for the first time heard testimonies of other businessmen who had received Christ and had heard an explanation of how one became a Christian as recorded in this chapter. Now, he had some doubts concerning his relationship with God. "I am 90 to 95% sure that I am a Christian — that Christ is in my life — but I am not absolutely sure."

It occurs to me that you, dear reader, may also be unsure. If so, I would like to encourage you, as I did this man, to offer the following prayer:

> "Lord Jesus, I am not absolutely sure that You are in my life and that I am a Christian. If You are not already dwelling within me, I invite You today to come into my life, forgive my sins, change me and make me the kind of person You want me to be. By faith, I thank You that You have now come into my life according to Your promise in Revelation 3:20 and will never leave me. I now know according to Your Word that I have eternal life and if I were to die today I would spend eternity with You in heaven. Amen."

This simple suggestion was all that my new friend needed. Immediately he responded and received the assurance of his salvation. I pray that if you, too, have doubts about your salvation, you will take this step.

1996 Templeton Prize Acceptance Speech

Dr. William R. Bright received the 1996 Templeton Prize for Progress in Religion. This is the acceptance speech that Dr. Bright delivered in Rome, Italy, at the Church of St. Maria in Trastevere on May 9, 1996.

Your Eminence Cardinal Cassidy, Viscount Brentford, Sir John Templeton, Professor Andrea Riccardi, president of the Community of Saint Egidio, distinguished visitors, ladies and gentlemen...

The prestigious Templeton Prize, to me, because of the nature of its objective, is greater than any other prize that could be given for any purpose. So I am deeply humbled and greatly honored to be the recipient of this 1996 magnificent Templeton Prize. I would like to thank and commend Sir John Templeton for establishing this prize, which emphasizes the most important aspect of life—the spiritual dimension—upon which all other considerations of life find fulfillment.

I receive this prize in the name of our wonderful Lord and Savior Jesus Christ, whom I have sought to serve for more than 50 wonderfully exciting, fruitful years, and on behalf of my beloved wife, Vonette; our wonderful sons, Zac and Bradley, who are here with us tonight and I am so pleased they could come; our dedicated and gifted fellow staff of tens and thousands all over the world; a great board of directors; and a mighty movement of literally millions of faithful and generous partners who have prayed for and helped to finance our ministry worldwide over the last 45 years. I feel I am the most privileged and fortunate man in the world to be associated with such a remarkable team.

The late Dr. Charles Malik, Ambassador to the United Nations from Lebanon and President of the United Nations General Assembly in 1959, was a very dear, personal friend for approximately 25 years, until his death. With an earned doctorate from Harvard University, and with over 50 honorary doctorates from many of the most prestigious universities of the world, Dr. Malik was truly one of the great intellectual, spiritual giants of our century.

It was my privilege to hear him speak to a group of world leaders in Washington, D.C. I was deeply touched by his strong witness for the Lord Jesus when he said, "Only those who stay close to Jesus Christ can help others who are far away. The needs of the world are much deeper than political freedom and security...much deeper than social justice and economic development, much deeper than democracy and progress. The deeper need of the world," he said, "belongs to the sphere of the mind, heart and spirit, a spirit to be penetrated with the light and grace of Jesus Christ." He went on to say, "I really do not know what will remain of civilization and history if the accumulated influence of Jesus Christ, both direct and indirect, is eradicated from literature, art, practical dealings, moral standards, and creativeness in the different activities of mind and spirit." Then he concluded with this profound statement: "The heart of the whole matter," he said, "is faith in Jesus Christ."

Following his address, I approached him to say, "Many political leaders speak of God, the Bible, prayer in a general way, but I have never heard one in your position of worldwide leadership who has spoken so powerfully and so convincingly of your faith in and your love for Jesus Christ."

His response moved me deeply. "I am sobered by the words of our Lord," he said, "'Whosoever therefore shall confess me before men, him will I confess also before my Father which is in heaven. But whosoever shall deny me before men, him will I also deny before my Father which is in heaven.'"

Like Dr. Malik, I too am very excited about our wonderful Lord and, in the words of the apostle Paul, "Everywhere we go we talk about Christ to all who will listen" (Colossians 1). Therefore, because of the nature of this gathering it seems appropriate that I use this occasion to describe to you something of my own spiritual journey, and how the sovereign unseen hand of our dear Lord has shaped and directed my life and ministry for His glory for over five decades.

As a young man, I was a materialist and humanist, so I can identify with multitudes of men and women, young and old, all over world, who have little knowledge of God. To me at that time, success in life was measured by the accumulation of material possessions, honors, applause, and praise of men.

I had the good fortune to be reared in a wonderful home by a good, though materialistic, nonbelieving father and a saintly mother who prayed for me every day of my life. I was vaguely aware of this, but wrongly assumed that all mothers were equally devout, so her beliefs did not affect my beliefs. However, her example did affect my morals, resulting in a high standard of ethics and integrity. But for all practical purposes I was an atheist.

The idea of God, or a Savior, or the Bible had little place in my life. All through high school, college, and in graduate school, on the extension faculty of Oklahoma State University, and later as a businessman in Hollywood, California, where as a young man I developed my own business, I was motivated by self-ish goals—materialistic pursuits.

Then one day—oh, I remember distinctly—I first sensed that unseen hand of God in my life. I can only describe it as a sovereign visit from God. Through the influence of an elderly couple, I was drawn to the First Presbyterian Church of Hollywood. It was there for the first time in my life that I heard about the great Creator God of the universe who, according to the Bible, spoke and all of creation came into being. Scientist have recently reported that the Hubble telescope findings confirm at least 50 billion or more galaxies were created. To better understand what that means: This planet Earth is like a grain of sand in our solar system, which is like a grain of sand in our galaxy, which is like less than a grain of sand in the vastness of all of creation.

Simultaneously, I discovered that my head had been in the sand—the sand of mundane, selfish interests and temporal pursuits.

But there at that wonderful church in Hollywood, I was moved to look up, beyond my microscopic world, at the wonder of creation, behind which was an obvious Creator. And one day I met this One who, according to the Bible, came to this earth disguised as a slave in the greatest act of love the world would ever has ever known. He revealed Himself to humanity with the appropriate Hebrew name of Yeshu'a, "salvation." Christians worship Him as Jesus of Nazareth; or Jesus the Christ, or the Messiah.

I discovered the amazing truth that this magnificent Creator, this all-powerful Almighty God, not only created the universe, but He loved me—little, insignificant Bill Bright, less than a nameless speck in space—and He devised and through His prophets revealed an elaborate plan to redeem me and all mankind by personally visiting this planet Earth as the God-man, Jesus of Nazareth, the only begotten Son of God. He even declared that He will share His eternal kingdom with me, and with all people of the world who will accept His free gift of love and forgiveness.

The sheer strength, power, love, and majesty of this man, Jesus of Nazareth, the Son of God, totally captivated me. And what I very quickly discovered was absolutely astonishing. I became aware that approximately 300 details of Jesus' life had been predicted by ancient Hebrew scholars and prophets hundreds of years before He was born, and they were fulfilled in His miraculous birth, life, teachings, miracles, death, and resurrection. Such amazing prophecies and their fulfillment had not happened to any other person in history, before or since. And these many prophecies with the details of His life and mission are a matter of impeccable record, with documentation.

But I also learned that this Jesus of Nazareth was His own authentication. In all of history, both before and since, He is unique above all men. Philosophers say that He spoke the greatest words ever spoken. He cleansed the lepers; He healed the sick; He cast out demons; He raised the dead; He performed miracles such as no one had ever performed. He claimed to be God in the flesh. He claimed to be the only way to the Father, and that He came to show us the way. And for this He was crucified, for heresy. He predicted His own death and resurrection, which happened just like He said. After His resurrection and before His ascension into the heavenlies, He was seen by the disciples on several occasions and by more than 500 people at one time.

Needless to say, as I continued my research, this Person, Jesus of Nazareth, began to capture my full attention. And one day I was driven to my knees in the privacy of my home, and in a most sacred moment I surrendered myself to Him and received Him as my Savior and Lord. From that magnificent, majestic moment for me, I was drawn to know Him better, and more personally. And this began a lifelong quest and exciting spiritual journey which continues to this day.

As I discovered more of the truth of the Bible and the identity and nature of this towering figure of all time—the Son of God, Jesus of Nazareth—I became more and more devoted to Him and His teachings, and more in love with Him. His many words of truth and eternal wisdom burned constantly in my soul. I wanted earnestly to build my life on solid rock and not on sand, as Jesus admonished his followers to do as recorded in Matthew, chapter 7.

Some of you know my beloved wife, Vonette, my partner in life for almost 50 years. We had both been very materialistic in our youth. But when we received Jesus Christ as our Lord and Savior, we discovered that there were other things far more important in life than making money, living in lovely homes, and enjoying "the good life," which I promised to her when I proposed to her. I said we would travel the world, that we would live in prestigious Bel Air, California. I promised her everything her heart could desire before we were married. And, you know, she believed me!

But within a couple of years our desires, our interests had changed. We had both fallen in love with Jesus. I studied in two internationally acclaimed theological seminaries, Princeton and Fuller, for five years. And I ran my business in the afternoons in California, and studied at the seminary in the mornings. Vonette was a vital part of everything I was doing. And it was together that one Sunday afternoon we came to the conclusion that knowing and serving Jesus were more important than anything in all the world.

So it was in that Spring of 1951, that memorable afternoon, Vonette and I, in our home in the Hollywood Hills, got on our knees and prayed, "Lord, we surrender our lives irrevocably to you and to do your will. We want to love and serve you with all of our hearts for the rest of our lives." And we actually wrote and signed a contract committing our whole lives to Him, relinquishing all of our rights, all of our possessions, everything we would ever own, giving to Him, our dear Lord and Master, everything. In the words of the apostle Paul, Vonette and I became that Sunday afternoon voluntary slaves of Jesus, by choice, as an act of the will. It was in his letter to Rome, chapter 1, verse 1, that Paul wrote of his love for Christ, and he said to the Christians here in this great city, not so great in those days, spiritually: "This letter is from Paul, Jesus Christ's slave, chosen to be a missionary, and sent out to preach God's Good News."

Vonette and I were deeply stirred, inspired also, and I guess primarily, by our Lord's challenge recorded in the eighth chapter of the Gospel according to Mark, where He said, "If any of you wants to be my follower, you must put aside your own pleasures, and shoulder your cross, and follow me closely. If you insist on saving your life, you will lose it. Only those who throw away their lives for my sake and for the sake of the Good News will ever know what it means to really live."

To really live! Vonette and I had known a very exciting life for two years of marriage, but here was a promise that exceeded everything we had experienced.

I have asked millions of believers in Christ all over the world: "What is the greatest thing that has ever happened to you in all of your life?" The answer is always the same: "Knowing Jesus Christ as Savior and

Lord is the most important thing that has ever happened to me."

Then I ask: "What is the greatest thing you could do to help somebody else?" The answer, of course, is obvious: "To introduce them to Jesus Christ."

Introducing others to Christ was an early passion of both Vonette and myself. Soon after signing that contract, God gave us a specific call—a call to do what we had done privately on a small scale, on a worldwide scale, by helping to complete the fulfillment of the Great Commission given by our Lord Jesus Christ shortly before He ascended to be with the Father in heaven, as recorded in Matthew, chapter 28. Jesus said: "I have been given all authority in heaven and earth. Therefore go and make disciples in all the nations, baptizing them into the name of the Father and of the Son and of the Holy Spirit, and then teach these new disciples to obey all the commands I have given you: and be sure of this—that I am with you always, even to the end of the world."

By God's grace, and with His help, Vonette and I and the wonderful team to whom I referred earlier have since had the privilege of helping to train literally millions of Christians in thousands of churches of all denominations and hundreds of missions groups. Together we have been able to share the gospel with more than 2 billion people. But, billions more are waiting for someone to tell them the most joyful news ever announced, the truth about God, like a young man, for example, whom I encountered some years ago.

I was speaking on a large university campus. This young radical student confronted me. I discovered later he was the head of the Communist Party on this big campus. He demonstrated his anger as he stood up before all the students and railed at me. He didn't like the idea that I was encouraging students to follow

Christ as their Lord and Savior. He had other plans for these students. Rather than argue, I invited him to come to our home for dinner, which he did. He was a very brilliant young man, articulate, and winsome. As we sat chatting through dinner, we talked about many things. I found him to be a delightful guest.

Finally, at the conclusion of our dessert time, I reached over and picked up my Bible and said, "I want to read something to you from the Bible." He reacted with obvious irritation. "I have read the Bible from cover to cover," he exclaimed. "It's a ridiculous book. It's filled with contradictions, lies, and myths. I don't want to hear anything from the Bible." I replied, "If you don't mind, I will read it anyway." So I began to read from the Gospel of John, chapter 1 (a portion):

> Before anything else existed, there was Christ, with God. He has always been alive and is Himself God. He created everything there is—nothing exists that He didn't make. Eternal life is in Him, and this life gives light to all mankind. His life is the light that shines through the darkness and the darkness can never extinguish it…To all who received Him, to them He gave the right to become children of God. All they needed to do was to trust Him to save them. All those who believe this are reborn!

Now remember—he had told me that he didn't believe the Bible but he had read it from cover to cover. And when I concluded reading this passage from the Gospel of John, he said, "Let me see that—I don't remember reading that." He read it thoughtfully, and handed the Bible back to me without comment. Then I turned to Colossians, Chapter 1, which records:

> Christ is the exact likeness of the unseen God. He existed before God made anything at all, and, in fact, Christ Himself is the Creator who made everything in heaven and earth, the things we can see and the things we can't, the spirit world with its

> kings and kingdoms, its rulers and authorities, all
> were made by Christ for His own use and glory. He
> was before all else began, and it is His power that
> holds everything together...

Again he said, "I never have seen that before. May I
read it?" I handed the Bible to him. Again he was very
sober. He handed it back to me. After reading a couple
of other passages from God's inspired Word, this
young man was obviously very moved. His entire
countenance had changed. We chatted briefly, and
after a time as he stood to leave, I asked him if he
would write in our guest book. He penned his name
and address, after which he wrote these words, which I
shall never forget: "The night of decision," a decision
to receive and follow Christ.

As you can imagine, in the past 50 years I have had
many moving experiences as I have sought to help others in their quest for peace with God, for meaning and
purpose in this present life. This meaning, peace and
purpose, I am so happy to report, are available to anyone and everyone.

I found it in one of the most infamous high-security
penitentiaries in America. Some of our Campus
Crusade staff been working with hundreds of inmates
in this prison in Atlanta, Georgia. Several of them were
convicted murderers. But as I sat listening, they gave
testimony of how they had been forgiven by God
through their faith in Christ. And even though in
prison, their spirits had been set free. I was deeply
moved by their powerful testimonies.

Suddenly my mind raced across the continent to
Hollywood. Two nights previously I was privileged to
be a guest at a great gathering of Hollywood personalities. They were among the rich and the famous of
America. I remember one world-famous actor sitting
on my left. He was inebriated, and very angry, When I

began to tell him about my work with students, he spouted at me, "Why waste your time on students. They are just a bunch of hot-headed radicals?" Then he said, "Why doesn't somebody work with older people?" Then he began to sob, cry. "Why doesn't somebody help me? I need help!" I was able to help him look to Christ. Later he was baptized in one of the leading churches in Southern California.

Sitting on the other side was the rich and the famous daughter of one of Hollywood's founders. She was wealthy, famous and lived in a palatial mansion, but she told me she had nothing to live for and was seriously thinking about suicide. But her countenance visibly changed as I shared the essence of Christ's love and forgiveness with her from a little book that I wrote called *Four Spiritual Laws*, which she asked to keep. She wanted to take it with her, she said, so she could read it over and over and over again.

Some years ago a seminary professor told me that his father was a great scholar who greatly influenced his own views. The father did not believe in the deity of Christ. He believed Jesus was a good man and had had a profound influence upon the world, but was not God. The professor continued, "About five years ago I began to reevaluate my personal beliefs and to study in earnest the writings of the church fathers and the original manuscripts concerning Jesus. The more I studied, the more convinced I became that Jesus is the Son of God." He concluded, "As a result of my research, I am convinced that no honest person who is willing to consider the overwhelming evidence proving the deity of Christ can deny that He is the Son of God."

God's pardon, God's peace, His purpose, and His power to change for the better are available for everyone, from prisoners to personalities to professors. Dear friends, sharing with others about my personal relationship with my Lord, my Master, my Savior and King is the driving force of my life. I want to live and walk and work in the same reality and power as the New Testament Christians, and to help complete the Great Commission given by our Lord before He ascended to be with the Father, and along with thousands of other Christian leaders and organizations, to do it by the end of the year 2000, December 31st.

Now, that does not leave us much time. As of May 9, 1996, we have four years, seven months, and 22 days—or 40,704 hours remaining to complete the task.

Because of our individual and national gross sins, the fulfillment of the Great Commission has been hindered. America and the world are increasingly coming under God's judgment, with severe discipline. The warning God gave to ancient Israel, centuries ago, as recorded in Deuteronomy, chapter 8, is also true for America and every other country. In essence, God says, if we obey God, He will bless us; if we disobey Him, He will discipline us, like a loving parent lovingly disciplines a child.

Unless there is a worldwide spiritual awakening and turning to back to the God of creation, His warning about national destruction is all too real in this age of nuclear and biological weapons, which are now falling into the hands of terrorists. Anything can happen. The modern-day potential for increased disaster upon disaster is too horrible to even contemplate.

I have been increasingly concerned about the spiritual condition and future of my own beloved country. Modern research has proven conclusively that America was largely founded on biblical principles and by committed Christians. And as a result, God has greatly and uniquely blessed America.

However, God's principles of blessing for obedience and discipline for disobedience are still in force.

And there is no doubt—because of the more than three-decade anti-God trend in media, government and society of America, our great country is losing God's former blessing and is now under His discipline.

What is a nation to do when it comes under God's discipline and is in danger of losing everything? America's great former president Abraham Lincoln was faced with a dramatic crisis during the bloody Civil War of the 1860s. Lincoln was a man who prayed. He read his Bible. He knew what to do in his hour of great crisis. And on April 30, 1863, he issued his famous proclamation for a national day of fasting and prayer. Here is an excerpt from that proclamation:

> We have been the recipients of the choicest boun-
> ties of Heaven…But We Have Forgotten God…In-
> toxicated with unbroken success, we have become
> too self-sufficient to feel the necessity of redeeming
> and preserving grace, too proud to pray to the God
> who made us! It behooves us, then, to humble our-
> selves before Almighty God, to confess our national
> sins, and to pray to the God who made us!

Lincoln and the nation honored the God of heaven. Through fasting and prayer, they petitioned God. God heard. God answered. The war was soon concluded, and the nation was set on a course of unprecedented prosperity and blessing.

But the crisis which America and the world face today far surpasses, in my opinion, the one Lincoln faced. For you see, ours is a crisis of spirit, character, soul, integrity, honor, right and wrong. But Lincoln's biblical solution still applies. Through the process of elimination, we know that nothing else or no one can help us humanly. There is only one hope, and that is the forgiveness, the love and blessing of God.

That is why I believe so strongly that God has led me to fast and pray for a worldwide spiritual awakening and the completion of the Great Commission, and to encourage millions of other believers to join me in fasting and prayer. During July and August, 1994, I felt impressed to fast and pray for 40 days. This was followed by an invitation and gathering of 650 Christian leaders to join me in Orlando, Florida, to fast and pray for national and worldwide spiritual awakening.

In November and December, 1995, I was led to experience another 40-day fast. During this fast, more than 3,500 Christian leaders met in Los Angeles to fast and pray for a great spiritual awakening to come to our country and the world. I have felt led of God to pray that 2 million believers in my own country and Canada—and I trust millions more throughout the world—will fast and pray for 40 days for God's grace, favor, and mercy on this world of darkness and sin.

Already there are scores of college campuses and, I believe, thousands of churches which are experiencing spiritual revival and renewal. And I am confident that these gatherings of Christian leaders to fast and pray have already contributed mightily to the current worldwide movement of God.

Please know that all the proceeds of the Templeton Prize will go to that God-inspired purpose. Through literature, seminars, radio, and television, I trust that we shall help to encourage and equip millions of Christians around the world to join us in fasting and praying for world revival and for the fulfillment of our Lord's Great Commission.

Some may wonder if the money could not be better spent by giving it to the poor, or to direct evangelism, in which I have been involved now for over 50 years. But the roots of poverty are spiritual, and the power for evangelism comes through fasting and prayer. In both cases, it is most important to seek God's face—that's what fasting is about, seeking His face—and ask

Him for Divine help and intervention. God can do more in one split second than all of us together can do in a thousand years in our own effort.

God's promise to Solomon for ancient Israel, recorded in 2 Chronicles 7:14, can be claimed by believers of all nations. God said to Solomon, "If my people, who are called by my name, will humble themselves and pray and seek my face and turn from their wicked ways, then will I hear from heaven and will forgive their sin and will heal their land." No other Christian discipline meets the conditions of God's promises to heal our land as powerfully as fasting and prayer. To me, nothing is more urgent. Nothing deserves greater priority, than that millions of Christians around the world would fast and pray to our holy and righteous Creator God, that we may become holy and righteous, conformed to the image of our dear Savior.

In closing, I urge all who hear this message to join with us—to humble ourselves before our almighty, loving, holy God and Father, to fast and pray, to seek His face, to ask Him for a great worldwide spiritual awakening, and to join with me and millions of other believers in the most exciting, incredibly fulfilling, rich and rewarding experience the human spirit can ever know—to help fulfill the Great Commission of our Lord, sharing God's love and forgiveness with every person on Earth, and at the earliest possible date.

Over half of the people who have ever been alive are alive today. Those who do not know Him desperately need to meet Him, to know our great Creator God and heavenly Father, who, according to John 3:16, so greatly loved the whole world that he actually "gave His only begotten Son, that whosoever believes in Him shall not perish, but have everlasting life."

Thank you, and God bless you all.

Response Form

☐ I have recently received Jesus Christ as my Savior and Lord as a result of reading this booklet.

☐ I am a new Christian and want to know Christ better and experience the abundant Christian life.

☐ Please send me **free** information on staff and ministry opportunities with Campus Crusade for Christ.

☐ Please send me **free** information about other books, booklets, audio cassettes, and videos by Bill Bright.

NAME _____

ADDRESS _____

CITY _____

STATE _____ ZIP _____

PHONE _____

Please check the appropriate box(es) and mail this form in an envelope to:

Dr. Bill Bright
Campus Crusade for Christ
P.O. Box 593684
Orlando, Fl 32859-3684

You may also fax your response to (407) 826-2149 or send E-mail to:

CompuServe: 74114,1206
Internet: newlife@magicnet.net